PENGUIN BOOKS

FIRST FEELINGS

Stanley Greenspan, M.D., is a practicing psychiatrist and chief of
the Clinical Infant and Child Development Research Center of the
Division of Maternal and Child Health and the National Institute of
Mental Health. A founder of the National Center for Clinical Infant
Programs, he has been honored with a number of awards, including
the American Psychiatric Association's highest honor for child
psychiatric research.

Nancy Thorndike Greenspan is a health economist who was formerly
connected with the U.S. Department of Health and Human Services
and with the World Health Organization, and is coauthor, with Stanley Greenspan, of *The Clinical Interview with the Child* and *The
Essential Partnership* (Viking). The Greenspans live in Bethesda,
Maryland, and are the parents of three children.

Stanley I. Greenspan, M.D.
Nancy Thorndike Greenspan

FIRST
FEELINGS

*Milestones in the
Emotional Development
of Your Baby and Child*

PENGUIN BOOKS

PENGUIN BOOKS
Published by the Penguin Group
Penguin Books USA Inc.,
375 Hudson Street. New York, New York 10014, U.S.A.
Penguin Books Ltd, 27 Wrights Lane,
London W8 5TZ, England
Penguin Books Australia Ltd, Ringwood,
Victoria, Australia
Penguin Books Canada Ltd, 10 Alcorn Avenue,
Toronto, Ontario, Canada M4V 3B2
Penguin Books (N.Z.) Ltd, 182–190 Wairau Road,
Auckland 10, New Zealand

Penguin Books Ltd, Registered Offices:
Harmondsworth, Middlesex, England

First published in the United States of America by
Viking Penguin Inc. 1985
Published in Select Penguin 1986
Published in Penguin Books 1989

10 9

This book was written by Stanley I. Greenspan, M.D., in his private capacity. No official
support or endorsement by the National Institute of Mental Health, Department of
Health and Human Services, is intended or should be inferred.

A selection from this book appeared orginally in *Self* magazine.

LIBRARY OF CONGRESS CATALOGING IN PUBLICATION DATA
Greenspan, Stanley I.
First feelings: milestones in the emotional development of your
baby and child/ Stanley I. Greenspan, Nancy Thorndike Greenspan.
p.   cm.
Bibliography: p.
Includes index.
ISBN 0 14 01.1988 4 (pbk.)
1. Emotions in children.   2. Child psychology.   I. Greenspan,
Nancy Thorndike.   II. Title.
[BF723.E6G74   1989]
155.4'12—dc19   88–29011

Printed in the United States of America
Set in Caledonia

To Phil

Acknowledgments

Many people have graciously read various parts of this manuscript and made valuable suggestions. We are very grateful for the support of Barbara and Korbin Lui, Milton Shore, Danielle Spiegler, Meg Robinson, Margaret Millstone, and Diane Feinberg. Our special thanks go to Bill and Chris Leahy whose detailed comments were especially valuable. We would also like to thank Vivienne Sernaqué Jaffe for her editorial assistance and Amanda Vaill for her helpful guidance in preparing the final manuscript.

Preface

This is a book about the emotional development of the infant and child. It is not a new topic, since parents have long recognized that their children develop emotionally. But most parents continue to be uncertain about when emotional development begins, how it happens, or how they can help their children along the road to healthy growth. *First Feelings* deals with these issues; it describes the larger emotional milestones of childhood and offers guidelines for helping parents translate their hunches and questions about their child's emotions into active caregiving.

Parents, like everyone else, get caught up in the emotional struggles of the moment. They tend to see the trees and miss the forest. Frequently, and understandably, a parent wants to know what to do when "Sally spits at a friend," "Johnny bites his brother," or "Bobby cries and clings to my dress all the time." But whether your parental concerns revolve around a power struggle, insecurity, sexual curiosity, or aggression, *First Feelings* will orient you to the broader issues that must be addressed before a solution to the particular drama or problem is found. Helping parents develop the ability to see the forest and the trees is perhaps the most important goal of this book.

Parents have questions about where they and their children are in the emotional joys, sorrows and struggles of each special developmental advance. Yet most parents have only had available information on their child's motor and intellectual development. Parents, in their interest in enhancing their child's competence, have gravitated to what is available as well as to hearsay on emotional challenges—from extreme indulgence to excessive discipline, from ignoring feelings to being overly sensitive to every expression, from teaching young infants and children overly structured tasks such as learning to read to ignoring early cognitive development. However, we have found that children actively progress through special emotional and intellectual stages, each with its own characteristics and requirements. And we have found that emotional and intellectual development cannot be separated; that these two functions come together as the child actively explores the emotional, social, and cognitive challenges at each of these stages.

This book was written for parents committed to understanding their children and themselves as complete human beings. As such, it makes demands of its reader. Taking up the challenge of understanding your child's first feelings, as well as your own, and of developing a sense of the major goals of your child's emotional life is one of the most important affirmations you will ever make.

Stanley I. Greenspan, M.D.
Nancy Thorndike Greenspan

BETHESDA, MARYLAND

Contents

FIRST FEELINGS

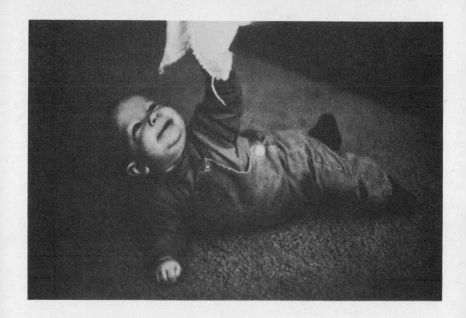

INTRODUCTION

At three months Josh was a sweet but somewhat reserved baby. He was generally peaceful and relaxed; he enjoyed snuggling into his mother's shoulder. His parents noticed, however, that he seemed to be missing that sparkle in his eye and glowing smile other babies are often gifted with. Occasionally he would brighten up, and his parents were excited by his joy. They very much wanted him to be a playful, cheerful baby. When their sporadic attempts to engage Josh in light-hearted play did not work, they became resigned that little Josh just wasn't a gurgly, bright-eyed baby. They focused instead on his pleasure in being held and cuddled. They tended to do things for him. They smiled for him, talked for him, even moved his arms for him to "pretend" he was reaching for his rattle. Josh became more passive and even a little sullen. He would sit with his arms folded, looking at his surroundings expectantly as his parents scurried around, trying to make him happy.

Two-year-old Sally had a different nature. When she was an infant she had been easily distractable; she seemed to overreact to many things and was difficult, if not impossible, to calm down. Her parents took some pride in this, calling her "independent-minded." But now, at two, she was becoming more verbal and capable, and wanted to do what she wanted to do. Her exuberance and impulsiveness were well-matched by her cleverness. Attempts at discipline led to Sally's breaking things, biting, kicking and crying. Her mother, feeling guilty about having recently returned to work, did not want to punish Sally. Her father, pressured at the office, didn't look forward to coming home to a willful child. At least twice a week he would end up carrying Sally, in full tantrum, up to her room. Both her mother and father felt helpless and overwhelmed. They were counting the days until Sally "outgrew" this phase.

Neither of these descriptions is extraordinary, either in its depiction of the child's behavior or in the conclusion of the parents. Children do seem to have basic personality characteristics right from birth, and they also pass through different stages as they mature. Often parents feel that they can do little about their child's "personality." Deep down, however, they often wonder if they are to blame, or if they could be doing more for their child. Even more upsetting is the sensitive parent's uneasy feeling that an infant seems "different" from his brothers and sisters.

In the examples we've just described, both sets of parents just kept hoping for the day when their child would somehow change. Josh's parents did not realize that some babies are particularly difficult to interest in the world—that the typical ways of playing with an infant wouldn't work for them. Sally's parents didn't know that some babies could be overstimulated by their environment and, therefore, needed to learn how to enjoy the world without becoming too excited by it.

In another case, Jason's development was unlike that of his gregarious older brother. As an infant he appeared totally uninterested in his caregivers. He would play with objects but not with people. He never smiled and would only glance occasionally at anyone who tried to engage his attention. He often stared off into space. As Jason grew older, he would sit alone in a corner when other children were available for play. As his father said of him, "He marched to his own drum from the time he was a few months old." His parents defended his "special abilities with things" and claimed to be convinced of his "superiority" and "great potential." But privately they worried. And, after Jason entered nursery school, his teacher confirmed their fears that he needed therapy to help him become more involved with the human world as well as testing to identify any possible underlying physical or cognitive problem.

Jason's parents had the sense that he was "different" but, like most parents in this situation, had no specific guidelines for testing their intuition. Instead of being able to take constructive action, they had little choice but to wait passively for confirmation of their assessment from an alert teacher or some other outside "authority." Unfortunately, by the time this happens, emotional development may be sorely lagging and disruptive behaviors firmly entrenched.

The Six Emotional Milestones

Until recently little has been known about how infants and young children develop emotionally. Most conventional information, especially concerning infancy and early childhood, focuses the parents' attention on observations of their child's physical and intellectual development. The implication is that if little Mikey can roll over by the time he is four months old, and if Jennifer knows all of the letters of the alphabet at age three, then emotional competence must also be on schedule. While this is sometimes true, it just as often is not. The absence of straightforward guidelines to the emotional development of the infant and child has created a gap in knowledge that is only recently being addressed. Advice has certainly been available on how to comfort a baby or how to discipline a child, but this advice has been based mainly on tradition or folklore, and any parent who has used such advice knows it is as unreliable as it is variable. Furthermore, it focuses on the parent's actions, not the baby's feelings— until now, scant attention has been paid to what the child experiences emotionally. But recently, as we have begun to understand the origins of emotional growth, we have been able to pinpoint childhood's earliest emotional milestones by closely observing babies' behavior, emotional reactions, and ways of relating to us. Doing this gives us entry into a dimension of our children's lives that has until now remained a mystery. This does not mean that from here on we will be privy to our child's every whim and desire. It does mean, however, that knowledge of these milestones and stages can be used to help us and our children experience deeper, richer, more understanding and more satisfying relationships with each other and the world.

A brief overview of the infant's six emotional milestones may help orient parents to the more detailed discussions in each of the subsequent chapters. As you will see, the time span for one milestone often overlaps with another. This is partly to acknowledge the variability in a child's mastery of a particular stage and also to indicate the simultaneity of the course of the milestones.

In the early weeks of life babies are confronted with two simultaneous challenges: to feel regulated and calm and to use all their senses to take an interest in the world. Suddenly, after nine months in the darkness and relative quiet of the womb, they are plunged into a new world of sights and sounds, movement, touch, tastes, and smells. The ability to organize these sensations—to feel tranquil in spite of them and to reach out actively for them—is the first milestone, which leads the way for the second, that of taking a highly specialized interest in the *human* world. The baby who is not interested in sights and sounds or finds them painful rather than pleasurable may be unlikely to progress to this next stage where the human world is seen as the most enticing, pleasurable, and exciting of all experiences. Once the relaxed and interested three- or four-month-old discovers the incomparable attraction of the world, you observe enraptured smiles and eager joyfulness as the baby gazes excitedly at your face, feeling your rhythmical movement, hearing your soft voice, and even, in his uncoordinated way, exploring your face.

Soon the special interest in the human world becomes the basis for the third milestone, the point at which the baby "says," "love alone is not enough—I now want a dialogue." And surely we observe the three- to ten-month-old baby enter into a dialogue with his parents. Little Johnny is not just smiling randomly or even in mimicry, but in *response* to his parent's smile as he reaches for an object that his mother or father holds out to him. He makes guttural sounds with his voice in response to his parent talking to him. Johnny is learning that the world is a cause-and-effect world; that his responses lead to reactions on the part of others. The emotion of pleasure produces a smile, which in turn produces a smiling parent. When he feels anger and protest, his tight grasp of the object in his hand and his refusal to give it up are testament to his feelings.

By ten to twelve months, Johnny shows his readiness for the fourth stage of development by taking his emotional dialogue with the world one step further and learning to connect small units of feeling and social behavior into large, complicated, orchestrated patterns. Toward the middle of the fourth stage, at fourteen or fifteen months, when Johnny is hungry he no longer has to sit on the couch and cry, as though expecting his mother to read his mind; he now can take his mother's hand and walk her to the refrigerator, bang on the door, and point to the food he wants. He is showing an amazing ability to organize a complex social, emotional, and behavioral pattern that contains his wishes (i.e., food), his intentions (i.e., taking mother to the refrigerator), and even his sense of satisfaction (as he eats some cheese with great pleasure). As his abilities for organizing complicated social and emotional patterns advance, Johnny also shows that he knows the "meanings" of things. He picks up the toy telephone and holds it to his ear. He takes the brush and seems to be brushing his hair. This is the beginning of a "conceptual" attitude toward the world. Objects now have functions. Most important, Johnny is coming to recognize that his parents have functions, such as storyteller or diaper-changer. Parents also take on attributes. They can be sweet, angry, playful, or they can demonstrate a number of other attributes that Johnny begins to recognize. Even though he cannot yet say words, he seems to understand the "functions" of the important things and people in his world. He also can communicate more effectively across space as he uses visual and vocal gestures to stay in touch with his mother from across the room, feeling secure with her prideful glance. Gestures across space help him practice his independence and initiative with confidence. It is astonishing to consider that all this occurs before age two.

The fifth stage or milestone seems like a huge leap in Johnny's capacities, yet it is really a gradual maturing of his ability from the last stage. Johnny learns to go from understanding how objects function to being able to create these objects in his own mind's eye. He can now create an image of his mother in his mind even when she is not there—a picture in which he sees her, hears her, smells her, remembers interactions with her, and so forth. He can do the same for his favorite teddy bear or red ball. This ability to create his own experiences also leads, as most parents know, to the ability to dream in an adult way. Two-and-a-half-year-old Susie, during her fifth stage of development, can wake up in the middle of the night and say, "Witches are under my bed." Parents need no further evidence that Susie is able to construct her own ideas. This was not possible at fifteen or sixteen months. Although fifteen- and sixteen-month-olds also wake up at night, sometimes scared and worried, the ability to construct ideas or an internal life must still undergo successive stages of development before they can be communicated.

Children learn, during the sixth phase, to expand their world of ideas into the emotional realms of pleasure and dependency, curiosity, assertiveness, anger, self-discipline or setting their own limits, even empathy and love. Eventually they learn to separate make-believe from reality and are able to work with ideas and to plan and anticipate. Now three and a half years old, Susie can say, "I dreamed there were witches under my bed. Tonight I'm going to dream about kittens."

It is a thrilling experience to nurture your child's uniquely human capacity for emotional growth and understanding. You can see your infant's initial interest in the world, which is, after all, a "sensory interest," involving sights, sounds, and feelings, broaden to become an interest in people, particularly yourselves. This interest grows into love. The love grows into a desire to have an emotional dialogue, to communicate emotions and receive communication of emotions. This emotional dialogue grows into the desire to interact in ever more complicated ways, such as understanding more about people—how they function, what they mean—and eventually leads to the ability to construct an internal mental life—that is, to imagine experiences for oneself.

Understanding this logical sequence of emotional development can help you to see your child's progress from one stage to the next. Gradually, you will also be able to see what you can do to foster your child's development: how to determine when this progression is not occurring as it might, and how to help your child overcome difficulties and continue to grow.

The Dimensions of Human Emotion

Views of emotions differ. Some of the fundamental issues concern what an emotion is, how many there are, which are the basic ones, and when during childhood is each one first experienced? Some researchers identify emotions by their expressive characteristics, such as facial expressions. Using this approach, they have identified basic emotions expressed in the early months of infancy—pleasure, distress, surprise, disgust, joy, anger, and—by eight to nine months—fear and sadness; in the second year they have identified more complex emotions, such as organized affection and shame. Other researchers focus more on the cognitive characteristics of emotion. Here, empathy is the intellectual ability to put yourself in someone else's shoes. Another view is that thoughts and emotions organize other aspects of behavior, that emotions determine what you remember. Being sad helps you remember other sad feelings. Still another view stresses the physical or physiological aspects of emotions. Many others define emotions only in terms of subjective experience, where it is the inner feelings and their associated fantasies or behavior that are important.

In this book we view emotions as complex, subjective experiences that have many components, including physical, expressive, cognitive, and organizing, as well as highly personalized, subjective meanings. With infants, only expressive features can be observed, and what their subjective experiences are have to be intuited. What we are most interested in is how the child combines these elements to organize and eventually to recognize his feelings and emotional experiences. We believe that a child's feelings cannot be separated from her experiences with herself and others, that emotions are both a part of as well as a help to define and organize all experiences.

In order to discuss a child's emotions, we have compartmentalized (albeit artificially) the child's experiences into a number of emotional areas that have been clinically useful in accounting for the full range of distinctly human experiences. It is all too easy to admire the child who is assertive and competent and ignore her private worries about being close and about having her dependency needs met. It is even easier to admonish the cautious, shy child for not being like her assertive older sister, even when this child may, once she has warmed up to a situation, be assertive as well as loving and may feel the full range of her distinctly human potential most profoundly. Therefore, we have found it useful to have an overview of a number of important emotional areas that highlight what is uniquely human.

As we learn more about emotional development, we also learn more about individual emotions and can appreciate the subtleties and levels within each of the emotional areas which accounts for the differences between us. If we as parents want to support the full range of our child's emotional experience, we must consider all broad areas of emotional functioning, including dependency, pleasure, love and intimacy, curiosity, assertiveness and exploration, protest and anger, and self-discipline (and, eventually, self-punishment), as well as emotions related to these broad areas such as (the various types of feelings of) loss, sadness, anxiety, fear, shame, and guilt. These seven areas cover a wide range of human emotions that characterizes not only children's functioning, but also a large part of adult functioning. Babies, children, and adults all operate emotionally in these areas. Dependency can be seen in the way a baby holds on to and cuddles with his mother, the way a young child seeks out the protection and security of his parents, and the way adults depend on one another for emotional and financial support. Pleasure is seen in the smiling and gurgling of the baby when stroked gently, in young children enjoying various games as well as the physical attributes of their own bodies, and in the adult capacity to enjoy sex play. Love and intimacy is evident in the enraptured gaze a four-month-old baby gives his mother and only his mother, in the special warmth the young child may have for parents and certain friends, and in the love relationships of adulthood. Curiosity, exploration, and assertiveness may be seen in the earliest behavior of the baby as he looks up, reaches for, and explores his mother's face as if to ask "Who is this strange but wonderful creature?", in the slightly older baby who searches under a blanket for a hidden ball, in the toddler who is finally able to explore his house, and in numerous activities of older children and adults. Protest and anger can be seen in the youngest infant who turns away and cries, the belligerency or temper tantrums of the toddler, the more organized hitting and yelling of the older child, and the various disguised—and not so disguised—attacks and destructiveness of adults.

By considering each of these emotional areas one can see the degree to which infants, young children, and adults are able to discriminate between the emotional subtleties of a particular situation. For example, a person may understand complicated interpersonal relations when it comes to loving but seem to have only very simple notions when it comes to anger. With regard to love, this person may understand that there are many shades of gray between liking and truly loving someone. However, when it comes to angry feelings, this same individual may see only two options: either a wish to hurt and destroy the other person, or no feeling of anger at all. In the same way, some adults are extremely sophisticated in the world of business: they appreciate the subtleties of the power structure, the balance between a friendly manner and a competitive one, and the trade-offs implied in every decision. However, when they return to their families, where more intimate and dependent feelings tend to be activated, they lose their sophistication and operate with all the sensitivity of a wounded boar. In other words, in one area there is more subtle understanding and more ability to fine-tune what we call "emotional intelligence"; in another area, emotional understanding is not as highly developed.

Like adults, children may also reach different levels of functioning in different emotional areas because of emotional constrictions or limitations. One young boy, for example, may be assertive, a leader of his peers, but unable to tolerate closeness or express tenderness or love. Or the opposite may be true. Another boy may be trusting and warm but quite scared of his assertive and angry feelings. These examples describe children who are able to reach a generally adequate level of functioning overall, but who experience setbacks in specific areas. There are also children who don't reach the general level of functioning expected of them: those who never learn to relate to people—for instance, preferring always to play alone—or those who cannot use ideas to express feelings, perhaps only showing anger and frustration through temper tantrums or destructive behavior rather than being able to talk or even scream about a problem. With help, many of these children can reach a good general level of emotional functioning in all areas and even achieve the ability to function in a highly adaptive and flexible way.

If you can appreciate the kinds of challenges your children face and the abilities they have to deal with these challenges, and if you know what to expect next and know how to encourage and guide your children along the way, you will find yourselves better able to support their emotional development with love and understanding.

A Positive Philosophy

A positive approach to understanding children must take two critical, and closely related, facts into consideration: each child is unique, and each child is a complex being.

These two principles may seem obvious; yet let us look at what they really mean. They mean that the individually different neurological, intellectual, emotional, and social dimensions of a child all interact to create a person who is more than the sum of his parts.

Add this to the maturing child's relationships with family members and caregivers within the larger social and cultural context that forms the basis of a child's "experience," and one can see how necessary it is to have an understanding of the dimensional approach we advocate. As your child begins, quite early in life, to derive a sense of self and of the world—a sense that will change continually through the stages of development—you should be able to monitor your child's development on all planes and offer the proper support and encouragement along the way. We help you to recognize your child's individual characteristics and also to recognize the unique and complex way the elements of your child's makeup interact to produce the human being he is.

The importance of your ability to "tune in" to your child's individuality and to recognize the need for an approach that will touch the various dimensions of your child can be seen in the two examples that follow.

Deborah's mother and father had read that stimulating their newborn daughter's capacities for seeing, hearing, and moving about would encourage her development of these senses. But Deborah's mother began to feel discouraged. Whenever she would cuddle her daughter and speak to her in the high-pitched singsong voice that mothers instinctively use to communicate with their babies, Deborah would turn away and begin to cry. "She doesn't like me" was the mother's sad conclusion, but she was determined to find ways to please her child. After much experimenting, both parents came to realize that while her father's low voice was soothing and interesting to Deborah, her mother's "baby voice" was an irritant. (Whether Deborah's hearing was overly sensitive or her nervous system immature, this small human variation posed a real threat to a loving relationship.) Soon after her parents' discovery both mother and baby were enjoying mother's new-found "low" voice.

A slightly more complicated example involves something that occurs even more frequently—focusing on one and only one aspect of development. This focus often causes parents to miss a related problem that could be resolved through early treatment.

Sara was slow in all areas of motor development. She was still on her back when other babies were turning over, and she sat up at a late date. When Sara's pediatrician recommended she see a specialist, her parents were apprehensive at first, then relieved when the doctor was able to give them exercises to do with Sara, and, finally, delighted when the exercises seemed to have an effect. Though Sara continued to be slower than her peers, her parents felt they had done all they could. What was overlooked, however, was that children like Sara may also have difficulty in regulating and controlling their feelings and occasionally their ideas. This is because a lag in sensory or motor regulation is sometimes part of a larger regulatory problem. After all, emotions are part of the body and are experienced and expressed through the muscles and the senses. In addition, since a child's first sense of mastery is often of her own body, when muscles can't be controlled and what is heard or seen is unreliable, the early sense of "self" may be affected negatively.

Sara did fine in terms of her motor and intellectual functioning with the help she got. But her unattended emotional development left her moody, prone to temper tantrums, and unsure of herself.

There is an unfortunate tendency to see difficulties in a child's development as important only if it is felt that these difficulties will lead to problems later on. It is as though the despondent-looking infant is somehow less a person and less entitled to help than the depressed adult. Infants and children are people with feelings. Significant and consistent deviation from normal development deserves attention no matter the age. And it is now clear that successive failures at each stage *are* associated with greater likelihood of difficulties in meeting the challenges of the subsequent emotional stage. Correcting problems as early as possible establishes a healthy foundation that will help your child adapt to the stage she is in and give her the capacity to cope with the challenges ahead.

In addition to my own clinical experience and research with many infants, children, and their families, there is an abundance of studies that support the descriptions that follow of the normal emotional and social landmarks for infants and children.

Chapter by chapter in this book, you will be able to see your child's emotional life developing; her awakening to the world and to you; her discovery of communication; the deepening of relationships; her developing sense of self; her ability to create new ideas and complex feelings.

Use these milestones to alleviate worries, to make vague concerns explicit, and to foster constructive action.

More important, understand your child's growth and appreciate the special qualities she brings with her as she discovers her world. The confidence that all is going well can be yours when you feel secure in the knowledge of your child's emotional life.

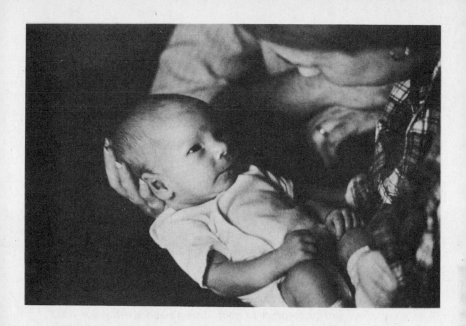

I | SELF-REGULATION AND INTEREST IN THE WORLD

— Birth to 3 months

Not so long ago it was thought that newborn babies were simply a jumble of reflexes, feeling little pleasure and even less pain; they were not yet entitled to be called "little persons." This view has changed dramatically over the years. Now it is well established that babies begin to experience sensations such as seeing and hearing even before birth. Shortly after birth they are able to follow their mother's face; to respond to different sounds, textures, lights and colors; and even to learn simple little tasks. We know all their senses function, though hearing seems to be better developed than seeing. We also see them smile, communicate their distress, or be absorbed by the new world around them. We do not know how newborns actually perceive and relate to their new experiences. But we can observe their different responses and wonder what they must feel. It is these responses—the infant's interest in a parent's smile or tone of voice—that parents want to encourage throughout the first few months.

Your newborn is faced with two fundamental and simultaneous challenges during the first weeks of life. The first is self-regulation—the ability to feel calm and relaxed, not overwhelmed by his new environment. The second is to become interested in the world about him. The way your baby becomes interested in the world is through his senses—what he hears, sees, smells, tastes, and touches, and what he experiences through his sense of movement.

Normally the capacity for regulation and interest in the world work together, each one supporting the other. The senses that help your baby become interested in the world also help him stay calm and organized. His ability to take an interest in your face, to listen to your voice, and to respond to your stroking and rocking are what calms him down when he is overexcited or uncomfortable. His ability to look outward helps him to regulate his own internal reactions. It is no different from an adult feeling better in the presence of a familiar face. This ability to focus the senses on the external world in order to feel calm and relaxed is perhaps the newborn infant's greatest asset.

At the same time the ability to be attentive and relaxed makes it possible for a baby to practice using his senses further. A baby who has a physical illness that "hurts," such as an ear infection, is often unable to practice using his hearing, his vision, or his experience of touch and movement. He is too distracted by pain. Similarly, a baby whose basic ability for regulating himself is not well developed may find it harder to use his senses to take an interest in the world. So we have a circle: the baby who is calm can look at, hear, and take an interest in his surroundings, and the baby who uses his senses well can help himself become calm and attentive.

This is not meant to imply that your baby will or should be this way most of the time or even a good part of the time. Fussiness and crying are often evidence of your baby's capacity to communicate that he wants to be fed, is tired, or that he has a gas bubble in his stomach. It is his way of letting you know that he isn't comfortable and needs something to be done.

At first, the interested and calm state may occur infrequently, for only a few minutes at a time. Gradually the episodes increase both in duration and number as your new infant matures. If you have a baby who is especially "tuned in" to his senses, early infancy will hold some unforgettable moments. Let's look at Joanne as an example.

Joanne was a robust, happy baby. She opened her eyes and looked earnestly at her mother within minutes of her arrival. Her first weeks at home were filled with respectable amounts of sleeping and fussing, and remarkable moments of communication when her mother saw Joanne looking at her eyes, almost smiling as she was talked to. Her mother even noticed that Joanne would try to move her mouth and arms to the rhythm of speech. At night, if Joanne cried, her father would hold her about three feet from his face, look at her, and say, "Oh, my little sweetheart, oh, my little sweetheart," in a sing-song voice. Joanne would stop crying, look at him, and brighten up. Joanne was unusually gifted in her ability to use her senses right away from the first weeks of life and to be able to take an interest in the sights and sounds around her as well as to calm and regulate herself.

You may wonder how the physical experiences of helping your baby to calm down by using his eyes, ears, and sense of touch aid his emotional development. This is basically because by using his senses, your baby learns to deal with both distress and pleasure. We have all seen adults with different capacities for dealing with stress or unsettling experiences. When feeling internal disharmony, some people can easily return to a state of focused attention and deal with the challenge at hand. Others, when faced with anxiety or internal conflict, immediately panic and their fragile sense of "organization" is upset. This is often because they are either not able intuitively to avoid overwhelming situations, or they become easily overwhelmed and confused, or they lack a sense of caution and hurl themselves headlong toward danger like a moth toward a flame. The security in one's own capacity for regulation, as you can see, is a fundamental ability that is at the very foundation of human emotional experience. And this capacity for self-organization and regulation is being learned for the first time in early infancy.

The capacity to experience the world as richly and deeply as possible through one's senses is also a foundation for emotional development. The person who early in life tunes out many of the messages he receives through his senses begins a pattern that, if it continues, will later rob him of the full range of emotional experience. Everyone knows and wants to be the adult who embraces experience, who is intimately involved in love relationships, who asserts himself at work and play, enjoys contemplative activity, and experiences the spectrum of human emotion in depth. We also know the individual who has "shut himself off" and seems to experience only the surface of life. He is not fully able to enjoy or experience such basic feelings as intimacy and love, or competitiveness and assertiveness. You will see in your child that a basic orientation toward sensory experiences begins in the first months of life. You can also help orient your baby toward a world that is rich and deep by helping him regulate his senses and by providing him with opportunities to experience a wide range of feelings.

Interest in the world in general sets a foundation that encourages a special interest in human relationships. Your baby's initial interest in his environment leads to his becoming interested in people and forming those first relationships that are the basis for all emotional learning to come. Each step is the foundation for the next one. Good mastery of the first steps can strongly influence the climb to the next. But if for some reason this is not possible at first, there are always opportunities later on to go back a few steps and rebuild.

Observing Your Baby

How well do you know your baby? You are probably aware of obvious physical traits: big or small, a chin like mommy's or daddy's. You might also recognize that, just as babies have differing physical characteristics, they are also born with individual personality differences: withdrawn or excitable, for example. But how well do you *really* know your baby? Which of her senses are unusually well or not so well developed? Which of her physical abilities are unusually well or not so well developed? Recognizing your baby's individual characteristics is the first step in supporting her emotional development. If you know your baby's traits and tendencies, you can begin tailoring your care to help your baby develop her capacities for self-regulation and interest in the world.

You can help your baby develop successfully through carefully

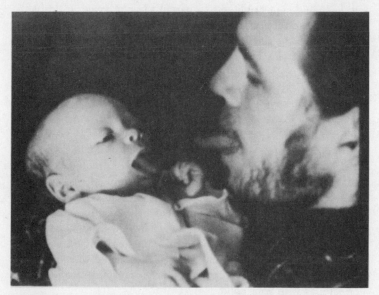

Only two weeks old and already he can look, listen, and even imitate his father.

observing her, yourself, and your baby's environment. Although these three items are inseparable and will overlap, for purposes of discussion let's first look at how to assess your baby and tailor your care to her needs.

Your first task is to assess your baby's capacity for being (1) calm and regulated, and (2) interested in the world. Ask yourself this series of questions during your baby's first two months. How much of the time does your baby seem tranquil? Does she sleep peacefully in a relaxed manner for a few hours at a time? Does she look at you, listen to your words, or brighten up when you speak to her? Are the times of focused attention—say, maybe, initially five minutes two or three times a day—getting longer and occurring more frequently as she approaches two months? If your answers are "yes," you may need to do little differently. Often, however, babies show unexplained and growing tendencies toward irritability, muscle tension, and back arching, or they do not brighten to a parent's face or voice. If this is the case, and medical reasons (including hunger or reactions to certain foods) have been ruled out, you may want to observe your baby's reactions more closely.

THE SENSES

In order to observe your baby's sensory reactions individually, you can play the following simple games, emphasizing first one sense and then another.

Vision. Look at your infant without talking. Make interesting facial expressions and see if she responds. Take an object, a bright ball, for instance, and put it in front of your baby. Move it slowly to the left and then to the right. See if the baby follows it. If your baby brightens to your smiling face and follows the ball to the left and to the right, you can rest assured that your baby is using her vision to take an interest in the world and to maintain her tranquility. Be sure to play these games only when the baby is calm and when she is not hungry, wet, or tired. You can make these and similar games part of normal play with your child.

Hearing. Next you may want to introduce sounds. Pitch your voice at the level you think your baby finds appealing. Say "goo," "da,da," or make other rhythmic patterns with a touch of novelty, such as "Bo . . . bo . . . bo . . . *ba!*" See if your child becomes bright and alert. When your baby is sitting in her baby seat, approach her at first slightly from the left and then from the right, making interesting sounds. See if she turns toward you a little bit. She may not respond with interest to every voice pattern or tone. This will enable you to determine which tones and patterns attune her to you and which either don't interest her or overexcite her.

Touch. Touch is an easy one. During a relaxed time, when your baby is not too sleepy, gently stroke the different parts of her body. Start with the heels of the feet, work up the legs, through the abdomen, onto the shoulders, neck, and face, then to the arms and down to the hands. Watching baby's expression tells you which areas she enjoys having touched the most and which she may not like. If stroking one area seems to make her irritable, calm her down, then come back to that area and check for rashes or skin irritations. If there are none then that area of her body may be extra-sensitive. (You may also want to notice the different reactions to light touch and firm massaging or holding. Many babies who are sensitive to light touch enjoy instead being tightly and firmly held.)

Position. Hold the baby vertically, which most parents do instinctively when looking at their babies. If she brightens or becomes alert and smiles, you know that she likes this position. Do the same at a forty-five degree angle and then on the horizontal. You will be able to tell whether there are certain positions your baby finds either too arousing or not arousing enough. The best positions for her will allow her to be alert, interested in the world, and calm at the same time.

Movement. As you gently rock your baby, look at how she reacts. Most babies snuggle, relax, and then fall asleep. But some find the movement too stimulating and get tense. If your baby does, then you will know that rocking may be too stimulating for her. During times of play, hold your baby up in the air, then gently move her down to eye level. Almost all new babies will startle if moved too quickly, but by two to three months some babies show they love brisk movement, while others are still sensitive to it. Some prefer vertical movement, while others enjoy horizontal, circular patterns.

Smell and Taste. Little is known at present of the impact or importance of these senses on your baby's development of self-regulation or interest in the world. Certainly it wouldn't hurt to have her experience the pleasant aromas of cooking food, fresh air, or other suitable fragrances!

For those of you who prefer not to do things so systematically, you may find that together you can recall how your baby responds to voices, faces, bright objects, to having different body parts touched, to different holding positions, to your moving her fingers and toes, and to whether she prefers robust movement or slower, more gentle movement patterns. In other words, in the normal experiences of the first few months of life, most parents can describe their baby's routine interactions with them. Often this is the approach that is more reliable than any single attempt at a systematic observation, which is obviously dependent on the baby's mood and state on that particular day. The two methods are probably best used in combination, when the more informal retrospective picture of baby can be complemented by a more systematic observation of the senses that you are not sure about.

THE OVER- OR
UNDER-EXCITABLE BABY

Babies who have difficulty being calm and attentive and/or interested in the world usually fall into two categories: those who tend to be easily overstimulated by the world around them and cannot remain calm, and those who tend to be calm but hard to interest in their surroundings. Babies who become overstimulated—known as hyper-excitable babies—seem to be irritable much of the time. Sometimes these babies are described as colicky, but colic is a general term and has many different causes. An extreme example of the easily excitable baby is one who arches his back, stiffens his muscles, pulls away rather than toward his mother, and cries in a high-pitched shriek much of the time. Attempts to console him often increase his panic.

The second category of baby is known as hypo-arousable. This baby seems to be calm and well regulated, but it is hard to interest him in the world. This baby often has poor muscle tone. When his mother or father picks up the baby's arm, it drops right down again. When the parents talk in rhythmic high-pitched voices, the baby does not brighten up or look at them. When being stroked and held he does not snuggle. He just does not seem interested in very much.

Over- or under-sensitivity to sensory experience has recently been found to account for many instances in which babies find it difficult to be calm and attentive. Infants tend to be most vulnerable to experiences of hearing, vision, touch, positioning, movement, and muscle control. For each of these senses both the hyper-excitable and the hypo-arousable baby may show distinct reactions.

Observing the Hyper-Excitable Baby
Hearing. The normal high-pitched maternal voice is pleasing to most babies and captures their attention. But for the overly sensitive baby, it may be a painful experience, similar to hearing a fingernail scrape against a blackboard. The sound may send shivers up his spine. It is not surprising that an overly sensitive baby will tense his muscles, arch his back, pull away from the sound, and begin crying to express his discomfort.

Vision. Normal lighting in a room may cause irritability in babies who are hypersensitive to light. Also, animated facial expressions may cause such a baby to cry.

Touch.　　Stroking a baby gently around his tummy is a comforting experience for most babies. Others, however, experience such stroking the way an adult would experience a bruise being stroked.

Motion.　　Some babies love to be rocked vigorously or tossed up in the air. But, babies who are hypersensitive to movement may panic at this kind of rapid movement.

Positioning.　　Most babies like to be held in the nearly vertical position. They seem to brighten and look at the person holding them. Others, however, find this position too stimulating and do better in the horizontal position. When held vertically, these babies get irritable, arch their backs, and tense their muscles.

Muscle Control.　　Most babies also like to have their toes and fingers moved, but for a few babies, even this will be overstimulating.

Usually these hypersensitivities do not involve all the senses, but are limited to one or two. But when a baby cries and tenses up every time he is held, it is easy to understand how his parents might assume that their baby is irritable, throw up their hands, and hope he will outgrow it. Fortunately, most babies do outgrow these patterns. However, in some instances, these sensitivities can prevent a baby from learning to regulate himself and take an interest in the world—making the next stage, falling in love, more difficult. We'll suggest some ways to help shortly.

Observing the Hypo-Arousable Baby

Hearing.　　A baby who has difficulty responding to sounds (even though his hearing is good) may not look toward a voice, move his arms or legs in the direction of a sound, or brighten on hearing it.

Vision.　　A baby might ignore what he sees, remain somber and blank when looking at a warm, smiling face or interesting toy, or not be alert to his mother's mouth movements.

Movement and Touch.　　A hypo-arousable baby might show little reaction to movement or to being stroked. There may be no change in muscle tone, facial expression, or level of alertness.

Position.　　Playing with baby's toes and fingers, gently moving arms and legs back and forth, may not lead to any noticeable impact on the baby, either.

Babies who don't seem to be interested in their surroundings very much may, like their overexcitable counterparts, be affected in only one or two senses. If the sense happens to be one that the parent appeals to frequently, the baby may seem generally listless.

Tommy was a real challenge to his parents. The product of a seemingly normal pregnancy and delivery, Tommy nevertheless looked sleepy even when he was awake. His eyes seemed to look inward. His parents described him as a "flower that wouldn't bloom." Tommy's muscles were floppy. When his mother or father picked up his arm and then let go, the arm would just drop back to Tommy's side. Both mother and father tried endlessly to interest Tommy by talking and singing to him, using funny voices and altering pitch and rhythm. But the more they talked, the more droopy Tommy became. Mother also noticed that he was sucking less vigorously at the breast. At Tommy's four week checkup his weight gain was not as much as expected. Tommy's concerned parents and pediatrician observed and examined him. It was discovered that Tommy tended to "tune out" sounds, even though a hearing test indicated he was normal. Sound just wasn't the way to reach him. After some experimentation, Tommy's parents realized that he responded extremely well to physical touch. When tickled on his belly he would break into a bright smile, and his muscles would then firm up a bit. He loved vigorous massage as well and especially liked his feet to be stroked and rubbed. Tommy also responded to shades of light and varied facial expressions. His show of interest in shadows or facial expressions was always gay, accompanied by a firming up of his muscles and overall posture. While it was not known why Tommy did not respond to his parents' voices, they used this knowledge to help him become interested in his world and learn to regulate himself. His parents made an effort to become more visually and tactilely oriented. They appealed to the senses Tommy seemed to favor.

While appealing to his favorite senses, Tommy's parents realized his perception of sounds, even in terms of rhythmic sequences, was probably less well developed than that of other children his age. They tried lowering their tone and talking more slowly, combining this with lots of physical touch and facial expressiveness. Tommy began responding to their voices. By three months of age he was the kind of baby every parent wants—gurgly, bright, with good muscle tone, gaining weight nicely and responding through all his senses.

Luckily, both parents and pediatrician actively searched for the ingredients that would nurture this child's growth. Rather than remaining uninvolved with his world and, later, perhaps less involved with people, Tommy began experiencing the joys and comforts of his surroundings. Unfortunately, not all situations are this straightforward and easy to resolve, but Tommy's example serves to show that when a baby is not sensitive to even one kind of stimulation, he can appear completely nonresponsive.

The preceding descriptions of the hypo- and hypersensitive babies presume that these babies were born this way. However, some babies who are not born with any special sensitivities may develop the same reactions. A serious illness or unsupportive parents or babysitters, such as those who are either very anxious or very depressed, can be the cause. It is important to recognize that your baby's reactions may be quite specific. By creating an especially supportive environment for your baby, you can often reverse the difficulties.

CARE OF THE OVER- OR
UNDER-EXCITABLE BABY

The main principle in determining a special pattern of care for either the over- or under-excitable baby is to encourage regulation and alertness through the receptive senses and then slowly work on improving those senses that are over- or under-responsive. In other words, don't ignore the senses that your child finds difficult. To help your hyper-excitable baby, for example, try to be sensitive to your baby's reaction and encourage use of the sense very gradually and in combination with pleasurable and comforting experiences. To help the hypo-arousable baby, try to make the experience of using the sense more interesting, perhaps by introducing novelty while continuing to help the baby stay regulated and engaged, using his other senses.

Let's look again at Tommy, our example of the hypo-arousable baby. He did not respond to sounds but did respond to vision and touch. His parents offered lots of stroking and visual experiences to comfort and interest him. In this way he became interested in the world and practiced using the senses that he found pleasurable to calm himself when he felt irritated. At the same time his parents experimented with interesting sounds, using voices, music boxes, and other devices to find just the right cadence and range that interested him. Of course, one baby may respond to very high-pitched sounds and another may respond to low-pitched sounds. Still another may respond best to sounds of uneven cadence, such as *clap-clap-clap-pause-clap*. If you are willing to experiment and keep trying, chances are you will find the right formula for your hypo-arousable baby.

The formula is similar for babies who become hyper-excitable from certain sounds. You can try speaking softly to your infant while rhythmically rocking him or while walking with him held securely in your arms or in a front carrier. In this way he experiences auditory stimulation but is soothed at the same time. With time and with sensitive help, your baby will usually develop more normal tolerance in any of the senses that may be difficult for him now.

Babies who have difficulty with movement may also respond to gentle encouragement combined with pleasure and comforting. For example, if your baby has very jerky arm and leg movements, you can help him feel more in control by moving his arms and legs smoothly and gently in rhythm with your own vocal cadence and body movement. This exercise will help your baby enjoy the smooth flow of his movement and learn that his body does not have to feel out of control. If your baby has very stiff muscles, help him bend his arms and legs and pull his knees up to his chest. Combine this activity with rhythmic movement or other sensory experiences that help him to be calm and regulated. He may learn that having relaxed muscles is pleasurable.

Although your efforts may be discouraging at first, perseverance and sensitive exploration of what works will usually pay off. At the same time, playing to your baby's strengths allows him to master the tasks of being involved in the world and regulated. For those babies who seem to be generally under- or over-excitable and are difficult to comfort or get involved, you may want to seek a professional consultation. A professional may be able to help you work out a pattern of care that will help your baby regulate himself and get him involved.

BABIES WHO DON'T USE
A PARTICULAR SENSE

A more subtle stumbling block to your baby's involvement in the world and ability to regulate himself is a seeming inability to use a particular sense to orient himself or to "take in" the world. For example, at around two to three months a mother may notice that her

Helping Your Child . . .

1. REACT TO SENSORY EXPERIENCE

— play simple games that emphasize each of the senses individually and in combination with one another: hearing, vision, touch, smell, taste, position, movement, muscle control
— be sensitive to your baby's reactions

2. OVERCOME OVER-EXCITABILITY

— gradually and gently introduce experiences in combination with other pleasurable and comforting experiences, help baby become self-regulated and alert using other senses

3. OVERCOME UNDER-AROUSAL

— make experiences more interesting; introduce something new while continuing to help baby be self-regulated and engaged in using his other senses

4. USE A PARTICULAR SENSE

— appeal to those senses that seem to help him become calm and alert while providing very simple stimulation to the sense he does not seem to use

baby, who is basically alert and relaxed, has a perplexed look on his face when she talks to him. The baby may also seem to have difficulty finding where the voice is coming from and perhaps looks past or away from mother. This reaction to vocal signals is a fairly subtle one and not always easy to recognize. Fortunately, "mother's intuition" is usually good at picking up on baby's missed signals.

The problem here is slightly different from that of the baby who is either over- or undersensitive to sound. Instead, the problem concerns the baby's inability to use or make "sense" of what he is taking in through his senses. If there is a problem with any of your baby's senses, your goal is to appeal to the senses that help him to brighten up, be alert, and be focused. At the same time continue to direct simple stimulation to the sense that seems to be having difficulty. For example, if your baby doesn't seem to hang on your every word, make a less complex cadence of sound while continuing to appeal to his senses of touch and vision. If the look of confusion continues, a professional consultation may help you pinpoint the problem more clearly.

Every baby has an individual rate of growth and development.

Differences in growth rates among different babies are usually quite normal. What is important is that you recognize your baby's individual rate of growth and take it into account when you care for him. Your child's individual rate may even become an asset. For example, an infant who is overly sensitive to high-pitched sounds may turn out to have an exceptionally discriminating ear. Only when your baby's sensitivity interferes with his self-regulation and alertness, or if his under- or over-sensitivity does not improve with time should you seek professional help.

Creating a Supportive Environment

The emotional climate surrounding your infant should support self-regulation and encourage interest in the world. In order to make this happen, you must be willing to *invest* whatever it takes to help your baby use her senses to be calm and alert. This means you must really get to know your infant by observing her different personality characteristics, encouraging her where she needs support, and experimenting with new ways to foster her developing abilities. Know what soothes your infant, what fosters her interest in the world, and what you need to do in order to help her pull her balancing act together.

By helping your baby calm down, for example, you are teaching her what it feels like to be tranquil and relaxed. Through experiencing and becoming familiar with this calming sensation your baby will begin developing ways to do it on her own. In fact your baby will probably model her tactics after what you do for her. The mother who talks in gentle soothing tones and periodically looks in her baby's eyes, letting the baby see her calm face, is giving her baby a picture of calm. Later on, this baby may learn that when she is upset, she can regain a feeling of calm by looking at her mother's face or listening carefully to her voice.

Parents sometimes equate this kind of investment in their baby with "spoiling" her. They think that babies who have their needs met will grow up to be demanding and never learn to cope on their own. But many babies first need to experience being calm and feel your support before they can begin to practice this on their own. You can't "spoil" your baby in the early months of life as long as you are helping her develop her abilities.

Similarly, you can invest in your baby by providing all the interesting sights and sounds for the first few months of life without fear of spoiling. Once baby realizes how interesting what she sees, hears, and feels can be, she will take an interest in the world on her own. To be sure, some babies may show a passive rather than an active interest, merely observing what you have provided—rather as if they have been given a ringside seat. If this is the case, starting at around four or five months, when your baby has greater muscle control, you can encourage her to take more initiative. As we describe in Chapter IV, you can achieve a balance between the baby's and your initiative by planning activities that require her participation.

You may be wondering, "But *how much* should I invest in my baby—that is, hold my baby, talk to my baby, be entertaining for my baby?" The answer is, "As much as it takes to help her stay calm and interested." In some cases your investment may escalate to heroic proportions: carrying your baby around in a front carrier, walking the floor through the night, trying to sleep with your baby relaxed on your abdomen. (Don't give up! These efforts should not be necessary for more than two or three months.) In other cases it means having some idea of what might interest your baby and then being alert to a response from her. Those silly faces and ridiculous sounds may be the highlights of your baby's day.

Even for babies who are naturally able to balance themselves between self-regulation and engagement, parents will want to invest time and energy to encourage them to continue. Your infant may become alert and take in the world on her own. She may find delight in interesting sights, sounds, and movements, but she will show even more delight when her mother and father are a part of these experiences. Take advantage of your baby's natural abilities, and support her continued development.

In addition to investing in your baby, there is another basic principle for creating a supportive emotional climate: Help your infant involve all her senses when she takes in the world. For example, when you offer her interesting sights, sounds, and rhythmic rocking simultaneously, she has an opportunity to practice connecting what she hears and sees with what she feels in the context of a special relationship. In other words, her world becomes more organized. A sight here, a sound or touch there, becomes a coordinated pattern of experiences as all the sensations come together. If one sense tends toward hyper- or hypo-arousal, involving the other senses can also help create a balance.

Reviewing Your Support

So far we've looked at a number of your baby's characteristics and his environment. Your own characteristics as a parent are of equal importance. Your ability to recognize who you are and what you do is extremely useful in making sure you support your baby's development to the fullest.

Though the meshing of the complexities of babyhood with those of environment and adult personality approaches fine art, there are successive steps that you can take to ensure that your infant's needs are met. These needs fall into three broad categories that apply to all of the stages of your baby's emotional development: education, introspection, and the use of professonal consultation. Education and introspection are parts of the process you can do on your own. Professional consultation can help when the other two are not enough.

Education is, by far, the simplest task ahead of you. Basically it involves becoming more aware of your baby's needs. For example, a mother who does not know that helping her baby use her senses is important may allow her placid infant to spend her waking hours watching a mobile. Should she become fussy, she feeds her or changes her diapers. Once this mother learns that it is important and appropriate to be more involved with her baby and recognizes that she is not doing this, she can change her behavior. In other words, parents sometimes need to become aware of the things they can do to support their infant's emotional development.

However, intellectual education is not always sufficient. Over time, we all develop in ways that can interfere with supporting our baby's emotional development. Introspection allows us to determine what we do, why we do it, and how we might change.

To begin, you may want to keep a diary, either in your mind or on paper. In it would be thoughts about the baby—your reactions to the baby and the baby's reactions to you. By sifting through your thoughts and actions you will be able to see where you are helping and where your feelings may interfere with her mastering the tasks of self-regulation and interest in the world. For instance, you might note when your play tends to make her fussy and when it makes her alert. Or you might discover that you do not hold your baby very much because you have a nagging worry that you may drop her. In focusing on teaching self-regulation you might examine how well you are able to calm your baby. Do you try different methods if one does not work? Are you able to use relaxed, rhythmical approaches? Do you try eye contact, voice, touch, and movement as parts of a calming pattern? What effect does the baby's irritability have on you? When considering your baby's interest in the world, think about the time you spend trying to get your baby to be bright and alert. Do you enjoy "entertaining" your baby? Are you animated and imaginative with your baby? Have you experimented with various pleasant sensory activities? Do you give your baby opportunities to use all her senses? Do you know what the baby prefers? Do you find yourself able to stop an activity before your baby becomes overstimulated? As uncomfortable as it is for any of us to look at ourselves, it is often easier to do when we realize that our baby's well-being is at issue.

If you feel somewhat constrained or anxious when comforting or interesting your baby, the problem may be in one of the following areas: a current disruptive life experience, a long-standing personality style, or a particular fear brought on by your baby's current stage of development.

YOUR FAMILY SITUATION

Strains and stresses of life that have little to do directly with your baby may also prevent you from providing him with the care he both needs and deserves. If you find that you are having trouble being involved with your baby, you may find that a family situation could be the problem. Look for conflicts with an older child, your spouse, or other family-related problems. Any of these can make you less available to your infant. And, since all families are in a constant state of flux, you will most likely find that, at one time or another during your child's development, you will be able to trace the difficulty you are having with your child to your broader family situation. If nothing surfaces within your nuclear family, examine the other major relationships in your life: important friends, work relationships—and don't forget your own stage of development (e.g., an approaching birthday or an identity crisis). Constructing a systematic profile will allow you to uncover an area of stress, anxiety, or depression that ordinarily would go unnoticed.

You will also want to take special note of the situations and relationships that you consider last. Generally, people think last of what bothers them the most. If something interferes with your relationship with your baby, it is probably because you are unaware of it. On the other hand, if you are aware of a stressful element, it probably does not interfere with your relationship.

Stressed people often focus on issues that aren't crucial to their problem. They substitute one concern for another. For example, a woman is preoccupied with proving herself at work when actually she is doing well. When she examines her various relationships, she discovers she is unhappy in her relationship with her spouse, who is somewhat withdrawn and doesn't offer the interest and support she needs. Rather than facing her lack of satisfaction in this relationship, she seeks satisfaction at work and becomes obsessed with impressing her boss, who is already sufficiently impressed. In the same way, your concern about your infant can become displaced to another area of life: you may tell yourself "my husband is too demanding," when really it is your baby's demands on you that are wearing you down. Once you systematically examine each of your relationships, however, you can root out the real issue, get to work on it, and make not only your relationship with your baby a better one, but also make your entire life more satisfying.

PARENTAL PERSONALITY STYLES

Without your knowing it or meaning for it to do so, your natural personality style may not be totally suited to your baby's development at one time or another. Though we can't always expect to be the "perfect" parent, we can identify areas within ourselves that need improvement for our baby's sake. As we support the efforts of our infant to be calm and alert, love and concern, as necessary as they are, sometimes aren't enough. We need to take into account our general styles of interacting with the baby.

You may recognize some of your own tendencies in the following descriptions. Everybody contains some elements of each of these

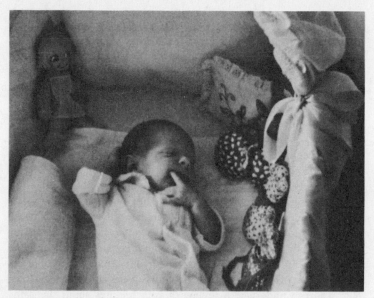

The challenge of finding your mouth—the reward of nature's pacifier.

personality styles. If you think that a particular style may be interfering in your relationship with your baby, try to step back from the
situation and think about it. (Specific suggestions follow the sections).
Try not to dwell on the most immediate and human reaction—guilt.
If you can realize that there is no such thing as the perfect parent,
and that you are far better off knowing you have a certain tendency
than not, you can then get on to improving the situation. Remember,
the seemingly perfect parent is likely to be so contrived and controlled
as to be missing the critical ingredients of spontaneity and real emotional warmth. Being human means being emotional, and being emotional means that some of your infant's needs will be easier to meet
and some more difficult. In struggling you are conveying your most
important quality: your humanness.

You should not expect every moment with your baby to make you
feel wonderful, nor should you blame yourself when you don't. The

utter helplessness of a newborn baby, which lasts for the first few months of life, can leave even the most attuned parents, especially mothers, in a mild state of shock. The baby must not only depend on your care for his every need, but he is also as yet incapable of letting you know what those needs are. And, if you happen to have an especially fussy baby, one who is particularly dependent on you to calm him down, help him eat, look, or listen—you may have the common parental feeling that the merry-go-round has not only speeded up but that the horses have started to run amuck.

If you begin to feel overwhelmed by the task of parenthood or at the sight of your helpless infant, you are not alone. Like many others, once you recognize what is going on, you can do something about it. First you need to acknowledge that life has changed—at least temporarily. You will be even more overwhelmed if you think you still need to continue your normal routine—whether that be maintaining a regular work schedule, cleaning the house, cooking special dinners, or entertaining. You should review all of your activities and omit the nonessential. Just having more time and rest can make coping easier. Next you can undertake a review of your feelings about the baby. For instance, if you are nursing and nervous that the baby isn't getting enough milk, you can talk this over with your pediatrician or someone from the LaLeche League. Once you figure out what is bothering you, you can seek out the right person to ask. Often other mothers of young children can be an invaluable source. They have recently been there themselves. If your husband is also overwhelmed, make sure you get some time together to listen to each other and be supportive. Soon enough your baby will be smiling and crawling, becoming communicative and independent, and the issue of "helplessness" may not be an issue at all.

Withdrawal or Depression.　　Depression is the most common reason for parental withdrawal. Depression can cause a parent to be emotionally unavailable and treat the baby in a mechanical way. When this happens, that baby is being undernourished as surely as if he were not getting enough to eat. In the absence of emotion babies will not "fall deeply in love" with the world, their next important milestone. For example, a first-time mother may dwell on not knowing what to do in an emergency. Feeling worried and inadequate, she may withdraw in depression. The spark of excitement for her newborn baby is extinguished—he becomes a source of anxiety, rather than joy, for her. Giving birth can also be related to depression and a semi-withdrawn state. Mothers frequently experience a short-term post-partum depression, which is physiological but can be aggravated by psychological factors. If you are depressed for more than a couple of months, however, psychological factors may be playing a large role in your state of mind.

Fathers may also become depressed after their baby's birth. After all, the introduction of a third person into a relationship, especially a baby, which requires so much attention, can be pretty disruptive to a couple's communication and intimacy. A father's feeling of being odd man out can be further increased if his wife is nursing the baby. Not only does the father not have the warm experience of feeding the baby but he must also watch as mother and baby enjoy this particularly intimate and warm experience. It is very important during this time of emotional adjustment for husband and wife to share their feelings with each other and to be sensitive to each other's needs, both for the baby's sake and for each other's—a depressed father is less able to help the mother recover from the birth and to care for the baby.

Being Overly Subdued. A personality style that seems similar to withdrawal is being overly subdued. Although they may be neither depressed nor withdrawn, people who are very subdued do not exhibit much expression or emotion. When they talk to their baby or look at her, their faces lack expression or their vocal tone may be monotonous. Obviously, this sort of behavior will give an infant a rather monotonous idea of what the world is like, but with active effort such parents can nonetheless help their baby to see the world as an interesting place. Fortunately, a consistently "flat" environment is rare. More often it is temporary stress or depression that causes a parent to become particularly unemotional. With a little effort, excessively subdued parents can still show they are emotionally available to their baby.

Overstimulation. A baby not only needs to be engaged in the world, he also needs to be relaxed and calm so that the world is seen as both an interesting and a peaceful place. Some parents' temperament and style may be such that they have to make a conscious effort to relax. For example, one working couple in high-pressure jobs were conscientious about allowing evening time for their new baby. They would rush home and play frenetically with their two-month-old son. They shook him and tossed him around, constantly making noises and changing facial expressions. Naturally, their over-wrought style left the baby irritable and crying. When they were able to understand this, they were able to find a solution: by simply giving themselves the opportunity to unwind before attending to their baby, they were able to meet their baby's need for calm but active play. They took time for the hello hugs and cuddles; they softly stroked him; they made their silly faces and noises but brought a gentleness to their motions.

OVERCOMING PROBLEMS
IN YOUR PARENTING STYLE

Don't hesitate to ask your spouse, another family member or a close friend to help you see if you have any of the personality characteristics we have noted here. Simply identifying your style may guard against its influencing your behavior with your baby. But if your personality style is more pervasive, you can take active steps to overcome it.

Even if you cannot understand why you react a certain way—and this understanding can be very difficult to gain—acknowledging your style allows you to practice a new approach. For example, if you realize that you tend to overstimulate your baby, you can try, hard as it may be, to be more patient. When you're tempted to poke or bounce your baby to get a reaction, gently stroke her and wait for a smile or a muscle movement instead. Try to get and hold your infant's attention by talking quietly. It's a challenge worth taking up.

Learning new patterns of behavior is not easy. When practicing a new approach, your old feelings may emerge and make you anxious, depressed, or frightened. This is when it is most important to tolerate your discomfort. Don't use your typical strategies, such as withdrawing or becoming overly excited, in order to minimize your discomfort. Discomfort usually means that you have found the problem. Once it's found it can be overcome. Clues as to what makes you feel uncomfortable may be found in examining typical parental fears.

COMMON PARENTAL FEARS

The common fears that parents experience at this stage in their baby's development usually stem from feeling overwhelmed by their baby's helplessness. These fears can exist consciously or unconsciously, in the extreme or in moderation. Most parents will experience at least some of these fears and feelings without necessarily interfering with their baby's growing capacities for self-regulation and interest in the world. But parents also realize that babies have very sensitive antennae and react to their moods and changes. If you are tense or anxious, your baby will experience this. So, even though it may be difficult for you to address your fears or anxieties concerning your baby, the payoff in the long run will be both a healthier baby and a healthier you.

Fears of Hurting Your New Baby.   This is one of the most common fears, especially with a first baby. Your fear may not be so unrealistic, either—your baby is small and helpless, and you are inexperienced. Your fears, however, may go beyond the fact of your baby's vulnerability and into your own background. For example, a mother may harbor resentment from having had to care for her younger brothers and sisters. She may be unaware that she fears taking out her resentment on her new baby. Your fleeting or unconscious thoughts do not mean that you are likely to harm your infant. In fact, most parents are very harsh on themselves for having such thoughts. This leads to the exaggeration of fear we are talking about. As we've said, having periodic fears of this kind can be quite routine and natural, and need not interfere at all with your basic tasks of engaging, providing a regulating environment, and taking a special pleasure in your new baby. However, if such fears cause you, for example, to hold your infant infrequently, your baby's interest in the human world and the quality of calming experiences can be compromised. To build your confidence in caring for the baby, you could find an experienced person (relative, friend, nurse) to help you. Just having someone with you to bathe the baby, clip her fingernails, or change her clothes a few times can settle your fears. A baby is not so fragile that with a little practice you shouldn't feel comfortable in caring for her.

Fear of Inadequacy.   Another common fear is the feeling that "I won't have enough to give." This is a frequent fear of mothers who are breast-feeding and may surface as the concrete concern, "I don't have enough milk to give my baby." Sometimes this may actually be the case, and if so, it must be dealt with. At other times it represents the general worry of "not having enough." Mothers who have this fear may also observe it in other areas of their lives. They may feel, "I won't do this job well enough, I won't be able to take care of my husband well enough, or I won't be as sexually giving as I ought to be." It is very common that such a fear, even if ordinarily only an occasional part of your life, may become more intense with a helpless, dependent, and demanding new baby to care for. If you notice that this fear intensifies greatly as your baby becomes more demanding and needy, you may be denying some of your own needy feelings— "I'm giving too much; I don't have any time for myself; I don't want to give any more." Some mothers think it's wrong to have such "selfish feelings." However, sometimes if a mother permits herself the luxury of such feelings, her fear may be reduced. She will also realize that becoming aware of her feelings means that she can choose when and when not to give in to them.

For instance, one mother, who finally had a baby after trying for several years, had tremendous fears of inadequacy. She feared not having good breast milk for her daughter and not having enough of it. She became depressed and began to withdraw from her baby. After a while she realized that, even though she had waited a long time for her baby, she was resentful about being tied down after so many years of independence. When she finally permitted herself to enjoy an occasional selfish feeling, she was greatly relieved to realize that having the feeling did not compromise her ability to be a loving and competent mother. While she occasionally felt that she did not have enough to give—to her baby or to herself—the feeling no longer dominated and depressed her. The irony of this feeling of inadequacy is that sometimes it becomes true—the preoccupation actually leads you not to give enough.

Fear of Being a Bad Parent. Another fear that is related to "I don't have enough to give" is "I am a bad mother (father)." You may feel that what you have to give is not good, or is not the *right thing*. If your baby cries, you feel that you are at fault. Every discomfort your baby suffers becomes further proof of your bad parenting. If such a fear becomes more than a fleeting feeling and begins to interfere with your ability to interest your baby in the world or help her learn to regulate herself, take some time to reflect on the underlying cause.

Perhaps the following example will help. A somewhat tense mother found herself so preoccupied with feeling she was a bad mother that she felt no joy toward her baby, causing the baby to show little joy toward her. On reflection she admitted that part of her feeling stemmed from the fear that someone else might find fault with her. By calling herself "bad" first, she felt she could avoid criticism. Though there were also other factors operating, including her own childhood experiences, her initial realization enabled her to be more flexible around her baby. Her tendency toward self-accusation was still obvious in other areas of her life, but she was able to untangle her baby from its effects.

Fear of Losing Independence. A common fear, particularly of mothers who have developed a career of their own, is the fear of losing independence. Unconsciously, a mother may fear becoming too dependent on her baby or too close to her, thereby losing what she has worked so hard for. This is a natural concern, particularly for independent women. However, some mothers begin to resent the closeness of their ties to their baby. Their fear of losing their independence interferes with the pleasure of their new relationship with their infant.

All parents must make a personal decision about working and how they can meet the needs of parenthood and a career. If you want to return to work full-time, try to ensure that there is a special person to care for your baby when you are not there and that when you come home you have free time for the baby. If you are working late most of the time and barely have time for the baby, then you need to reassess your motives. Sometimes you can fall into old work patterns as a means to deny your feelings of closeness to your baby. That is, it may be easier to deny temporarily your love—"out of sight is out of mind"—than to struggle with two important personal needs, your baby and your career.

Fear of Being Controlled. This is a fear that is related to the fear of losing one's independence. Mothers frequently report "my baby controls my life, I can't stand it!" How a helpless little individual, who can do nothing but cry, is able to control a grown adult is often an enigma to mothers who feel controlled; this may even increase their resentment. Yet, most parents experience these feelings. They are natural unless they begin to interfere with warmth, love, spontaneity, or the ability to comfort.

One young mother who had such feelings found that she had a tremendous desire to control her little baby. If her baby cried and she was not in the mood to give comfort, she became furious. If her baby was alert and playful when she wanted to read the newspaper, she reacted similarly. Anytime her own schedule was upset, she became annoyed. However, when she discovered that she was more controlling than her baby, she was able to see her own tendencies in perspective and become more responsive to her baby's needs. She realized that she was expressing her helplessness, not trying to control her.

Fear of Sexual Feelings. Another parental fear involves sexual feelings toward babies. While there are ample incidences of both physical and sexual abuse of babies, by and large, considering the population as a whole, these are rare phenomena. More common are uncomfortable "sexual feelings," which sometimes interfere with tenderness, engagement, and relaxation between parents and babies. For example, one father discovered that when he nuzzled his one-month-old daughter, he experienced sexual excitement. This made him very uncomfortable. As a consequence he stopped picking her up, holding her, or cuddling her altogether. Most parents feel physical pleasure toward their babies. For some, these pleasures are translated into fleeting sexual feelings. If such feelings begin to dominate to the degree that they make you uncomfortable, try to become aware of their source. The husband in our example learned he had never been comfortable being completely intimate and close to another person, even his own wife. His sexual feelings and fantasies, which were often impersonal in nature, were a way to distance himself from the more basic dependency needs and fears he felt about closeness. Once aware of this, he was slowly able to become more relaxed when comforting and enjoying his daughter. If he had an uncomfortable sexual feeling, he would reflect on the more basic issues involved.

Resolving fears is not easy. Sometimes the embarrassment we feel leads to *denial,* anxiety, and an inability to put our fears into perspective. Therefore, the first and most important step is to recognize and accept the fear. Recognition leads to the ability to think about fears and put them into context. Acceptance allows us to talk about them to our spouse, close friends, and sometimes, professionals. Fears need not become actions, if we stay aware of them.

A newborn baby is unique. Even parents of many children will tell you that each new baby has her own particular strengths and weaknesses, and needs different approaches for soothing, comforting, and engaging her attention.

Your support is invaluable to your baby during those wonderful moments of early interaction—calm, alert periods when your baby is relaxed and looking at your face, listening to your words, or moving in response to your rhythmic stroking of her body. It is your sensitivity to your infant's needs and your ability to provide the special patterns of care that will allow her to grow and flourish over these first few months. It is your help in comforting her that shows her how to be soothed and relaxed. She cannot do this for herself—yet. You must guide her. But she will learn. Treasure your baby's growing ability to be calm and alert; from this foundation she will take the leap into love.

II | FALLING IN LOVE

— 2 to 7 months

Ellie was a beautiful, dark haired, blue-eyed baby, who, from the first days of life, looked intently at her mother and seemed to take an active interest in her very attentive father. By the time she was four months old, she would look around, brightly interested in all that she saw. And when her mother or father talked to her or stroked and cuddled her, little Ellie would coo and smile so broadly that her parents were led to comment, "We can't believe little babies can express so much love." Even other adults were amazed at her intensity; she virtually lit up the room. Ellie and her parents were clearly involved in a mutual love affair. Warm, positive, and at times very intense emotional engagement took place between them. Ellie's infectious delight in the world, and especially in her parents, was a beautiful beam of love.

As your newborn moves along into the second, third, and fourth months of life, she will begin to show selective interest in the most special part of her world, namely, you. You will see that when you look, smile, and talk to her, she will begin to smile, open her eyes wide, and focus her attention on you. This is part of a general pattern of social alertness. Your baby is now becoming more responsive to external social interactions, whereas earlier she was more influenced by her inner physical sensations (e.g., hunger, gas bubbles). It is a very common experience that, sometimes earlier but usually by the second or third month, a parent will say, "She knows me—our little Jill is looking/smiling at me." From the womb, to birth, and now to recognition, the special relationship between you and your baby reaches new heights as her capacity to respond to you increases.

Now that your baby is beginning to be selective in her responses, there is a basic and delightful task that you can undertake to help her—you can encourage the loving relationship between your baby and you. This task involves encouraging a range of rich, deep feelings between the baby and you, wonderful feelings you may remember from your courtship days. There will be special moments when your infant appears enraptured with you and looks longingly into your eyes. There will be times when she brightens at your sound, mimics the movement of your mouth, relaxes to your gentle stroking, and, most important, creates an emotional presence that makes you feel unique and valued.

It is at this stage that your baby shows a growing intimacy with the human world and appears to learn what a loving relationship is in a way that you can appreciate. All of your baby's subsequent human learning depends on a human relationship; the importance of this stage cannot be overestimated. The question is, how do you encourage a deep, rich human relationship that contains the range of emerging human feelings and is, for the most part, pleasurable and positive? How do you also encourage an attachment that is rich in its physical as well as emotional contact? How do you and the baby develop that special gleam in the eye just for each other?

Observing Your Baby

The basic approach to "wooing" your baby is no different from the approach you used for helping your baby to become regulated and engaged in the world. First, identify specific strengths and weaknesses of both your baby and you, then do your best to provide the emotional climate and patterns of care that foster a deep, loving relationship.

Also remember that while we are emphasizing loving interaction between you and your baby, he needs time to just play with his toes, watch his mobile, or take in his world. Be sensitive to your baby's availability and interest. After all, babies differ in the amount of interaction they can absorb. If he enjoys 10 minutes of interacting with you but then tires from the stimulation, he has earned a rest. Even if he is difficult to woo, try to choose opportunities that seem to mesh with his mood. Wooing should be a rewarding experience for both of you, not an overwhelming one for your baby.

As with any stage, there are issues that are special to the task at hand. The four major areas for parents to observe at this stage are:

FORMING RELATIONSHIPS, ESPECIALLY WITH PRIMARY CAREGIVERS

Is your baby starting to reach out emotionally and respond to you and others? Is your baby beginning to show a preference for mother, father, siblings, or babysitter?

Many babies at this stage show that they want to be involved with other people. They study your face as you talk, return your smiles with a special glow all their own, and cuddle softly into your shoulder—you woo each other and learn about love together. For many babies these responses come naturally or with little effort on the parents' parts. Others require some special attention. It is at this point that you can teach your baby what falling in love is all about. After all, how can he learn what love *is* unless you show him?

If you notice that your baby does not demonstrate a special reaction toward you, the solution may be as simple as spending more time with your baby, being a little warmer, or making more of an effort to interest her. If your baby does not sustain a period of loving attachment with you for more than a few minutes, even after you have become the world's most fascinating person, try to anticipate the baby's attention span for intimacy. Just before the fussiness begins, shift the activity to something more physical or less intimate. Afterward, return to the wooing posture. Try to make each wooing interval slightly longer, gradually increasing your baby's interest in emotional closeness. Starting with a few such intervals a day gives your baby an opportunity to fall in love without being overwhelmed with constant wooing.

Should it become difficult to make loving contact with your baby, either because he withdraws or becomes overexcited, first be patient and position yourself so that your baby is held securely, can see you, and can touch you. Then, if the baby is still withdrawn, patiently respond to his actions—a brief look, a smile, or vocalization—with a loving reaction that emotionally pulls him to you. Although you may be tempted to jiggle, bounce, or tickle your baby, or to raise the volume of your voice, it will probably frighten him away and may even result in his stiffening his muscles, turning away, and looking every place but at you. If your infant provides no initial "opening" (look, smile, or movement) to build your loving on, then try gentle, interesting vocalizations, glances, rhythmic movements, or interesting objects to provoke a reaction. You may have to be fairly persistent and ingenious to help get things started. Once your infant is involved with you, you can gently explore his or her special likes and dislikes in greater depth.

If your infant tends to be hyper-excitable, your task is to be soothing and wooing simultaneously. For example, first use only facial expressions that are calming. Reserve your more expansive vocal tones for when you have established a wooing rhythm with your baby. Once he has discovered a calm, loving harmony, you can experiment with new, more lively expressions.

After three or four weeks, you should begin to see some progress— a baby that returns your smile and brightens when you woo him. If your baby remains withdrawn or hyper-excitable and continues to be emotionally removed, or if his fleeting, loving gaze does not gradually mature into a more rapturous glow, you will probably want to seek a professional consultation.

Remember, a loving relationship does not have to be limited to parents. If another family member or a babysitter routinely cares for your baby, that person should also try to elicit a special attachment. It is sometimes hard, especially for a working mother, to watch her baby be affectionate with a babysitter. She may be resentful of the other person or not encourage the warmth between baby and sitter.

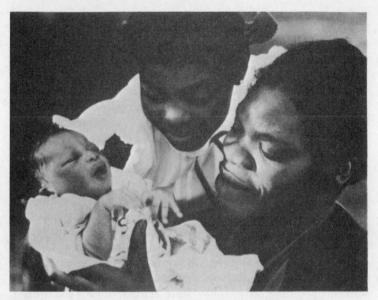

Falling in love begins with the love you give your baby from the beginning.

However, your baby has more than enough warmth to share. Her emotional exchanges with another person do not mean that you have been replaced. And without the sustenance of a loving relationship with her caregiver, her day would be empty indeed. Assuming that your baby does not become overwhelmed by too many people, a few close relationships can be enriching. Each new person provides a different way of interacting, and stimulates different interests.

QUALITY OF RESPONSE

Are your baby's reactions emotionally rich and full? Is she gradually increasing her capacity for warmth and physical affection?

The quality of your baby's response to your engaging smiles should contain some feeling of warmth, need, and interest. Although your three-month-old infant's smile may not embody total enrapturement, it should hold the promise of more to come. If your infant's smile seems imitative and/or if her look is not focused on you, she may be missing out on the emotional connection. Helping your baby move toward a deeper emotional attachment requires fine-tuning your wooing efforts. Either become more expansive and emotional if your baby is a little hard to reach, or become less so if your baby becomes overwhelmed by facial gestures, cooing, or movement. Over three or four weeks your efforts should result in a deepening emotional response. If she remains only semi-involved it may mean you are not wooing her in a way that appeals to her. If experimenting with different wooing methods doesn't work, you should consider the sincerity of your feelings and whether you are tired or preoccupied when you are with your baby.

STABILITY DURING PERIODS OF ATTACHMENT

When you and your baby are looking, babbling, nuzzling and loving, is the interruption of a sneeze or a gas bubble easily overcome?

Over time, your baby should be showing an increasing capacity to maintain a loving exchange. The interchange that lasted for a minute or two should grow to five or even ten minutes. When the wooing is interrupted by a loud noise or a jostle, a baby whose attachment is stable will quickly be able to return to a state of involvement with you. This stability reflects, in part, the baby's capacity to cope with stress and maintain his or her developmental accomplishments.

With a baby whose attachment is less stable, you may have to spend more time, first wooing baby, then letting the baby woo you. Pay special attention to what helps your baby recover after stress— for instance, a calming smile, soothing voice, gentle massaging, or rhythmic motion. Knowing this, you can practice helping the baby as needed—then see if she can gradually become more assertive. For example, woo your baby with a pattern that works—say, smiling calmly—then stop and see if she tries to copy you and woo you back. "Practice makes perfect" may be an overstatement, but it does help considerably.

USE OF THE SENSES

Does your baby look at people, like to move rhythmically, and use her other senses, such as touch or hearing, to foster a loving relationship?

Your baby will experience a loving relationship more fully if she

45

can relate to another person by using all of her senses. If your baby doesn't seem to use a sense, you can encourage her by combining an activity she enjoys with one that uses the sense she ignores or that irritates her.

For example, Jamie, at four months, would smile and show pleasure but purposefully avoid eye contact with her parents. She seemed frightened and overstimulated by a human face. She responded well to sounds, rocking, and touch, but without the special visual communication between parent and child that usually develops around this age, her parents began to feel rejected. "She shows more interest in her red music box than she shows in us," Jamie's parents lamented. Fortunately, they did not give up on Jamie by waiting for her to "grow out of it," nor did they leap to the conclusion that something was terribly wrong with their child. Instead, they assumed that Jamie was a baby who simply took longer to warm up than most, and they set to work, finding ways to help her respond to them. Since they knew she responded to their voices, her parents held her upright, facing them. When Jamie began to look away from them, they could encourage her to look toward them again by making interesting sounds. Babies particularly enjoy a vocal cadence that has novelty at the end, a "dum, dum . . . da!" Over time, the "look and talk" game increased the amount of time Jamie was able to look directly at her parents.

Another approach also used the principle of combining Jamie's pleasant and unpleasant sensory experiences to accustom her gradually to using the sense she found unpleasant. Jamie's red music box played a central role. Her father would use the music box to capture Jamie's attention. As she gazed at the toy, her father would gradually move it in front of his face, so that Jamie had contact with a smiling face while she looked at the toy. After a while she became more comfortable with her father's face, then intrigued by it. The toy was then used in a simple game of peek-a-boo. The day that Jamie finally smiled directly at her father was a day of triumph and celebration. After a sustained effort her parents had finally managed to "break the ice." Though Jamie still took up to fifteen minutes to begin to respond while another baby might take only a few seconds, their continuing support and pride in their daughter's breakthrough eventually turned her tentative smile into a broad and welcoming one. From there she learned fast and was soon studying her parents' facial expressions, babbling away to them, returning their smiles with sparkling pleasure, and moving her body in rhythm to theirs.

Looking back, Jamie's parents knew she didn't have particular difficulty with any of her senses. She seemed to hear well, see well, experience touch comfortably. It was as though her interest in the human world did not develop as rapidly and spontaneously as did her other interests. The new sense of warmth and relatedness Jamie's parents felt with their daughter was proof enough that they had chosen the right course to follow.

Incidentally, the principle of combining a pleasant activity with an unpleasant one can be useful in many practical situations. Let's say you are nursing your baby and at five months you want to wean her to a bottle. When you give her the bottle, she cries and turns her head. Chances are, she can be convinced to take the bottle if the atmosphere is sufficiently "wooing" and engaging. For example, lie her on your lap between your thighs so that she can make eye contact with you and can watch your changing facial expressions. In addition you can softly sway your legs and talk to her sweetly. Once she is relaxed and enraptured, she will probably try the bottle if you offer it to her gently. As with many of us, extra inducements can make an experience less offensive. Gradually she will begin to drink from the bottle, have her diapers changed, or agree more readily with your other cooperative ventures.

If your baby has become more involved with you and others, if she has developed a special relationship with you and her other caregivers, if she feels and expresses warmth and responsiveness, if she can maintain her loving exchanges despite interruptions, and if she seems to reach out to you with all her senses, she is well on her way to "falling in love." But it may be hard for you to tell if she is *not* doing these things. We are often unaware of how good an infant's bright smiles, cooing, and animated gestures make us feel, so we often do not recognize our reaction to a baby who is unexpressive. Billy was a passive but sweet and comfortable infant—he responded to rocking by nuzzling closer; he "purred" when sung to. But at six months Billy had trouble focusing on his parents' faces and looked right past them when they beamed at him. Like most of us, his parents felt discouraged at not receiving a response but didn't identify the discouragement for what it was. Instead they "pulled away" from him emotionally. They began to be more self-involved—to talk more on the phone to their friends and to feel they "needed" to go out more. They lost the emotional spark from their relationship with Billy.

Parents should use this change of interest in their baby as a clue that his developmental pattern may require a thorough evaluation. In some instances, for example, a baby's unresponsiveness can be a signal of a delay in motor development. Some parents of children who evidenced motor delays (such as abnormal lags in sitting up, crawling, and walking) recall that they did in fact gradually pull away from their baby at that time. Your own change in interest may signal that the baby is having some difficulty which may be a physically related motor lag as well as a primary emotional problem. Pulling away from an infant with a motor delay will often accentuate the lag. He needs extra practice, not less.

As mentioned, a change in attitude toward your baby can result from many circumstances: work problems, family patterns, problems with other children. While it is critical to explore these areas, you must also always ask whether your baby may be contributing to your feelings. As a clue to the answer, pay attention to your feelings. Watch to see, as you try to interact with your baby, if the two of you find a rhythm, or if, as you vocalize and gesture, the baby can't quite follow you and respond. Particularly between two and ten months, when babies are falling in love and learning to communicate, parents may be the first to recognize that something is interfering with their mastering this ability, and that the baby may need some help with coordinating his muscles and senses.

An evaluation can determine if your baby needs special exercises to help develop muscle tone and motor skills. Your pediatrician may recommend an occupational or physical therapist who can prescribe these exercises and even show you how to practice with the baby. These practice sessions can result in enormous progress, for babies are extremely flexible and love to practice new challenges.

Creating a Supportive Environment

If there is one basic principle for parents to remember during this important stage of emotional development, it is this: woo your baby. You provide your infant with his first experience in a relationship,

Helping Your Child . . .

1. FORM A RELATIONSHIP WITH YOU

— be warm and interesting
— be patient, position yourelf so the baby can see you and is secure
— anticipate your baby's attention span for intimacy; before fussiness begins, switch to another activity, then later return to wooing
— for a withdrawn baby, look for and respond to baby's fleeting gestures
— for a hyper-excitable baby, soothe him and woo him with calming gestures

2. RESPOND TO WOOING

— fine-tune your wooing efforts
— for a withdrawn baby, become expansive and emotional
— for an excitable or fretful baby, become calm and subtle

3. MAINTAIN STABILITY

— pay attention to which patterns help your baby recover after stress
— use these patterns, then stop to see if the baby tries to continue on his own to woo you and calm down

4. USE HIS SENSES

— integrate an unpleasant sensory experience with a pleasant one

and you can make certain it is a fulfilling one. Many of the steps for creating a supportive atmosphere are similar to those described in Chapter I: be sensitive to your baby's individual differences, provide interesting experiences, involve all your baby's senses and take advantage of those activities that provide particular joy. In addition, in the "falling in love" phase, you must also foster mutual engagement, attachment, and fascination that is emotionally rich and stable. This is a need quite distinct from your baby's earlier requirements.

For example, consider a baby whose parents worked and who was cared for by a babysitter. During the first few months, the baby learned to be soothed and also to be bright and alert. The parents spent some time with their son in the evenings, and the sitter played with and comforted the baby during the day. However, the sitter was used to performing the activities of engaging and comforting the baby somewhat mechanically. Although her efforts were good enough to get the baby to be alert, she emanated little personal warmth. As the baby developed and became ready to form deep attachments, his sitter was not emotionally available, and his parents, who loved him, did not spare enough time to develop a deep, pleasurable rapport. Even though the same people were caring for him that had cared for him before, this baby's needs had changed, and he did not have a person with whom to develop a rich relationship.

Although parents or other caretakers often project a deep, warm feeling even before the infant is able to reciprocate, this does not always happen. Falling in love may not happen naturally on your baby's part, and wooing may not be natural for you or your baby's other caregivers. Especially if your baby is difficult, it may take "work" to achieve these joyful interchanges that can be felt but are hard to describe.

In order to help your baby fall in love, you must set aside time when you are not preoccupied or distracted, for pleasure and loving. Involve your baby's senses and motor coordination with activities such as eye contact, talking, looking for imitative mouth movements, nuzzling, and giving your baby an opportunity to explore your face. (He'll pull your hair or nose, or try to put his little fingers into your mouth.) Don't be discouraged if your infant is unresponsive or irritable. It will always be your task to be more innovative, expansive, and patient with your baby and to reach out as far as it takes.

Although joyous expressions of love are incomparably pleasurable for parents, all loving relationships also involve the other side—frustration and anger. Don't stop your wooing as soon as your infant begins to protest; stay engaged and show him how supportive a loving relationship can be. Your baby may push you away, seem to reject you. This is not exactly delightful behavior, on top of which you will have to put in the time and effort to soothe him. However, it is important to tolerate his anger so that your baby learns that it is acceptable to be assertive in protest. Your attitude of invested interest heightened by the desire to develop a loving relationship will help see you through.

Reviewing Your Support

As your baby grows, the specific questions you ask yourself about your support of her growth will naturally change—different babies have different needs at different times. To assess your support for

---

Creating a Supportive Environment

1. Woo your baby, let him learn about love from you
2. Set aside time for pleasant and loving exchanges
3. Tolerate and continue to woo a baby who is upset or protesting

---

this milestone—your baby's "falling in love"—begin by examining your loving relationship with your baby. Do you woo your baby and attract her attention? Do you try to woo her even when she is fussy? Do you take deep pleasure in developing a loving experience for both of you? Does your baby have a special, bright look for you? Do you address all of her senses and motor abilities, and use a range of emotions to woo her? If you are keeping a diary, look over your thoughts and reactions with these questions in mind. Knowing that your goal is to encourage your baby's interest in people, and in you in particular, you should be able to spot any obstacles. Also keep in mind the different areas from which trouble can spring: your own strong reaction, a family problem, a personality style, or a fear evoked by this stage of your baby's development.

YOUR FAMILY SITUATION

Joan had practiced law before her daughter Beryl was born, and when Beryl was six months old, she planned to return to work. She carefully checked around for child-care options until she found a woman close by who cared for children in her home. After finding the woman both warm and emotionally nurturing, she gradually introduced Beryl to the woman and to the new setting.. At first she stayed there with Beryl. After a few days Joan was able to leave her with the woman for a few hours. She gradually increased the time over the course of two weeks until she was certain that Beryl felt secure with the woman. Joan went back to work. For the first weeks everything went well. Then suddenly Beryl began waking up at night and clinging to her mother. Even though Joan had been very sensitive to Beryl's adjustment to their new pattern, she had not recognized a common pitfall for working mothers, and had fallen into it.

When Joan came home from work at night, she tried to make up for lost time with Beryl. She tried to squeeze a day's worth of inter-

Four-month-old Johnny and his mommy showing the joy of falling in love.

action into a couple of hours. To do this, Joan tended to become overly controlling, intrusive, and hyper-stimulating. There was no time for simply relaxing together, though Beryl longed for a quiet, soothing time with her mother. Her midnight wakings were an expression of the anxiety caused by the frantic "quality time" with her mother.

It's not unusual for working mothers to go in the other direction as well. Some mothers deny feelings of guilt or deprivation about not being with their child. They may withdraw and become aloof, taking the existential position "We each live in our own space." Many working mothers do not realize (perhaps because they feel they can't) how much they miss their children and how much they feel they are sacrificing in order to have their careers. (This is not to suggest they should not do both.) Rather than tolerating the fact that they miss their children, they may feel competitive with their babysitters. In order to make the emotional burden easier, they distance themselves from their children.

If you are, or plan to be, a working mother, try to identify what your natural patterns of coping with emotional stress tend to be. Do you become anxious and disorganized, withdrawn, hyper-excitable? If you know what signs to watch for, you will be better able to identify if you are feeling stressed, so that you can work on the problem and observe any potential impact on your child. With a clear head and fewer unnecessary emotional burdens, you'll be both a better mother and a better worker.

As we have already discussed, your current relationship with your spouse, other children, parents, friends, or work associates may influence the love relationship with your baby. A sudden change in the relationship with your baby or in your baby's established patterns could indicate outside interferences. For example, a disruption in your baby's sleep pattern could be related to your being too preoccupied with some other relationship to give adequate attention and love during the day. Your baby may feel insecure and rejected. (Always consider your infant's physical health and normal maturation when you notice behavioral changes.) Since a stress in one area of your life can be displaced onto another area, examine *each* relationship honestly and systematically to be aware of any hidden feelings or changed behavior.

PARENTAL PERSONALITY STYLES

As we've already seen in the phase of self-regulation and interest in the world, there are some parental personality styles that are not naturally complementary to a specific stage of development. In the case of the potential love relationship between a parent and infant, the same overall styles that might interfere with self-regulation and emerging interest in the world can also hamper a child ready to "fall in love." Only now, at this new stage of development, these "styles" create a new challenge for the infant.

Withdrawal or Depression. When a mother is depressed, she may find that all her energies go to provide physical care for her baby. She feels she has no emotional energy left to smile, coo, and effectively woo her baby. With a baby who is very animated, the mother may not need to woo very intently. But with a baby who is herself a little withdrawn, the mother's inability to be persistent would hamper the baby's capacity to fall in love. When the baby is at last ready to *respond* to emotions, the mother is spent; she cannot gurgle in response to her baby or return her smile. After a while the baby may begin to reflect the mother's look and tone—somber and emotionless. Babies can have their own form of depression when they reach out for love and are not met.

If a mother is at home full-time, providing a daily continuum of support and care, the father is then the one who adds a little spice to the baby's life. He may go away to work in the morning, but his return gives a lift to the day. Even if the father is not the only working parent, and unique in that respect, he broadens the baby's experience, because most people favor one form of interacting over others—maybe cuddling and holding over animated movements—and having both parents involved with the baby enriches the baby's life. The father is also the one who gives the mother support, both emotionally and physically. If the father is depressed and can't be supportive, the mother could find the baby trying and overwhelming. A depressed father can be just as critical as a depressed mother.

Being Overly Subdued. Being very subdued may be related at times to fears of being assertive. A parent may think, subconsciously, "If I reach out, I may either hurt someone or be rejected." Some babies are so wooing that they can help a parent who is feeling subdued to reach back. A passive baby, however, needs a parent who can recognize his laid-back style and do the reaching—the very thing the subdued parent has trouble with. A stand-off won't work. Someone has to reach out. Often, if one parent is very subdued, the other one can lead the way.

Overstimulation. Sometimes, when parents feel anxious or frustrated, or are frightened by gentle intimacy, they are tempted to get a reaction from their baby by aggressive means. Especially when "revved-up" parents are matched with babies who are "slow to warm," parents may "playfully" shake and poke, aggressively tickle, or even butt the baby in the chest with their heads. If these temptations overtake you on occasion, try to replace them with patience and wooing. If you want to prod, make a facial expression (and not a scary one!) instead. Should you get the urge to shake, try a soothing voice pattern. Your challenge is to keep your baby from recoiling or withdrawing from you by meeting him on *his* level of intensity.

There are other styles to watch for as you develop a love relationship with your baby. Most of us will recognize these feelings within ourselves to some degree, but most will not act on them consistently. Only when these traits are strongly present must you take a hard look at your relationship to your baby, and take steps to improve it.

Seeing Baby as a Plaything. Let's take the extreme example of one mother who liked to call her baby "my little doll." At times the mother found her baby amusing and would smile and play with her, enjoying her smile in return. At other times, however, she ignored her baby's attempts to communicate. When the baby showed anger, her mother simply left her in her crib. The mother thought that her "doll" was there only to bring her satisfaction. She herself felt she had never been treated as a person while growing up; consequently, she had never learned to relate to other people as people. Deep down, however, she worried about hurting her baby: thinking of her baby as a doll who "couldn't be hurt" diminished the painful fear. So she functioned at the level of either having or not having her own needs met, ignoring her deeper fears that she could not meet others' needs. For example, in conversation she would listen until she heard the answer to her question, then would interrupt and talk about something else.

As her baby developed and demonstrated a personality and special needs of her own, the mother became frustrated and discouraged. She began to leave the baby alone in her crib for hours at a time. The baby, who had begun to smile, interact, and show pleasure in the world, soon turned into a baby who became irritable and unpredictable. It wasn't until the baby showed a lag in motor development—an inability to sit up—that her pediatrician asked some questions and suggested professional counseling for the mother.

The Baby as an Extension of the Parents. Although many parents indulge in fantasies of what they would like their child to be, they recognize these fantasies for what they are and do not let them intrude into their nurturing. Some parents, however, become so involved with their ideal that they actually expect their baby to accomplish the things in life they have not. Sometimes this is related to a difficulty in dealing with feelings of loss and disappointment. A mother who relates to her baby only to "show" others what "the two of them can do" might be an example. Should her baby smile gleefully, the mother might return a mechanical smile, then quickly turn to a friend for admiration. When the baby becomes fussy, the mother might put her down so as not to "spoil" her. A "spoiled, temperamental" baby might mean that she is a baby who cannot carry out all of her mother's plans.

Difficulty Experiencing a Wide Range of Emotions. Sometimes a parent may be able to engage the baby and offer a loving relationship but have trouble helping the baby experience a variety of loving, playful, or assertive interactions. Babies are capable of showing a full range of emotions, which might be overwhelming to some adults. They may react to anger and protest by getting overly upset, to extremely joyful play by withdrawal. Your baby will soon learn to restrict his display of emotions to those that receive the most satisfying responses, a loss for both child and parent.

OVERCOMING PROBLEMS IN YOUR PARENTING STYLE

The personality styles just described can result from varied emotional conflicts. But at this particular stage of your baby's development, conflicts with closeness and intimacy are the most prevalent reason for these personality styles. Although you may not understand the source of the conflict, you can still change your approach to wooing your child. Just recognizing that something is interfering with joyful wooing is the first step toward correcting the problem. The second step is to establish a pattern of mutual wooing; baby and parents can work as a family in this challenge. Discover your uncomfortable feelings, what you tend to do about them (avoid, overstimulate), and then experiment with more adaptive patterns. If you can do these things, you've won ninety percent of the battle. Don't hesitate to call on family and friends; they can be very supportive and instructive. If you find yourself unable to adapt to the needs of your baby, take advantage of professional help to learn about feelings that you may be avoiding. Often the identification of your fear may provide the clue to a personality trait you have been wondering about.

COMMON PARENTAL FEARS

A number of parental fears are common to the stage of falling in love and may occur in mild form in many normal healthy mothers, fathers, or other caregivers. In exaggerated form, however, they can begin to interfere with a close relationship with your baby, and so it is useful to consider them.

Fear of Closeness. The fear of closeness is often related to underlying fears of losing your sense of self. To identify this fear, examine how you feel when being intimate with your baby. If you experience discomfort, think of similar intimate situations and your level of comfort or discomfort. Awareness of discomfort with a basic feeling such as closeness can sometimes free you to engage your baby in a deep, rich attachment. Awareness alone may not cure your worry or fear in all relationships, but it can provide a foundation for resolving the problem.

A basically well-intended mother did well in the first few months of her baby's life, but was unsure of her sense of self when "in love." In her past, intimate relationships led to her losing her sense of who she was and who the other person was. While this sense of fusion or merging comforts some people, it made her very uncomfortable. She would immediately assert her independence. Similarly, she responded to her healthy, robust baby and his affectionate longings for her by prematurely trying to teach him independence. When he reached out for her and tried to nuzzle, she would move away, rationalizing that she was teaching him to be strong. Underneath, it was her fear of intimacy and closeness that caused her to do this. When her husband noticed that their baby was becoming less responsive, they discussed the baby's reactions. After some reflection the mother was able to identify her discomfort with closeness. Although she was unable to remove the feeling completely, she found that by focusing on her baby's smallness and helplessness, she could begin to respond to his desire for closeness and gradually initiate some reaching out on her own.

Fear of Rejection. Another frequent fear is that of being rejected. To some people, sensitivity to rejection, which is perfectly understandable, is seen as a trait to deny. Meanwhile, underneath a calm exterior lurks a mother, father, or other caregiver who is ready to interpret any action on the baby's part as a lack of love. Parents may become particularly sensitive as their baby becomes more socially interactive and capable of warm human contact. When she is fussy, frustrated, or simply tired, they immediately conclude "she doesn't love me." Such a thought may be only fleeting and can be excused as "meaning nothing"—in most instances it does, in fact, mean nothing. But, if you are such a parent and your anxious and uncomfortable feelings during your baby's frustrated moments hamper effective comforting, try to determine whether fear of rejection is a prominent concern of yours. Ask yourself whether you experience this fear in your other relationships? If so, then there is a good chance it may also be playing a role in your relationship with your baby.

Fear of rejection may become aggravated by babies who are especially irritable and have trouble focusing attention on their mothers or with babies who are apathetic and withdrawn. Babies who cannot give enough to make their mothers feel loved and accepted require a mother who is very secure and who can pursue and woo them. The mother who is sensitive to being rejected may find it extremely difficult to be the *wooer*. She expects wooing and comforting herself.

Occasionally the mother who is sensitive to rejection "overwoos" her baby. In other words, instead of admitting her sensitivity, she says, "Me, afraid of rejection? Never—I take what I want and I get what I take." Her aggression and intrusiveness are symptoms of her underlying fear. Her baby, on the other hand, may often feel overwhelmed.

Let's complicate our poor mother's problem with a daytime babysitter. The mother, who is away most of the day and feels guilty about it, sees her baby cuddle and nuzzle with another mothering figure. Feelings of rejection, betrayal, and jealousy are all stirred up. The mother's reaction might include "giving the baby up" to the babysitter or competing for the baby's signs of affection. But the baby can be quite comfortable with a strong attachment to more than one caregiver. With a few close relationships, your baby can experience a variety of ways of interacting. A babysitter is no different from a relative with whom the baby is very familiar. But *you* are special.

Feelings of Envy. Envy is perhaps one of the most difficult feelings to deal with, and it is not uncommon that it is stirred up as parents watch the emerging abilities of their growing baby. As your baby becomes a person and develops his capacity for social interaction, he often shows great joy and contentment. Some parents may secretly envy their baby's calm, carefree, and cared-for state. One mother dealt with these feelings by trying to "overdo" for her baby; she was at her infant's beck and call. Another mother dealt with similar feelings by vacillating—one day she was tuned in and in love with her baby, the next day she saw her baby as selfish and greedy.

If you are envious of your baby, certain clues may show up. Excessive teasing of the baby is one. You start, for instance, to give the baby a toy and pull it away abruptly. Excessive anger is another. Although babies can be very frustrating, some patience needs to go with the job. If the baby is always irritating you, something more must be riling you. And lastly, there is feeling competitive with the baby. If you find yourself thinking, "He or she (your spouse) gives her more attention than me," this reflects on your attitude toward the baby. It may be that your spouse is not being supportive of you, but talk to him or her about it. Don't take it out on the baby.

If you find your feelings veering in the direction of envy, the first thing you can do is to recognize and accept what you feel. Awareness lets you see the feelings in the perspective of other emotions. Also, look to see if *you* are getting adequate emotional support. Maybe your husband could be more admiring of your job rather than complaining that the baby wakes him up at night. Talk to those friends or relatives who will make you feel more esteemed. You need some stroking, too. Then there will be less competition with the baby.

Fear of Hurting Your Baby.   Your baby's helplessness, size, and dependence can easily evoke the fear that you might hurt her. This fear, however, can lead to an overprotective, overintrusive attitude or, at the other extreme, an attitude of emotional withdrawal and physical distancing. A parent's preoccupation can intrude into loving moments between parent and baby. For example, a mother may suddenly become anxious as she playfully sways with her baby, and will hastily return the baby to the safety of her crib.

If you fear your baby will be hurt, examine your other intimate relationships for similar fears. A fearful person might, for example, stand by the window, watching for her husband's return, and wondering whether he has been in an auto accident. If you see that fears of hurting your baby are part of a common pattern, try to put them in perspective by realizing how seldom your fears come true.

Fear of Sexual Feelings.   The sexualization of the relationship with one's baby is another common fear at this stage. As we've mentioned, some mothers and fathers, when they feel deeply affectionate, quickly

Once you've established a loving relationship it's time to move on to dialogue: there's more than one way to tell Mom it's time to go.

translate their feelings into adult-type erotic and sexual longings, and may even experience sexual arousal. Having such feelings toward your little baby may frighten you and cause you to withdraw. But remember that such a feeling comes out of a context of special intimacy with another human being. This can reassure you that it is normal, and, at the same time, inhibit you from acting inappropriately. Your awareness can keep your special relationship with your baby from being dominated by this fear.

In fact, identification of the main emotional issue can remove at least some of the anxiety around any experience and allow you greater flexibility with your baby. If you are able to pinpoint precisely the moment that your anxiety begins, you can defuse it and maintain a rich, intimate attachment with your baby. This is a great deal to do, and it comes more easily to some than to others. If you, with family or peer support, cannot seem to alter your pattern of reactions, professional consultation may be your best solution.

The quality of your baby's first relationship is not only important in its own right but also for the building of his other relationships in life. Fostering your relationship requires an understanding of your baby's individuality and of your own emotional response to entering into a rich and loving attachment. Don't be afraid to acknowledge that certain aspects of your relationship with your baby, or even your baby's presence alone, can make you anxious, depressed, or withdrawn. Some negative reaction to your baby is common and need be considered a problem only if it interferes with your being intimate and relaxed with him.

What is most important during this phase is that you woo your baby when he is happy as well as when he is fussy. In this way you will encourage a relationship that has emotional range and depth. Be imaginative in your wooing, especially if your baby is irritable, withdrawn, or under-responsive. Should you have a difficult baby, much effort will be required on your part. But your reward will be your four- or five- or seven-month-old, looking with eyes only for you, lighting the room with a joyful smile.

III | DEVELOPING
INTENTIONAL COMMUNICATION

—3 to 10 months

Between his third and tenth month, it may seem as if your baby is changing from a one-man band into a three-ring circus. No longer a little bundle of instincts and reflexes whose focus is solely on himself, your baby is reaching out to the world—physically, mentally, and emotionally. During these next few months your three-ring circus will feature communication in the center ring. But make no mistake, this is a family affair. Your part will be to foster intentional communication with your baby.

You can do this by responding to your infant's signals reciprocally, which means returning your baby's smile with your own or reaching out with your hand when the baby reaches out with his. In short, your two-way interchange begins taking on a cause-and-effect quality. Your baby realizes that his actions can elicit a response from you, that what *he* feels and does makes a difference. What a step forward that is! Your baby's capacity for responding has already begun to develop throughout the first two stages, but it now takes on a quality of intent that wasn't there before. Mother and baby are not just vocalizing or smiling at each other randomly; each is responding to the other's signals. Your look of surprise will get a look in reaction. As your baby begins to babble, your responsive sounds will keep him going. At seven or eight months he may pat or stroke a stuffed toy in imitation of you.

As your infant's capacity for complex interactions begins to emerge, your goal is to read his communications or signals and systematically respond to them—that is, to be a good communicator. You'll feel your mutually loving relationship become even richer as it begins to include more complex "discussions." These discussions, which may be silent, involve *responding* to your baby's signals through *any* of the sensory-motor systems that your baby uses and *initiating* communication via any and all of these systems.

When you read and respond to your baby's specific emotional communications, he is learning that his actions and emotional expressions result in reactions from the world. For example, when your baby is gleeful and happy and you vigorously return these emotions, the baby begins to realize that his joy can cause your joy. This link gives him a beginning sense that he can have a pleasurable impact on the world—a most important foundation for optimism and trust—and also that there is a relationship between what he does and how "the world" responds. This cause-and-effect understanding is the essence of reality testing. Your baby is not born knowing he can cause something to happen; he must be taught by your reciprocation of his emotional responses.

Reality testing—that is, learning about cause-and-effect relationships—begins to develop gradually after the first few months. For example, early in the first half of the first year, if you give your baby a string with a bell on it, he will pull the string and hear the bell. If the bell is removed your baby will still pull the string. He does not yet connect the pulling of the string with the sound of the bell.

However, as your baby begins to show the capacity for interactive communication, removing the bell from the string will cause your baby to stop pulling the string, because pulling the string is no longer an end in itself; it is done in order to make the bell ring. Your baby has a beginning appreciation of causality. This logical relationship to the world will not be fully organized until middle childhood (from ages four through seven). Nonetheless, the earliest foundations are set in place through these initial encounters with cause-and-effect relationships.

In the world of objects, cause-and-effect relationships are fairly straightforward. If your baby hits a bell with his hand, he will hear a sound. If he takes a block and bangs it on the floor, he will feel pressure and hear a sound. In these situations he readily experiences that his action causes something to happen. In your baby's emotional world, predictability is not so easy to come by. He may smile at you, but you may be preoccupied and not return the smile. His smile has not brought any reaction on this occasion. He doesn't learn the effect of showing happy feelings—that is, pleasurable signals in return. If he receives no reaction repeatedly, he may become confused and gradually stop showing these feelings. On another occasion you may smile back. If you smile back at him enough times, he will come to feel that, in the world of human interaction and emotions, he has a reliable impact. Do not expect to reciprocate each of your baby's overtures. He can figure out your general tendency. He also needs to learn a little "modesty." Let's look at the example of William.

William was a robust eight-month-old. When his mother called to him, he usually answered with a loud assortment of babble. When she handed him a block, he reached for it and took it. Sometimes he raised his arms and gestured at his mother while he made all kinds of noises. His mother would hand him a toy and he would grab it and then relax, as though he had been trying to tell her that was what he wanted. If it wasn't what he wanted, he would push the toy away and continue gesturing. (Not acknowledging that he really wanted another toy but instead insisting that he wanted the first one would confuse and understandably anger him.) He made loud noises to get attention, then dazzled his parents with a gleeful smile to which they couldn't fail to respond. When William was mad he screamed and waved his fists. There was no question that William experienced a range of emotion, from pleasure and warmth to anger and protest, that he was assertive and curious and that, most important, he was able to orchestrate his feelings to promote a "dialogue." He was intentional. He both expected and got responses to his overtures.

When William's father came home in the evening, William's face brightened. He would crawl over to his waiting father and give him an adoring look. When picked up, he would nuzzle in close to his father's neck. William's father was amazed at the way his son communicated with him. He would frequently say, "I feel like we are talking together. He's like a little person, not a baby."

William was particularly gifted in communicating a range of feelings. Usually children excel in some areas—say, assertiveness—and need some support to develop others—perhaps pleasure. Since each child will have his own individual differences, you may need to experiment with how to elicit the various emotions from your child.

Observing Your Baby

Observing the ways in which your baby communicates and the extent to which she is *able* to communicate is useful for knowing where she is in relation to this third milestone of her emotional life. As with all other stages, your observations can help you find ways to foster your baby's development in this area. Your patience and love will welcome her as she enters into her "dialogue with the world."

RECIPROCAL INTERACTION

Does your baby reach out emotionally and respond to you?

You can encourage a reciprocal interaction between you and your baby by finding a behavior such as a smile, frown, arm movement, or sound that is easy for baby to do, then using this behavior as the basis for interacting. This interaction may happen either naturally or with just a little prodding from you. In some cases, you may first have to concentrate on gaining your baby's attention before the interaction can begin.

Scott's parents had known for a while that Scott was a somewhat hypo-arousable baby. For example, he seemed to be a little bit on the lazy side. He opened his eyes and looked but did not respond to his mother's look. When she smiled and cooed at him to try to get him to smile back, he either closed his eyes, looked away, or simply looked at her in his lazy way. At the same time he did not seem to generate much action on his own. If his mother did not bother him, he did not bother her. Scott's pediatrician had characterized him as a "low-sender."

Scott's parents had worked hard to bring him along, with moderate success so far. They knew that helping him develop in this new phase would involve more of the same techniques they had been using. They already knew that a reasonable number of times a day they had to find a way to get his attention, and their efforts were similar to those they had used when engaging and wooing their baby—that is, they experimented with different kinds of experiences that might appeal to Scott in terms of what he heard, saw, or touched. What they had to remember when experimenting this time was that the goal was to get Scott to *communicate* with them. The bright blue pencil they showed him to gain his attention was not the end in itself. Nor was his paying attention to it their goal. They used it so that Scott would eventually shift his attention to them. Once they had their baby's attention, they made funny noises and facial expressions in order to initiate interaction. They also remembered to be particularly sensitive to the tone of their interactions with Scott. They knew interesting vocal cadences could be of immense value to their lethargic baby.

Once Scott was interested, they worked on his sensory and emotional interactions. They waited for him to do something, then reacted to it. If he made a sound, they responded with the same sound. If he nuzzled them, they held him in a more secure way so he could feel a bodily response to his bodily signal. They took advantage of his smiles by smiling back at him, showing him what happened when he communicated his feelings of pleasure. Scott's parents used even his protesting and unhappy moments as a basis for interaction. When he was upset, they showed him that they could comfort him and make him feel better. Without overwhelming Scott, they watched for openings to respond to him—as well as sometimes initiating interaction. Reacting to his actions served to reinforce the cause-and-effect understanding they gradually introduced to their son. To his parents' pleasure, Scott soon became more active and interested as he realized that he had the ability to affect what went on around him. Having impact seemed to be its own reward. Scott enjoyed being assertive now that he could make things happen.

In contrast to babies who are on the passive side, you'll remember the hyper-excitable babies, who are very active and easily distracted. They seem to overreact to every stimulus. Their behavior appears to be random and chaotic—how can you respond to it? They smile or frown or move their arms or legs independently of the signals they are sent. They need your help first to focus on your signal, then to respond to it in a purposeful, coordinated way.

You can begin by soothing your infant with rocking, with your voice, or with a calming facial expression. Once the baby is fairly calmed down or even moderately focused, you can help her see that interacting with you is more fun than simply marching to her own drum. Be as inventive as you like. For example, by four or five months many babies enjoy making cooing sounds. They are also capable of making a sound in response to yours, especially if you can copy the tone and quality of theirs. By first involving baby in a "cooing" game, then gradually changing the pattern or cadence of the sound or slightly varying the pitch, you and your baby can enjoy a conversation! At a later age, maybe ten months, try a game with an object the baby likes—for instance, a simple game of give-and-take with a ball. Once the baby is willing to do this, vary the game by covering the ball with your hand and inviting her to find it. Soon your baby may expand this game to other objects.

This may all sound fairly routine, but remember that Step One— helping your infant calm down, focus, and get that first purposeful interaction going—may be the most difficult part and could take hours of time and patience. If you can hold out for four to six weeks, your infant should begin to use purposeful communications to calm herself and focus more easily. If, after this time, either your "low-sender" or distractable baby shows no beginning improvement of her level of interaction, a professional consultation may shorten your period of frustration, and result in your child's improvement.

INTERACTION IN ALL EMOTIONAL AREAS AND WITH ALL SENSES

Does your baby reciprocate through a range of emotions and through his various sensory and motor systems?

As we've seen, by three or four months your baby is capable of a wide range of emotions—pleasure and excitement, protest and rage, assertiveness and curiosity, dependency, love, and security, demandingness and stubbornness—as well as the capacity to calm down. You will also begin to see what may seem like new emotions related to these broad categories. Your baby may appear disappointed or even sad should you miss his overtures for closeness. Or you may see cautiousness or even fear if an introduction to a new person or, perhaps, a moving toy dog is not "properly" combined with the security of his mother or father's presence. Watch your baby over a period of two weeks to see if he interacts by using these emotions. Your baby's natural preferences may mean that some emotional interactions are more developed than others; but all should be present to some degee. If you notice that your baby does not express a full range of emotional interaction, you can help him work on the ones that give him trouble. Let's say your baby doesn't seem particularly happy. Babies must experience happiness and pleasure before they can respond to it in kind. A special facial expression, voice, or movement may do the trick. Mild novelty or surprise, such as covering your face and then uncovering it to show a smile, often works. Or teach your baby to anticipate: get the baby to look to the left and right in a rhythmic manner, then change the rhythm. Interacting can be involving and fun. Once you start, the interaction should keep itself going.

Let's take one other example, that of the hyper-excitable infant who needs help to harness his assertiveness in a purposeful cause-and-effect manner. In this case, the previously mentioned game of give-and-take may be expanded. Have your active infant reach for an object, such as a favorite toy, then offer him an even more interesting object. Helping him give you the first object while you offer the second is one example of a "purposeful" interaction.

These are suggestions for babies who do not use their full range of emotions. There are also babies who do not use all of their sensory motor systems to interact. Whether your baby has a different readiness time clock or needs a special pattern of care to correct slow development, practicing his new abilities will have a positive effect. If your infant has minor difficulties using his muscles to sit up, crawl, or coordinate his senses with his movement (such as looking and reaching) you can offer exercises that will serve the larger purpose of

Stop! Joanna has an important message for the world.

helping him learn "cause-and-effect" and at the same time help him practice using his senses and his motor system. You can focus the exercises on fine motor coordination (picking up food), gross motor coordination (sitting, crawling, or beginning efforts to pull up and walk), as well as the baby's senses (seeing, hearing, experiencing touch, motion, movement, smell, and taste).

For example, to improve your baby's coordination, hold up a toy that the baby particularly enjoys and encourage him to reach for it. Gradually move the toy further from the baby. If the baby is crawling, place the toy just out of reach to give him an incentive to practice coordinating seeing, reaching, and crawling.

Having your child experience movement while in your arms can also be helpful. Your baby will respond to being whirled around or gently raised and lowered. Some children may startle easily; others gurgle happily and want an even quicker pace. For the child who seems unsure of himself in space, make his experiences gradual so he is not overwhelmed. Hold him in different positions; close then far, up then down, but at a pace that he finds pleasurable. At first he may need to be held close to you while you move gently. Feeling secure in space could take months to accomplish, but it can help your baby gain better control of the muscles that must be coordinated for crawling, reaching, and walking.

As your baby progresses from one milestone to the next, remember that he doesn't really leave any of them behind. In order to grow and develop to his full potential, he must continually build on and strengthen all of the steps that have gone before. Your involvement in fun games that help your baby practice using his senses and motor system at a pace that he can enjoy and that serve the broader purpose of social interaction is your greatest challenge—and will be your greatest pleasure—at this stage of development.

Some parents find it hard to see how their baby's senses or his ability to crawl, stand up, and eventually walk have much to do with his emotional life. So what if he learns to crawl a little later—what will that have to do with how he feels about himself? In some instances it has little to do, but in others it can alert you to a potential problem.

A baby who has a problem integrating what he sees, hears, or touches with his motor behavior may also have a problem either in processing information (taking information in through the senses and making sense of it) or in integrating information (connecting information from the senses and combining it with appropriate motor behavior). Just as there are seven- or eight-year-olds who have trouble learning how to spell words or who rotate their letters when they read, it is possible, though still a matter for speculation, that babies can have related difficulties. After all, even though babies don't read or write, they do have their own ways of figuring out the world. A baby figures out how to get to an object he wants, how to hold it, how to put it into his mouth. He figures out how to respond to his parent's sound with a sound of his own.

When babies are slow to develop their capacities to coordinate their senses with their motor planning, it is reasonable to consider that the problem can either be the "figuring-out part" or the ability to use and coordinate their muscles to show what they want, such as crawling for an object they see.

Helping Your Child . . .

1. RECIPROCATE INTERACTION

— gain your baby's attention
— determine a behavior that is easy for your baby to do
— use this behavior for interacting
— for baby who is a low-sender, react to *any* signal the baby sends
— for an excitable baby, relax him and then make interaction relaxing and enjoyable

2. INTERACT IN ALL EMOTIONAL AREAS
   AND WITH ALL SENSES

— help your baby experience the emotions of pleasure and excitement, protest and rage, assertiveness and curiosity, dependency, love, and security and the capacity to calm down
— react to your baby's expression of emotion
— help your baby practice interaction in all emotional areas

3. INTEGRATE ACTIVITIES

— begin with the activity your baby does best
— gradually add on activities that encourage your baby to use other senses and motor systems

In addition, it is reasonable to speculate whether the baby who has difficulty figuring out, for example, whether a sound is coming from left or right, can figure out complex emotional signals. Can this baby distinguish his mother's smile of pleasure from a frown or even an annoyed "stop that!"? Given these possibilities, we think it is worthwhile to be on the safe side and give a baby who is a little slow in sensory-motor areas extra practice across the board. By helping your baby practice using his senses, movements, and feelings, you can help him develop these functions, which will serve him the rest of his life. And do not forget that emotions play an important part in how interested a baby might be in practicing his motor skills. The coordinated infant who will not crawl because everything is brought to him or because his father is anxious that he will hurt himself is not uncommon. Or the infant who crawls everywhere but toward his father may be trying to tell you something.

INTEGRATION OF FUNCTIONS

Is your baby able to integrate all of his sensory-motor systems for interacting?

We mentioned integration of the senses briefly above. Some babies can interact emotionally and can interact with each of their sensory-motor systems but must be taught to put the whole range of possibilities together. They need to learn that they can do more than one thing at a time. For example, take the baby who plays a peek-a-boo game but doesn't make a sound or reach out with his hands at the same time. Such a baby can be helped to coordinate his various senses and motor capacities. Begin with what the baby does best—say, playing peek-a-boo. Once the game is well established, encourage the baby to pull your hands off your face and add a sound, such as "ah *ha*" at the end. By doing this you are helping your baby bring together what, for him, are disconnected experiences into a purposeful pattern.

Creating a Supportive Environment

Since no parent is able to read and react to every signal (nor should this be expected), infants must learn to accept delay and frustration as a part of life. It's important that your infant learns this fact in a supportive environment. The following four principles can help you to establish a home atmosphere that will encourage a rich communication system.

First, read and respond selectively and appropriately to each of your baby's signals—from pleasurable ones to those of protest. This is the way your baby learns to differentiate her internal needs and feelings one from another. Parents who can appreciate the differences in their baby's signals throughout the spectrum foster their infant's natural capacity to appreciate subtle differences in their own and others' emotions.

There is no "right" way to respond—each family has its own natural and intuitive responses—but it is important for you to look for and concentrate on reading the different emotional signals your baby is capable of producing. You can help your baby to become a good sender, reader, and responder.

A second principle for encouraging communication is to respond in an empathetic manner. In order to read emotional signals effectively, you must be able to feel what your baby is feeling. The mother who sees her baby finally find the teething ring under her hand and, at that instant, feels some of the joy her baby is feeling, is reading her baby's signal on a deep emotional level. What the baby receives is the sense that she is understood emotionally. If, on the other hand, the mother is continually bored or distracted, she becomes like the person who says, "Yes, I understand" while shuffling papers or looking for a pen. There is little sense of emotional engagement or understanding from such a person. Similarly, and even more profoundly, a baby who feels her signals being read impersonally does not receive feedback or a sense of emotional communication. In a sense, your empathy is a shortcut to reading your baby's signals. You will not have to *think* about what a signal means, you will *know*.

A third general principle is to notice how many of your baby's sensory and motor functions she uses in her evolving intentional communication system. In general, the greater the number that she uses in a coordinated manner, the better the system that evolves. Your baby can have a rich, multifunctional system, along with the understanding that both parent and baby may have their preferred ways of communicating.

Some babies, for example, are very visual. Sensitive parents will be very visual in response, perhaps by introducing their baby to peek-a-boo games. Other babies love sounds, and their experimentation will encourage their parents to talk to them a great deal. Still other babies use movement to create their own special rhythmic communication with their parents. At the same time parents might unintentionally exclude certain modes of communication. For example, parents who are very visually oriented may neglect oral communication. As a result language development may be slowed. The optimal situation is one in which all ways of communicating are used in an integrated manner.

Obviously, as you interact with your baby you cannot and need not be aware of all that is happening; using different sensory-motor functions is usually spontaneous. However, in a quiet moment, reflect on the different ways in which you communicate with your baby to see if you can identify interactions using each of the following functions: hearing, vision, touch, taste, smell, motion, fine and gross motor skills, and combinations of these.

The fourth principle is to continue to support your baby's earlier tasks—those of self-regulation and falling in love. It is against a background of comfortable harmony and love that your baby's intentional communication system will flourish. In most cases integrating the tasks of the past with the task of the present will occur quite automatically, but since this is such a stimulating phase for both parents and baby, remember that your infant still needs quiet comfort, too.

For example, Susan's parents were intent on enhancing their baby's new communication abilities. They became so involved in buying her more and more complicated toys—each one designed to expand her sensory-motor accomplishments—that they lost sight of her need for comfort and help in regulating herself. They bombarded her with stimuli and encouraged her to play adeptly with her new toys. Their persistence changed the quality of their interaction. Susan was forced to do her "homework." Because her parents forgot that Susan's communication system should develop *as part of* the more important system of mutual love and mutual regulation and interest, both parents and Susan became chronically irritated with each other, and the relationship appeared strained. She continued to develop cognitively, showing interest in inanimate things and in playing complex games, but became increasingly aloof and withdrawn from her parents and other people.

It should also be emphasized that at this stage your infant is learning about making things happen. Excessive structure or emphasis on passive learning right now may not prove as useful to your infant's emotional or cognitive development as active experimentation and freedom to take the initiative.

Reviewing Your Support

Occasional feelings of confusion about what your baby is trying to communicate or occasional boredom or fatigue that might prevent you from being your baby's ever-sparkling companion are natural and to be expected. If, however, you find that you are often anxious, overwhelmed, or confused by your baby's sounds and gestures, so that you're unable to respond to him or to see whether he responds to you, you'll want to discover why. Your support of his ability to communicate is especially important now. During the last two stages he has learned to take an interest in the world and to fall in love with you. He is poised and ready to step into the world and take part in life's two-way give-and-take. You are his guide and model.

Ask yourself how well you communicate generally: Do you often have difficulty reading and responding to people's signals and emotions? Do you feel sure you know when your spouse is angry, whether you understand what your friends mean, whether you can tell when your boss likes your work? If you do not, then ask yourself if understanding what people mean makes you anxious. Do you handle fear and anxiety with the ostrich approach—preferring not to understand a comment or look? If a person looks at you, do you automatically assume he or she is being critical of you?

These questions may lead you to discover, for example, that you have always been concerned that people will not like you, or that people will be too demanding of you.

If your general tendency is to react this way, you may transfer this reaction to your baby. His crying may make you feel rejected or his look of puzzlement may make you feel that you must have done something wrong. Even partial recognition of the cause can give you the resources to overcome your particular block, at least with your baby.

By recognizing your tendency, for instance, to be confused by and withdraw from ambiguous signals, you can try an alternate strategy. You can be more persistent. Push yourself to sort out the ambiguity and tolerate the anxiety. Although your anxiety or desire to control will return, awareness of some of the underlying issues can provide you with the ability to cope with uncomfortable feelings caused by your new challenges.

YOUR FAMILY SITUATION

Babies between six and ten months who are leaving the infant stage and becoming more capable are often seen as a renewed threat by slightly older brothers and sisters. Young ones who can reach and grab, follow their siblings everywhere, and get the lion's share of mother's attention can stir up some negative feelings. Squabbling siblings can keep you from the pleasant interactions supportive of your child. With less time given to policing the children, you can spend more energy supporting your child's communication skills. Let's look at an example of ingenuity born out of desperation.

One mother and her ten-month-old, Ellen, had developed a searching game. Her mother would "hide" Ellen's fuzzy bear behind the arm of the couch, and Ellen would "walk," mostly holding on to the couch, to find it. Once found, her mother would ooh and ahh with surprise. Through this game Ellen, a somewhat timid child, was learning about curiosity, surprise, and excitement. All would go smoothly for the first trip to find the bear, until Gina, Ellen's three-year-old sister, would decide to become involved. Gina had perfected the knack of "accidentally" brushing against Ellen just as she dared to let go of support and tried to walk on her own toward the bear. Plop on her bottom she would go, and then begin to cry. This commotion would effectively end the game. Although her mother had warned, threatened, screamed, stomped and even separated the two, it was to no avail. For Mother to be able to interact with Ellen, she needed to involve Gina in the play as a helper. With her mother's help, Gina "taught" Ellen to play Ring-Around-the-Rosy. Ellen not only got to practice a few steps with her sister's help, but also to anticipate the surprise and excitement of falling down, and Gina got the satisfaction of helping her sister "fall down" without a push or punishment. From there, Gina began to take pride in Ellen's ability and accomplishments. "I'm teaching her how to walk, Mommy," "Look at the block tower we built, Mommy." Her mother had helped Gina become Ellen's partner in learning to communicate around certain emotions, especially assertive exploration.

PARENTAL PERSONALITY STYLES

During this, as with other stages of your baby's life, your personality traits or tendencies will have an effect on your baby's development.

At this stage of your baby's development he needs you to respond to him by reciprocating his communication and doing so in a systematic way. If you tend to be, say, overly protective, or if you find it difficult to be attentive to people's feelings, your baby may not receive the necessary support for learning to communicate. Though you may find some of our parental "examples" overstated, they at least still help you to become aware of possible tendencies.

Withdrawal or Depression. Let us consider a mother (or father) with an underlying depression. She (or he) is not visibly depressed but is lethargic in movement and slow in speech. There is little vocal range when she talks and little energy, interest, or variation of emotion. Her interaction with her baby consists primarily of watching him, occasionally stroking his back, and rocking him. It does not involve reciprocating his overtures. Although these actions are soothing and comforting, the baby needs more by this age. The mother's actions were probably sufficient to help baby fall in love with the world and even with her, but not enough to encourage him to reach out and communicate purposefully. This mother is likely to find that her baby, who is not getting his new developmental needs for purposeful communication met, is increasingly irritable and frustrated.

Intrusion. Sometimes a parent will misread his baby's signals, at least in certain emotional areas. Unwittingly, such parents project their own desires, feelings, or thoughts onto their baby. For example, many parents enjoy tickling the baby and playfully tossing her around. Such games can be fun, but at some point baby usually signals she's had enough. The parent, still enjoying himself, might interpret the baby's signal as one of pleasure and continue to tickle and toss. Another example of parental intrusiveness is the mother whose baby squirms in her lap. The baby wants to get down on the floor, but the mother thinks the baby is angry with her. Mother proceeds to hold the baby closely and rocks him until he gives up and goes to sleep. In this instance the mother misread her baby's desire for greater freedom and instead projected her own concern that the baby was angry. Based on her misreading, the mother then forced her baby to sleep. It's possible that the baby would learn from this experience that the desire for independence, or any kind of self-initiative, was an emotion to be denied or held in check. With continuous misreading, a baby may give up and become very passive, or respond with increased irritability, frustration, and negativism.

Overcontrol. Parents who tend to be overly controlling often believe their children should be a certain way and try to see that they are. For example, parents who believe in physical and mental "toughness and control" may establish a Spartan regimen for their son or daughter. They might deal with protest by setting limits, but this would not balance discipline with pleasure.

Marilyn was a good example of this. She thought children should be tough. She often said, "Pampering children won't prepare them for the cruel, hard world out there." Her regimen included a very strictly adhered-to schedule (up at 7:00, breakfast at 7:30, etc.), no choice of what to eat or wear ("If you don't like lunch, dinner is served at 6:00"), and no tolerance of fears ("If you're afraid of the dark, you'll just have to get used to it.") If the children were playing a peek-a-boo game and dinnertime arose, they weren't allowed five extra minutes to finish up their game. Nothing was allowed to interfere with the schedule. The three-year-old was unwilling to endure the punishment and displeasure required to rebel against this system. He found it easier to be passive and forgo any show of emotion—positive or negative. The twelve-month-old—who had just learned to walk—wasn't willing to give in so easily. The power struggles that ensued lasted from morning to night. Marilyn's relationship with her children was increasingly an exercise in assertiveness and aggression—not an exchange of pleasure.

A baby who does not have his pleasure signals read will soon start either to inhibit himself and so not know that it is possible to cause pleasure, or he may begin finding his "pleasure" in being provocative.

Overprotection. Overprotection stems from the worry that your baby might hurt herself. In order to ensure that no harm befalls the baby, a parent might overcontrol the baby's actions. An overprotective parent may have a generally anxious manner, which is often communicated through voice and emotional tone. The baby, sensing this anxiety, may become hesitant and insecure about exploring and trying new activities.

The overprotective parent may notice a general feeling of apprehension regarding the baby's well-being: when she suddenly goes out of your sight ("she could get into things"); when she climbs onto a chair ("she could fall backwards"); when she picks up a stick ("she could poke her eye"). Although these could all be potentially dangerous situations and may require you to intervene, most of the time they don't call for such a panicky, apprehensive approach. Greater involvement of the other parent (who hopefully is not overprotective) can help. Perhaps you have a small indoor slide but don't like the baby to play on it because he could fall. If the baby plays on this while your spouse is present, you can rely on your spouse's judgment for what is safe as well as become more aware of what your baby is able to do. Another helpful avenue can be a toddler group, where you can share some of your apprehensions, get feedback from peers, and see what other babies are doing.

Random Responses. In addition to checking your own general personality style, take a hard look at your own communication systems. You may be reading your baby's signals and may be involved and interested in your child, and still respond randomly rather than reciprocally. You may be neither intrusive, controlling, nor withdrawn, but nonetheless you may have difficulty paying heed to your baby's feelings. On the surface all may look fine. You may pick your baby up, toss her around, snuggle with her, and rock her rhythmically. However, you'll need to ask yourself if you are acting in response to a signal from her. In other words, some parents must be taught to give more consideration to their baby's needs. Adults can cope with others who are inconsiderate, but a baby may begin to become sober and expressionless or negative and avoidant as her signals go unheeded.

Anxiety from Certain Emotions. Some parents experience anxiety in the face of certain emotions, which interferes with reading their baby's signals correctly. Many people have difficulty with emotions such as aggression, intimacy, or rejection. Should your baby communicate an emotion that causes you to be anxious, you may respond by becoming stiff and unnatural. Take, for example, a father whose infant daughter likes to cuddle and coo. Intimacy makes him anxious. He transmits tension rather than pleasure back to his daughter. Her new cause-and-effect understanding tells her that intimacy causes tension and anxiety. A similar reaction may occur if parents are uncomfortable with signs of displeasure. A protesting infant causes his parents to withdraw in confusion. With little response to their baby's organized signals of protest, the baby's ability to protest in an organized way may be impaired, resulting in disorganized and nonassertive behavior.

Understanding Subtlety. Finally, understanding subtlety is a parental communication skill that will foster the same skill in your baby. Your ready response to blatant protest or cheerful giggling is important, but don't miss the gradations in between—mild curiosity, flirtation, disappointment, and pouting, for example. When babies have their subtle signals responded to, they, too, can mature with the ability to read similar signs, either in others or in themselves. Remember that your child knows herself, in part, through her understanding of others.

COMMON PARENTAL FEARS

Each stage of your baby's development tends to bring certain "stage-specific" fears to the surface. In earlier stages we saw fears about protection, comfort, interest, and also intimacy and love. Fears during the stage of intentional communication deal with being understood and understanding, and with interacting and being assertive.

Fear of Being Uninteresting. "My baby doesn't find me interesting" is one fear which may arise when the mother is not able to read her baby's signals well. Since a good communication system is not being developed, the baby may not tend to brighten up or interact with his mother a great deal. The mother may think, I'm uninteresting, I'm unappealing, I'm *boring.* Mothers who think this way often feel they are generally uninteresting. They may become depressed and withdraw from baby even more. But when mothers consciously and persistently try to read their baby's signals and begin to communicate better, they find that their babies respond and interact more. Once the mother's attempts are encouraged, she finds she is neither boring nor bored, and mother and baby roll happily along.

Fear of Doing Things "Wrong." As complex communications become more important, the attitude of "I can't understand him and I can't do anything right" often rears its head. This reaction, like the fear of being uninteresting, often fits in with the long-standing self-image of never being able to do anything the "right way." It can be part of an underlying lack of confidence, or even underlying depression. If this fear was present during your baby's first stage of emotional development, it may become more prominent now, since the demands for functioning are greater; your baby is a more complex communicator, asking more from you.

Let's look at a baby and his mother who had formed a loving attachment. When Paul began to communicate in a more complicated manner, his mother became worried that she was "misreading" him and that she would respond incorrectly. Needless to say, Paul's mother's worries began to make her prediction come true. Her fear of "doing everything wrong" led her to do nothing at all. Instead of responding when Paul moved his arm out to her, she wondered what to do. Instead of responding to his angry protest with attempts to amuse or comfort him, she worried, "Will I spoil him?" Even though she could read his cues and signals and had instinctual responses she could trust, her lack of confidence interfered with her ability to help her baby develop.

Fear of Being Passive. In the same way, the fear of being passive can interfere at this stage of development. A fear of being passive can make some parents read and respond to their baby's signals almost before he makes them. They want to be perfectly attuned parents, but they could use a little patience in order to read their baby's signals accurately. Unfortunately, responding in a less impulsive manner makes them feel anxious. They often view themselves as "inadequate." Realizing what causes their anxiety can often lead this type of parent to be more relaxed and to wait and see what baby is trying to communicate.

Fear of Being Empathic. As we've mentioned, appropriate empathy is necessary in order to read your baby's signals and emotional level. However, some people have a tendency to overempathize—that is, once they step into the other person's shoes, they never get out, which makes them unable to cope with the situation. In an effort to correct this, they then try to *avoid* feeling what the other person feels. They do this because, in a sense, they are frightened of losing themselves. Unfortunately, when the "other person" is their baby, the result can be the infant's loss of a full range of emotional experience.

Awareness of the fears we've illustrated can lead you to relate more fully to your baby during this crucial phase of his growth. Even if you are not fully aware of certain fears, a balanced approach to interaction—including use of all the emotions, of all the senses, and of all the motor capacities—can insure your baby the full range of experiences so vital to his continuing growth.

You can be a good communicator with your baby if you have two basic capacities: the capacity to read your baby's signals accurately and to respond to him reciprocally with empathy. If you do these two things, you will support your baby's ability to differentiate among various feelings and desires and also provide the foundation for sound reality testing. The beginning of a communication system between you and your baby is one of the most exciting and gratifying phases of both parenthood and babyhood.

IV | THE EMERGENCE OF AN ORGANIZED SENSE OF SELF

—9 to 18 months

The transition from babyhood to toddlerhood takes place gradually between the ages of nine and eighteen months. During this time, your new "little person" is developing so many skills, activities, and behaviors that you may at times want to say, "Stop! One at a time!" It is also a phase when the more flamboyant skills your baby learns— crawling, standing, and walking—may overshadow the immense gains in overall social and emotional development that are also occurring. These gains could be even more important for understanding your baby's development at this age than his or her motor accomplishments. The emerging ability to piece together many small activities and emotions into a pattern, known as the ability to organize, is crucial to the development of higher-level thinking and planning. Becoming more "organized" in behavior *and* emotion is the major challenge facing your toddler.

During the earlier stage of learning to communicate, a baby might respond to a sound or smile by making a sound or smile of his own, or to a hand reaching out with a reach of his own. But in the present phase, the baby begins to string a number of behaviors together. For example, when a mother comes home, she might notice that the baby toddles to her, smiles, reaches up with his hands, and makes pleased and contented sounds when picked up. The baby can now say hello, not just with a smile, a sound or an arm gesture, but with all three together. This is a demonstration of a complicated emotional and behavioral system. Similarly, a toddler does not just cry or get frustrated at this age, but might look away from her mother and crawl or run into another room. When her mother tries to approach, the baby might make a noise that sounds quite nasty and scoot even further away. When the same angry toddler returns to a loving mood, she may seek out her mother for a hug.

The emotions already evident in earlier stages now are more organized. Love is expressed with more tenderness, including hugs and kisses. There may even be a pat on the head for an older sibling who has hurt himself. Anger may be more deliberate, including throwing a toy or hitting an older sibling in the nose. And disappointment may be expressed poignantly, with forlorn looks that tug at your heart, sometimes followed by unforgiving coldness or aloofness for a brief spell. The fears and anxieties related to dependency or curiosity are also organized, such as with separation anxiety in which your toddler holds on for dear life when you are going out, or when new company comes over and you want to show off your wonderful toddler before he has explored them on his own time and on his terms. Yet there is also greater assertiveness accompanied eventually, toward the end of this stage and at the beginning of the next, by a look of pride in a tower well built or a word well said. You shouldn't expect, at this stage, to see the more advanced forms of empathy, shame, and guilt, even though hints of some of these capacities are beginning to emerge. Your child simply hasn't developed a sufficiently organized sense of self.

But there are many little bits and pieces of emotion and behavior that your child will now begin to link. The most important of these can be put into categories: imitating, understanding functions and meanings, developing originality, reconciling emotional polarities, and becoming a unique personality. You'll see your child learn to take a piece of imitation, add some originality, perhaps a bit of initiative and, presto! There you have a series of linked feelings and actions—perhaps a little shaky, certainly not long. Nevertheless, like a new cook, your child is beginning to experiment with the ingredients of emotional development. The calm baby looking at pictures who all of a sudden, with a prideful twinkle, is wearing the book as a new hat is an example.

Toward the end of this phase of learning to combine and express feelings and action in ways that are both understandable and acceptable, your child's abilities to talk and to accept limits will add even more to his capacity for social and emotional development.

Emotions and Cognition

Many of the toddler's emerging skills may seem to be both cognitive and emotional at the same time. The difference between the two may not always be clear. In fact, during these early years, there is a great deal of overlap between these aspects of development. However, one might characterize emotional development as the application of mental processes to the world of feelings, interpersonal relationships, and inanimate objects to which the child is attached—at eight months learning that a smile begets a smile; at four years, realizing that angry thoughts are different from angry behavior. One could characterize cognitive development as the application of these same mental processes to the impersonal world—at six months, learning that hitting the crib slats makes a sound; at four years, saying the alphabet. In essence, it is our view that infants and children learn to understand all kinds of experience according to the developmental principles outlined for each stage. But it must be realized that while a child can learn for himself that he has impact on his impersonal world (banging a piece of wood with a toy hammer), he can only learn from another person that loving feelings lead to holding and cuddling or that angry biting leads to a "no no." In a sense, emotional development is the more challenging to parents.

EMOTIONAL PARTNERSHIP
AND COMPLEX IMITATION

A child learns to organize her behavior through experiencing herself as a partner. She reacts and interacts to the emotional tones of the other person whether they are tones of love, admiration, intrusion, control, or firmness. For example, a fourteen-month-old is playing with some pans and a spoon, making noise and experimenting. Her father, seeing the baby try to stir, talks admiringly of the child's prowess. The child grins broadly and tries to move the spoon in the pan even faster. Feeling both competent and masterful in reaction to her father's praise, she communicates an organized response. She links her behavior—smiling and stirring more vigorously—with the competence and mastery she feels inside.

Another example is a seventeen-month-old looking at a picture book with his father. Father thinks that pointing and naming the pictures from left to right will eventually help the child to read, so he refuses to acknowledge the child's own pointing at his favorite pictures. Having his intentions ignored in this "pleasurable" interaction, the child decides to be belligerent and throws the book down. He is reacting to his father's control by being rebellious. He is learning an organized response to his father's rigidity and is experiencing himself as a rebellious child.

The emotional partnership also encourages complex, organized imitations of both behaviors and emotions. Parents are quick to notice that from early in life babies try to copy what their parents do. Between nine and eighteen months, you will see a dramatic increase in your child's ability to imitate complicated emotions and behaviors. The nine-month-old may mimic a parent's shaking his head or a special facial expression or even a special smile. Later, she advances to hugging her daddy just the way her mommy does it, or to picking up a newspaper and "reading" it, playing with the pots when she sees her mother cooking, or "talking" on the telephone. At first the imitation has an artificial quality. It is obvious that the toddler is "just playing" when she looks at the newspaper or talks on the phone. After a time, however, even without a parent to copy, a toddler will initiate a warm tender kiss or sit on the couch, pick up a book, and begin to look at the pictures. What has begun as mimicry ("I'm copying Mommy") now becomes emotions and behavior (reading for pleasure) that is a part of the child's personality.

EXPRESSING NEEDS AND INTERESTS THROUGH TAKING INITIATIVE

The capacity to imitate and to reciprocate behavior and emotions makes way for a toddler's budding self-definition through initiative. He is beginning to instigate behaviors based on his own needs rather than just copying your activity. Observe a hungry fifteen-month-old who takes her seated father by the hand, pulls him, and then takes him into the kitchen and bangs on the refrigerator door until he opens it. Some precocious toddlers can even point to what they want to eat—and will assertively push away what they do not want. This pattern of organized behavior is very different from the passive toddler who, when hungry, cries and expects the parent to know he is hungry. Another example of a self-starter is a child who initiates a favorite game. One twelve-month-old girl, who loved to play peek-a-boo, would peek around the corner of the couch at her mother, giggle at her, and then disappear. Upon hearing her mother say, "Where's Suzie?" she would peek around again and continue the game. The sense of one's self as an initiator who can get needs met and explore emerging personal interests is important.

INDEPENDENCE AND DISTAL COMMUNICATION

An emerging trait that complements that of initiative is independence. Developing independence frees the curious toddler to explore and experience her world and further define herself. Typical is the ten-month-old who scuttles through the rooms of her house and even those of others, as greater mobility and curiosity propel her to new adventures across greater reaches of space.

In order to leave her mother's side and still feel comfortable, however, the toddler must begin to develop an ability to "feel attached" not only through being held and touched but also from a distance, through looking, gesturing, and using her voice. This may be termed "distal communication." By developing the ability to communicate over distances the toddler can have her cake and eat it, too. She takes her mother with her by looking and talking even though she still returns for the kiss and the hug that are always the ultimate security and pleasure. Parents will see their child become freer, more flexible and daring once she is able to feel as secure and loved while exploring as she does when being stroked and cuddled.

Using vision, hearing, and gesturing to communicate across space allows the child to take you—his "security blanket"—with him. As we often see, toddlers also literally carry their security blankets around with them to attain the same aim of feeling secure. The most famous, Linus's blanket in the comic strip *Peanuts*, has become part of American folklore. These "transitional objects" may be anything that has come to be associated with early feelings of closeness—a blanket, a bottle, a little pillow, a piece of cloth, a doll. Remember, it is often the special touch, smell, or look that is important to the child. Washing or changing the object in some way may not be met with eagerness.

ORIGINALITY

You will also notice that along with more organized emotions and behavior and "secure" independence, you now have on your hands a little inventor who combines what he has been shown with what he has experienced, adds his own twist, and comes up with an "original" approach to life's emotions, be it a special new way to be cuddled or an ingenious tactic for getting even with an older sibling.

An eighteen-month-old, Janet, exhibited her budding originality by expanding a game she played with her father. The game involved Janet's taking a piece of paper, holding it in front of her father's face, and playing peek-a-boo. One day Janet put the paper on top of her head as though to make a hat and somewhat precociously said "me Mommy." They were soon experimenting, giggling and laughing at their masquerade, and Janet was thoroughly enjoying her first attempt at a new self-definition, "being Mommy."

UNDERSTANDING FUNCTION
AND MEANING

Advanced play—a child using a telephone or pots and pans for their intended purpose—is imitation that includes a partial understanding of the object's use or function. Your child will apply this functional understanding to all aspects of his world, including his interactions with you, and to his body. For example, the eighteen-month-old child who hurts her foot and gestures to father to kiss her "boo-boo" has a sense of her father as a person with a function, that is, he can "make it better." The child who builds a block tower and is praised by mother sees her as a person with the function of admiration. In other words, the child is able to recognize the abstract emotional quality or function of the person.

It is natural for the toddler with an emerging sense of himself and of others to view his own body in a more understanding way. Children around eighteen months seem to have the beginnings of a sense of themselves as a complete physical entity, which is suggested by their ability to recognize the image in the mirror as their own. They might notice differences in the anatomies of boys and girls, or mothers and fathers. They may become curious about their dolls' bodies. Their curiosity about and sense of their own bodies are natural derivatives of systematic behavior and a beginning understanding of the uses and meanings of people and things.

TODDLER-TO-TODDLER
RELATIONSHIPS

Not long ago, toddlers were thought capable of only playing with other toddlers side-by-side or in "parallel" play, that is, of not interacting during play. Now it is well established that toddlers can enjoy the company of their peers through interactive play. However, at a birthday party of three or more toddlers you are still likely to see each child go his own way: playing independently with toys or running around. Interactive play does not occur until a group of children gets to know each other. Usually, a group or subgroup of two or three children is most conducive for interaction. The larger the group, the more difficult it seems for the children to form subgroups of two or three.

Recent research which involved observing toddlers who met regularly has led to an unusually detailed account of the natural unfolding of toddler relationships. These observations, together with clinical work, suggest the following sequence in their relationship patterns. First, toddlers seem to find something about another toddler that attracts them—a red shirt, a pretty ribbon, long hair. Not infrequently, there is then mutual exploration between the two. Aggression, such as pulling the ribbon, or passivity, such as allowing the ribbon to be pulled, is the basis for this exploration. During this time, the toddlers can also use an available adult for collaborative interaction—exchanging food through the adult or trading a car between themselves and rolling it to the adult.

If supported, this "buffered" or "refereed" play leads to opportunities for sharing experiences. Humor is often an element of these experiences, as they laugh together at some spilled milk or at a toy car knocking over a tower of blocks. Not long after these experiences of shared emotions, the toddlers often go off, playing in the sandbox together, making funny faces and gestures at each other, or helping one another knock over the clown punching bag.

This sequence may take from weeks to months to develop. It is, in part, based on new cognitive skills but it also suggests that, with familiarity, interpersonal relationships can occur. This pattern provides toddlers with an opportunity to use their capacities for behavioral and emotional organization, emotional partnerships, imitation, and an understanding of the functional meaning of objects not only with adults but also with their peers.

RECONCILING EMOTIONAL POLARITIES

Just as toddlers are learning to understand the functions of objects and see the meaning in patterns of behavior, they are also applying this new ability to their emotions. They are beginning to learn that even when they are angry at their mother they can still trust and love her. Early in the second year this was not the case. The "bad" mother was all bad and the "good" mother was all good—and they weren't the same. Now they are starting to see that a person—including themselves—is composed of many emotions. Throughout the next two stages they come to understand more fully that a person is a combination of many sensory and emotional elements.

The only documentation for this at this age comes through "clinical empathy." When playing with a twelve- or thirteen-month-old, one gets the sense that should he become angry with you, you're in for an all-out, no-holds-barred attack. He seems to have no reservation about or hesitation in seeing you as his total enemy. By eighteen to twenty months the same toddler, similarly angry, conveys perhaps a sense of threat, but his "feeling tones" and gestures say he also knows you are a person of security and trust, even during his angry spell.

Children of this age and stage of development are entering into the lifelong, and very human, struggle to reconcile the emotional opposites they feel. And those who can accept that love and hate, passivity and activity can co-exist in the same person, will gain an appreciation of life's emotional complexities and a richer understanding of human nature. Their sense of themselves will be a full and integrated one.

ABILITY TO
COMMUNICATE WITH WORDS

Toward the end of this phase of development, parents will see the emerging capacity of their child to use words. Although talking increases greatly after two, toddlers as young as sixteen months can name favorite people or objects. Often the child can use words to make a request or voice a reaction, saying "bottle," or "all gone," or "no." Even if words are not used, sounds will be used as a means of expression. So, using arm and facial gestures and sounds—like a foreigner who cannot speak the language but can make himself understood—the toddler communicates in an ever more complex way. Expressing himself with gestures, sounds and finally words greatly enhances a child's ability to make his wishes known and to connect a gesture, sound or word to an inner emotion.

ACCEPTING LIMITS
AND USING THE "DISTAL MODES"

Little by little your child has been gaining in his capacity to accept limits. The understanding of gestures, sounds and words permits you to say no in a hundred different ways and for him to understand it— and all from a distance (some of the time). If you can succeed in this milestone of using "distal modes" for setting limits, the twos can indeed be joyful. The ability to accept limits set for him by his parents helps a child understand reality by teaching him what he can and cannot do. Perfection is not the goal here. Any toddler with a flawless record of behavior is a highly suspicious case. But parents should begin to see an ability to follow some basic rules, suggesting the youngster's ability to make "setting limits" a part of himself.

This is a wonderfully active and important time for your toddler. He or she possesses new physical, mental, and emotional abilities, and is now empowered with that heady concept: choice. Your baby can choose what to copy, what and when to initiate, what limits to obey. Now is when he or she will begin to show a fairly consistent emotional style, whether giggler, clown, or curious George. This is a time when your child's strengths will become more evident and also a time when you'll be able to gauge where support is needed in order to maintain a comfortable balance between various emotions and activities. The process of development is well under way, and your toddler will use and combine all of his or her abilities to shape a brand-new and unique personality.

Little Margot was an industrious eighteen-month-old. She would toddle away from her mother to get her little brush and pretend to brush her hair. Then she would find her toy telephone, put the receiver to her ear, and smile gleefully at her mother across the room. If her mother wasn't paying attention, Margot would rush back to her, grab her leg, and whine. If, on the other hand, her mother returned her enthusiastic smile, thereby making emotional contact with Margot from across the room, she was contented and went about making all kinds of interesting noises into her toy telephone. After she tired of this play, Margot would often take her mother's hand and lead her into the kitchen. Pointing to the refrigerator she would say, "Ba, ba." When her milk was given to her she voiced her satisfaction by saying, "Ah, ha."

At night when father came home, sometimes preoccupied and busy, Margot would give him an especially joyful welcome-home kiss. When he sat down to read the paper she would grab his knee, then run to the other side of the room when he looked up to talk to her. Falling for the bait, her father would pursue her, to her delight—and his. She was already learning to be coy and to tease her father into playing with her.

Margot, at eighteen months, had already achieved many of the milestones of her life stage. She used "distal communication modes" to stay in emotional contact, she experimented and understood the meaning of objects, she developed a range of complex emotional patterns, such as welcoming her father home, and even developed original and sophisticated emotional play to deal with her preoccupied

Behavioral and Emotional Checklist

1. EMOTIONAL PARTNERSHIP AND COMPLEX IMITATION: Your child is capable of reciprocating and copying your behavior and emotions

2. EXPRESSING NEEDS AND INTERESTS THROUGH TAKING INITIATIVE: Your child begins to instigate activities based on his own needs and desires rather than by imitation alone

3. INDEPENDENCE AND DISTAL COMMUNICATION: Your child leaves you for short times in order to explore; he feels connected with you from a distance by using his hearing and vision

4. ORIGINALITY: Your child adds his own interpretation to things he has been taught, and uses objects or toys in ways he has not been shown

5. UNDERSTANDING FUNCTION AND MEANING: Your child begins to understand the uses and meanings of people and things

6. TODDLER-TO-TODDLER RELATIONSHIPS: Your child can begin to develop a shared relationship with a toddler who is a regular playmate that goes beyond parallel play

7. RECONCILING EMOTIONAL POLARITIES: Your child begins to realize that people are composed of many emotions—that even though he may be mad at Mommy, he still loves her at the same time

8. ABILITY TO COMMUNICATE WITH WORDS: Your child begins to communicate with gestures, sounds, and a few words

9. ACCEPTING LIMITS AND USING THE "DISTAL MODES": Your child begins to respond to your setting limits verbally or with a gesture

daddy. Of course, her daddy's participation in these games helped Margot feel that all her efforts were worthwhile.

Observing Your Baby

How can you, as a parent, know whether or not your child is meeting the major challenge of this phase of development? Organizing behavior and emotions into a complex pattern is no easy task. Watching it happen leads parents to the appreciation of their baby as a "little person." But every person, big or little, is different, and each child will develop at a different rate in different areas. What is important to know is that in the great majority of cases, this unevenness in development is perfectly normal. For example, your child may be a master at peek-a-boo; someone else's child may not. Some children respond quickly to the setting of limits; others require more patience on the part of already saintly parents. What parents need to determine is this: Does your child show the basic elements of the new capacities? Does he or she gradually develop them? As you answer the following questions, look for age-expected patterns, but also for areas in which your child may be experiencing difficulty. Your sensitivity and willingness to act may allow you to help your child reach his maximum potential.

ORGANIZATION OF BEHAVIOR

Is your child beginning to string several behaviors together? Does he show intent and originality in his play? Is he capable of reciprocating and imitating emotions and behavior?

As we've learned, the beginning of the second year is characterized by the child's gradual ability to combine small pieces of behavior to create a more complex one. For instance, a thirsty eleven-month-old might crawl over to get a bottle on the table, stand up, pick up the bottle, and hold the bottle out in the direction of the parent or proceed to drink from it. At fourteen months, on hearing the laughter of sisters and brothers, the child might toddle over to find them and then try to join in their game. One youngster, upon seeing his brother and sister lined up to race, quickly positioned himself behind the starting line and careened down the race course in the wake of his older siblings. By sixteen to eighteen months, a toddler might respond to a parent's question of "Read book?" by running to get his favorite book and then coming back to sit in his mother or father's lap.

On the other hand, let's say your sixteen-month-old seems to string together one piece of give-and-take at a time. She may take a toy you hand to her, for example. Or her play activity may look something like this: she points to a book, then finds her play hammer and hits a play workbench. Perhaps she then goes over to a toy car, picks it up, looks at it, drops it, and begins looking aimlessly out the window. After a few minutes she may walk over to you and pull at your clothing. In other words, there seems to be no organized pattern emerging from her behavior or needs—that is, from her emotional life. At sixteen or seventeen months, this kind of behavior signals a need for you to become more involved in helping your toddler link up actions so as to organize her emotions and behavior.

One way to help your child become more organized is to help create "bridges" between one response and another. In order to give your child the needed support, you will need to set aside adequate time and energy. Twenty to thirty minutes at a time, a few times a day, seems to work best.

Let's take the example of Andrew, a fifteen-month-old boy, and watch as his mother works to help him overcome typical "fragmented" behavior. During one playtime Andrew points to a book but does not get the book and bring it back; instead he begins to stare aimlessly out the window. He has provided his mother with an opening; an indication of a wish, but no more. His mother simply and directly verbalizes what Andrew wants, "Ah, book." Since he for some reason will not take the initiative to get the book, his mother offers a helping hand, saying, "Let's go get it together." But when his mother offers her hand, he turns away, refusing to help get the book. This happens frequently during their early playtimes together. The first few times mother shows him that she recognizes what he wants and gets the book for him, providing running commentary on what she is doing: "Oh, book—let's get it together. Well, Mommy will get it." Then they proceed to look at the book together. After this pattern is repeated many times, whether with a book, truck, or other toys, his mother tries to encourage Andrew to accompany her and sets up incentives for the youngster to participate more actively. She gets the picture book, for example, but then sits on the floor and invites him to join her. Further enticement comes from her making expressive facial gestures and saying, for example, "Wow, look at the picture of that truck." This behavior is finally enough to prompt Andrew to join mother in the middle of the floor. Although she has done two-thirds of the work, Andrew has agreed to meet his mother part way, which may indicate that his initiative and ability to link up two responses in a complicated social exchange is emerging.

In a later playtime, his mother offers a helping hand and, this time Andrew extends his tiny one to her. They walk together, get a book, and sit down to look at some pictures. But much more has actually happened. The patient and steady encouragement the mother has given her child may have helped him realize that it can be satisfying to take the next step. For whatever reason he had been reluctant to proceed, the offering of support and collaboration provided a bridge between thought and action that he could not have constructed alone.

Andrew, although it was difficult for him, at least gave his mother an indication of what he wanted to do. A child less able to organize emotion and behavior does not provide even this small opening, often leaving his parents with little idea of what to do. This is when parents most need to draw on their patience and originality.

For instance, a fourteen-month-old may grunt a number of times and then look blankly around the room. The parents' task is first to gain the child's attention, then try to understand what the grunt is about. They may begin by patiently offering different objects to her. She may react to these offers by simply turning her head or saying, "No." This is not a discouraging pattern; in fact, it's quite the reverse. Their child, who just sat there and grunted at first, is now involved in a complicated social interchange. She is both paying attention to her parents and what they are offering, and making a clear response to what is being offered. Now may be the time to build on those simple responses by using humor and creativity. Making comical faces, using a funny voice, or having the toys talk to one another may catch the child's interest and get her involved with both toys and parents.

The parents mentioned above worked very hard to help their child overcome her early difficulty with the milestone of beginning to organize her emotions and actions. They knew they first had to be available to their child, then offer her very specific encouragements. Initially it meant making one hundred percent of the connection, but slowly they were able to change the balance so that their child eventually did most of the initiating, while they offered support.

An occasional difficulty encountered by parents of children who have trouble linking actions is their ambivalence about encouraging their child's independence, rather than supporting his appealing passivity. Once ambivalent parents become aware of their mixed feelings about seeing their child grow up, however, they can give up their ambivalence, become sincerely interested in fostering their child's growth, and take pleasure and pride in his ability to link actions together, with their help.

If it seems to you that, after you make a reasonable effort, your child's difficulty in linking bits and pieces of behavior together persists, it might be wise to seek professional help. It is possible that

Ten-month-olds involved in organized interactive play.

your child's difficulty may have physical, neurophysiological, cognitive, and/or emotional elements.

ORGANIZATION OF EMOTIONS

Is your child beginning to communicate a variety of emotions in an adaptive manner, with clear intent—in other words, in an organized way?

Toddlers are capable of so many emotions: for example, pleasure and excitement, protest and rage, assertiveness and curiosity, dependency, love and security, disappointment, embarrassment and fear, demandingness and stubbornness. They frequently show strong emotional development in some of these areas, but need help in others. For example, Brad, at fifteen months, was a marvelously organized child, but only when he was being negative or refusing to do something that was asked of him. He just couldn't seem to be happy in the company of people. What he seemed to enjoy most was playing with his trucks, moving them back and forth. During this activity he would tolerate his father's presence as an onlooker, but he always grabbed the trucks away as soon as his father tried to become an active partner. The consistent defiance he showed by pulling the truck out of his father's reach and his complete lack of joy not only suggest organization and intent to be negative, but also an unwillingness or inability to interact with his father in a pleasurable way.

The goal for any parent whose child has the capability to express emotion in one or two areas is to help his child broaden his ability to cover areas he is less comfortable with. In Brad's case, these were pleasure and curiosity. Brad's father's first step was simply to be available for play. In this case, he had to be actively passive—he voiced an enthusiastic comment or two, occasionally offered to help Brad do something, or imitated Brad's play. In this way, Brad had the opportunity to take charge and direct the play he chose. After a few weeks of ignoring his father's presence, one day Brad suddenly banged his toy car into his father. A short time after that he would sit close to his father and lean on him—still in an aggressive way. From there he graduated to ordering father around a bit.

Brad had begun to make use of his father, even though he was still expressing negative rather than positive emotions. Though it was difficult for Brad's father not to get angry or discouraged, his desire to free the love and warmth he felt were in his child made him persist. He knew that if Brad could be drawn into a relationship with him, there would be an opportunity for Brad to experience the variety of emotions that emerge when two people are intimate—feelings of joy and happiness, excitement, discovery, and curiosity. Brad's father began to foster some of these feelings by gently introducing novelty into their play. For example, to help his son experience the pleasure of mild surprise, he rolled a truck toward Brad and then pulled it back. Brad brightened up and gave a little grin; he was interested in the unexpected. Eventually Brad imitated this pattern and tried to surprise his father. He was now gaining more confidence in his own initiative. The formerly unaffectionate Brad could now be wooed to sit on father's lap so they could examine the truck together—how the wheels turned, how the door opened and closed. Physical closeness, together with the excitement of exploration and discovery, further enhanced Brad's capacity for intimacy. Before he could interact emotionally, he needed to experience the feeling of intimacy for himself. By working long and patiently to show Brad he was there for him, and by gradually introducing him to a set of emotions founded on love, Brad's father was eventually able to reap the reward of his small son's climbing into his lap with trust and affection, and a toy to share.

At the other end of the emotional seesaw is the child who is well organized when it comes to mild, pleasurable activities, but could use some help with anger, assertion, and exploration. Such a child is often affectionate, passive, and compliant. This child plays well alone or with her mother or father and is able to use gestures and sounds to communicate her wants. On the other hand, curiosity, assertiveness and the desire to explore seem to be absent from her repertoire. Anger and frustration overwhelm her and lead to uncontrollable crying, leaving baffled parents to figure out the cause. She may be generally apprehensive about acting independently, and especially anxious and clingy anytime her mother is out of sight.

For this type of child, parents need to provide support for whatever attempts their youngster makes to link her feelings of assertiveness, anger, or protest to behavior. But first, parents must learn to tolerate their child's frustration. Doing this allows the child to see her negative feelings as acceptable, and the need to express them as appropriate.

For example, the mother of our affectionate but frustrated child may find her child's cry of hunger and discomfort frightening, but rather than responding quickly and anxiously by bringing a variety of foods to placate her, she can calmly suggest that baby show her what she wants. This type of parental behavior teaches two things: (1) bad or uncomfortable feelings can be tolerated and dealt with without undue panic or upset; and (2) the fastest, most effective way to deal with these feelings is to communicate needs and wants effectively including using gestures, sounds, and words as well as organized behavior. The "show me" attitude gradually encourages the child to link negative or uncomfortable feelings with solutions that require assertive (or angry or explorative) behavior, and which the child has the power to set in motion.

In addition to finding the parental tolerance to help a child face frustration, it is important to find opportunities for involvement with your child when she is relaxed and ready to explore. Parents of a child who is able to play well on her own need to be especially thoughtful about being involved in their child's pleasures. When needs for closeness and interaction are met during a time of pleasure, the pressure to have those needs met during a time of anger through enraged clinging may be reduced. This is also an especially good stage in your child's life to take some time away from other activities and sow the seeds for a close relationship with your child.

In all spheres of emotion, there are at least three principles that always apply.

First, respect your child's emotional intention by helping her find the behavior that expresses that intention in an appropriate manner. The problem for the hungry and upset child in our example was not the fact that she was expressing herself but rather that she was expressing herself inappropriately. Her mother supported her intentions when she encouraged the child to express them through assertive behavior. Out of the experience of frustration came the motivation for growth.

Second, create opportunities for unforced practice. Brad, the fifteen-month-old who gradually learned to play with his father, illustrates this principle. Father, as frustrated as he was at times, did not try to force the experience of play and intimacy. He knew that force could have undermined Brad's initiative and might have caused him to rebel against control.

Third, encourage the highest level of communication skills that your child has mastered. When possible, encourage an expression of wishes or limits through organized behavior and emotion, gestures, sounds, and words.

EMOTIONAL STABILITY

How well does your child recover from stress?

Along with your child's new-found ability to put emotions and behavior together, and his ever-expanding emotional and behavioral range, comes the necessity of regulating or stabilizing both feeling and action for oneself. Typically, children who experience a mild upset at this stage regain their composure on their own, or with only a little help from an adult. The child who becomes impulsive or withdrawn after only mild stress or frustration can often be drawn back with patient availability and an organized and pleasurable activity, such as looking at pictures, playing with cars, or making funny faces. Gradually he can learn to see an upset as a temporary interruption of a larger, stable pattern. Your child needs you to help him learn that he can get back to relating to you or others and feel secure and calm.

UNDERSTANDING FUNCTIONAL MEANINGS

Is your child beginning to use objects for their intended purpose? Does he come to you to perform certain functions?

Toward the end of this stage, around eighteen months, the child develops a conceptual attitude toward the world. He becomes interested in how things work and in what they do. He experiments with brushing his or your hair; he closely examines one of his brother's trucks. He also begins to identify certain roles he expects you to perform. Some of these relate to everyday activities such as tying his shoes, and others concern his emotions. When he gets a new toy, he comes to you to share his pleasure and excitement, to tell him how lucky he is to have such a nice new car. When he hurts his knee, the only thing that makes it better is a kiss from you. He begins to understand you as a setter of limits, too. After you have taken the book away from him, which he wants to tear up, and told him not to touch it, he watches you to see if he can sneak over to get it.

You can help your child understand functional relationships by identifying the functions for him. You can encourage him to comb his hair, brush his teeth, or wash his face. You can look to see how the toy choo-choo train works. And the same principle applies with helping him to understand your role. When he falls, you can say, "Let Mommy fix it" rather than just picking him up and physically comforting him. When he is excited, you can express your pleasure over his happiness. Parental involvement and encouragement always heighten a child's interest. In this case, it also teaches him how the world works, which is a very important step for his next stage of learning to create emotional ideas.

SEPARATION AND FEELING CLOSE FROM AFAR

Is your child interested in exploring or does she "cling" to your side?

Part of your toddler's ability to take initiative and do more is related to her ability to be independent. In a small way, independence surfaces when your toddler takes the lead in, or changes, a game she is playing with you. Independence surfaces in a large way when she decides to go exploring and starts crawling up the stairs on her own. Parents often remark that when their babies go exploring they come back periodically to make sure that their parent (or other caregiver) is there. Children practice independence but want to know that the apron strings have not been cut.

Many children are initially reluctant to leave a parent's side. Usually, however, as they become infected by the excitement of exploration, they need little encouragement to strike out on their own. Children who resist exploration may not feel sufficiently secure. Here is how one mother was able to help her timid child.

Mother had carefully worked out a plan to help her clingy, fifteen-month-old daughter, Michelle, become more comfortable with separation. First, she planned to accustom her child to communicating with her by means of voice, gesture, and eye contact. Then she would experiment with leaving the room for short periods of time, gradually increasing them until Michelle was able both to tolerate her absence and to find her own activity interesting. Mother also knew that she must be especially careful to remain loving and close during other times she and Michelle were together.

She began to put her plan into action one day when she and Michelle were playing on the floor with some blocks. After a few minutes Michelle became interested in a game of stacking two blocks and then knocking them over. As she continued this activity, her mother began to organize the toys on the floor close by—never moving too far away and constantly talking to Michelle about the block game. Each day a similar kind of scene occurred, with the mother gradually able to move around more freely. After a week or so Michelle was comfortable playing and exploring new activities by herself, while her mother, after having been involved in the play for a while, communicated verbally or by facial expression once in a while from across the room.

The next step was to begin to experiment with leaving the room. Mother would play with Michelle for a while, then say, "I'm going into the kitchen for a minute, I'll be back soon." If Michelle yelled, "Mama," her mother would yell back, "I'm in the kitchen." In this way she stayed in vocal contact with her. Initially, Michelle could only tolerate about thirty seconds alone before she ran into the other room to be with her mother. Each time her mother would stay away a little longer, using verbal communication more, always making herself available to Michelle when she needed her and always letting Michelle know where she was. Gradually, Michelle began to tolerate separation, was able to act independently, and could take more initiative on her own.

While encouraging Michelle's curiosity and independence, her mother continued to provide security and intimacy at other times. For example, she tried to increase their special "cuddle" times. Michelle began to blossom as she learned that there are times for closeness and times for more independent play, and that she could be close through seeing, gesturing, talking to or hearing as well as touching.

ACCEPTANCE OF LIMITS

Is your child beginning to respond to limits and making them a part of himself, or does he lack the ability to impose self-control?

At around twelve or thirteen months children usually begin to respond to authority. They may be quite selective about which limits they will accept, however. For example, your child may stop blasting you out of the room by turning the stereo dial after you have issued a few stern nos and some headshakings, but he may continue to put small objects in his mouth, no matter what you do. Children of this age may also wait until you are not looking to do the forbidden. Even so, they will begin to gain an appreciation of what they are and are not allowed to do. Your saying no, shaking your head or finger, or giving a stern, displeased look from across the room will begin to have meaning and impact. Through his increased functional understanding of the world, your child senses your seriousness. When it is necessary to take something from your child or to restrict his activity, accompany the action with a verbal explanation so eventually physical force can be replaced by words and gesture or sounds. When all else fails, going "eye to eye" and letting your child know who is boss and what the rules are is worth the effort.

Children who have trouble responding to limits usually need one or both of two things: more closeness and affection, and/or more practice with limits. In order for your child to respect your authority, there must be a foundation of security and intimacy and the development of purposeful communication. If these earlier tasks have not been successfully mastered by the child, both parents and child are bound to have a terrible struggle with the setting of limits. So, first ask yourself whether your child has established a good foundation of security and intimacy. If you have doubts, return to Chapter II and practice wooing your child. If the development of communication has been a little shaky, take another look at Chapter III and concentrate on responding to your child's actions in a reciprocal manner. With time, patience, and a liberal dose of these "special ingredients," your toddler should begin to follow your instructions. Gradually, he will be able to set limits for himself.

Practice can also help your child learn to follow limits. As tempting as it is, it is not wise to always avoid the difficult situation so that nothing is upset. Allow your sixteen-month-old child into a room where there is valuable property, but impose limits. Since you probably do care about your possessions, here is an opportunity for your child to practice following rules that are not set arbitrarily. He will also begin to realize that one behaves differently according to the context—he can be as rambunctious as he likes in his playroom, but in another setting self-restraint is more important. Remember, sometimes the best lessons occur during the real ball game.

Your assertive, organized child will probably offer some protest to the limits you set for him. Why shouldn't he? That china box may be a priceless antique to you, but to him it's made to be opened and shut. Crying, shrieking, and stomping around a bit are perfectly acceptable ways to vent some anger, and distraction can usually short-circuit a major blowup. However, your child may choose a more worrisome outlet and need your help to find better expressions for his frustrations.

Head-banging is an example of a worrisome outlet. Although repetitive motion is common between eight and sixteen months, repetitive head-banging can be harmful to the child and should be discouraged. Both ear problems and other physical difficulties can at times cause this behavior, so take your child to his pediatrician first. If no problem is diagnosed, there may be an underdeveloped ability in some area. For example, a child who uses his neck and trunk muscles to express frustration may not have tried using his hands and feet to bang or stamp or may not have used his whole body to experience motion by running or dancing. Perhaps he is providing himself with rhythmic experiences he missed in earlier stages of infancy. Whatever the basis for your child's behavior, you can help by giving him alternatives for venting his anger and for feeling motion that can aid his development. Teach him to wave his arms and legs, bang a toy hammer, or do simple tumbling exercises. Cuddling, rocking, and wrestling with an adult may also help. What he is learning is how to coordinate his whole body to meet the basic needs of feeling motion and expressing frustration.

What you are learning is how to help your child find alternative behavior that will enhance his development while meeting his basic interests and inclinations. It's always easier for a child or anyone else to give up an old habit if a better outlet is offered. Particularly at this stage, when your child is developing flexibility and a capacity for original behavior, your assistance will help him to use his emerging inventiveness to create a few alternatives of his own.

PERSONALITY DEVELOPMENT

Is your child developing his own inclinations and strengths? Is his unique personality beginning to emerge?

By twelve or thirteen months you will begin to see your child's distinctive personality emerge. One child may be an insatiable explorer; another may be teasing or playful; still another may appear very thoughtful and show great interest in picture books. The behaviors your child prefers demonstrate her emerging interests.

Sometimes, however, a child may display a personality style that does not seem to capture his uniqueness. Take, for example, the overly compliant child. This child seems to define herself only in relation to what her *parents* want. In the absence of parental wishes and demands there is little personality that is her own. Similarly, a child who can define herself only as the opposite of what her parents want may also have little else in the way of a unique sense of self. In both cases these children are not developing their own inclinations and special features. Though the traits of overcompliance and negativism play a role in normal development, they must not become the only pattern the child shows. If they do, you need to take a step back and help your child discover what makes her special. You can do this by setting aside special playtimes and other opportunities to be to-

Helping Your Child to . . .

1. ORGANIZE EMOTIONS AND BEHAVIOR

— spend enough time with your child to become involved in interactions—e.g., if your child is in an active mood, put a record on, dance together
— make connections between the interactions for your child—e.g., "Music's on. You want to dance? Let's dance"
— build on your child's responses—"I like your dance. Can you clap, too?"
— gradually shift the initiative to the child—"Would you like another record?"

2. BECOME ORGANIZED ACROSS THE FULL EMOTIONAL SPECTRUM

— respect your child's emotional intent—"My, you look angry"
— help give him alternative ways to express the emotion—"Don't cry, show me what you want"
— provide bridges to help him elaborate intentions in a more organized way; if your child has trouble expressing warmth—"Come sit in my lap and let's look at this toy"

3. HAVE EMOTIONAL STABILITY

— show your child how to return to a state of calm; When child is upset because he can't have more cookies, draw him back to you by offering pleasurable activity
— offer closeness and security

4. UNDERSTAND THE FUNCTIONS OF OBJECTS AND PEOPLE

— show your child how things work
— let him practice using a comb or brush on you
— explain how you will make his hurt better, or why you don't want him to do something

5. FEEL CLOSE WHEN SEPARATED FROM YOU

— make sure your child can communicate with you distally (across space) through facial expressions, gestures, and voice
— go into a different room from child for short periods of time, gradually increasing and use verbal communication
— give extra opportunity for hugging and cuddling throughout the day

6. ADHERE TO AND RESPECT LIMITS

— make sure you and your child have a close relationship
— allow your child to practice limits—teach him not to unroll the toilet paper, don't just remove it
— help your child channel protests into adaptive expressions; tell him "You may not hit me, but here is a pillow you may hit"
— teach the setting of limits by combining words and actions; before you take your child away from the toilet paper, say, "Don't do that"

7. DEVELOP A UNIQUE PERSONALITY

— set aside special playtimes
— support and admire your child's initiatives
— follow your child's leads

gether and by following your child's lead for clues to her "secret" person. Your admiring, supportive attitude toward your child's favorite games and ways of communicating will help your child express herself and gain confidence in her abilities and initiative.

Creating a Supportive Environment

Aside from the very specific things you can do to support your child's growing ability to organize his emotions and behavior, there are broader emotional characteristics and parental skills that are especially important to have during this phase of development.

One of the key emotional characteristics parents must have to encourage organized behavior is the ability to *admire* their growing toddler. This admiration for the toddler is more than simply the loving affection and caring of the earlier stages. Admiration invites the child to feel pride and investment in his new activities as well as feel affection. A toddler needs this pride and interest in his new physical, psychological and thinking abilities. As he struts and wobbles about, testing his new ability for walking, as he figures out how to take a toy apart, as he expresses complicated emotions in a more organized way, the toddler either senses admiration and pride or a lack thereof. When the admiration is there, the toddler feels support for his new capacities.

If parents are repeatedly indifferent, the toddler may suffer by feeling disappointed and not learning to appreciate his abilities. Even more troublesome is the parent who, consciously or unconsciously, feels envious or competitive with the toddler because of his emerging abilities. Sensitivity to his parent's envy, which is in many respects the opposite of admiration on the same emotional spectrum, might cause a child to feel conflicted about his abilities. If no one shows them how to show love and concern, how can they learn to do so?

A good opportunity for admiring your child is when you are playing with him, especially when you are following his lead. If you are a good follower, you can help your child achieve greater organization and complexity in his emotions and behavior. At this age, especially, your child wants to be "the boss." To be sure, there is much that a toddler should not be in charge of—using sharp scissors, stirring cooking food unaided—but in play and other relaxed activities, there are opportunities for you to be the follower. If your tendency is to overcontrol at this age, your child's tendency may be either to rebel or, on the other hand, to be overly compliant.

Following your toddler's lead and being a good partner is not necessarily easy. You may feel like you're trying to learn a new dance step with a partner who keeps changing the rhythm. Yet, if you can make yourself available to your child and can concentrate on her, she will provide clues to what she is trying to do or communicate. For example, one seventeen-month-old girl had a favorite book about a baby bird. Once, when her mother was about halfway through the book, the little girl grabbed it, threw it down, and smiled at her mother. Her mother scolded her, which led to a mild tantrum. The next day they read the book and the same thing happened, but in this instance, mother saw the larger pattern: her little girl was trying to help the baby bird learn to fly! She didn't need scolding, but encouragement. The mother made birds and a nest out of paper and helped her daughter act out the story as she read it. This mother's spontaneity, intuition, and an ability to see the pattern enabled her to see and support her child's clever interpretation.

While many of us would never have guessed "the bird wanted to fly," your admiration and ability to follow are fundamental characteristics which, if practiced persistently, can encourage growth in all the child's tasks—even with many "wrong" guesses. And there are numerous other ways that you can encourage your child's emotional growth.

The ability to bring your toddler back to a state of self-control after he's gone out of control is an art of great importance. This is similar to helping your child regain stability after a stressful situation. Let us take Eric, an eighteen-month-old, as an example. He brings a book to his mother and they begin looking at pictures together. After a few minutes, he starts to mess up his mother's hair and become mischievous. Taking Eric's lead, his mother engages in a little roughhouse with him, until he starts to become overly aggressive, kicking his feet and flailing his arms. Sensing that Eric is getting carried away, his mother attracts his attention back to the book by pointing out some pictures she knows he's interested in. Using this help, Eric is able to calm down and regain control of himself. The pattern is completed as Eric resumes looking at the book rather than getting completely carried away. Mother's behavior was exemplary: she was not overly controlling and tolerated her youngster's initiative up to a point.

In another instance a child who becomes playfully excited might begin throwing toys around the room. Before this activity becomes too chaotic, parents might call their child's attention to a specific toy, also showing their own interest in it. Once the child's momentum has been stopped, they can suggest other ways to play with the toy— perhaps, "Let's pretend to drink from the teacup," or, "Show me how the jack-in-the-box jumps out," or, "Love the baby doll." In this way, the parents help their child learn to shift from disorganized play, and from one activity to another.

Also important will be your capacity to help your child expand the complexity of her play. By expanding her play, the child brings in more behaviors and emotions. For example, a child may build the same block tower again and again. A parent can help expand this activity by building a tower next to hers and then suggesting they build a path between the two. The towers can even take on separate personalities, one which wants to clown and fall down and one which wants to be upright and solid. If the child is interested, the twosome will be off into new territory. Similar tactics can be employed for a variety of other games. After playing a chase game for a while, father could gradually interest his child in exploring the yard or house together. The theme, finding things, remains the same, but the context is changed. At the same time the child is encouraged to string together quite elaborate emotional patterns.

Throughout the establishment of this supportive environment the importance of your ability to provide security and set limits for your growing child cannot be overstated. Let us discuss security first. The combined feelings of new independence and continued security are basic to normal development. The need for this combination may be particularly strong when a child is angry with her parents. For example, Marissa, an eighteen-month-old girl, was very angry and frustrated when her mother couldn't understand what game she wanted to play. The following scenario took place: Marissa ran out of the playroom, walked back in, pretended not to see her mother, then walked out again. Her mother did not protest. Marissa continued to walk in and out of the room, but now glanced at her mother each time. Taking advantage of the contact, mother smiled and reached out lovingly. Finally, Marissa came over for a hug, and they searched for an activity that she enjoyed.

This mother's behavior gave her daughter the assurance that she could be independent and assertive and her mother would still be available when she was ready to reconcile. Marissa's mother did not run after her and try to control her daughter's independent action or shut her out because she was angry. She was able to remain warm and available, which encouraged Marissa's exploration by providing a comfortable balance between her need for independence and her need for security.

Sometimes it seems hard to provide security and independence with an angry child. A good example is Judy who, when leaving for work, was always faced with a very cold shoulder from fourteen-month-old Tommy. She very much wanted Tommy to give her a warm hug and kiss goodbye, but Tommy just turned his head away. Not only did he make her feel guilty about leaving but also distressed about leaving without a feeling of closeness. After being troubled by the situation for a few days, Judy realized that she had to allow enough time in the morning to play with Tommy and also a few extra minutes around departure time. With this change, she made Tommy feel included in her morning routine and also gave herself time to woo him back to her—to cajole him and run after him—once she announced she was leaving. When Tommy finally gave her a hug, it contained the warmth and closeness she needed to let her know that Tommy, although sad to see her go, wasn't angry with her. It showed that he felt secure in her affections and would tolerate the separation.

You may also face the cold, silent treatment from your child if you are busy running in and out, not having much time for contact. This is a little different. Children use this response as a protective mechanism. They don't want to warm up when you don't have time to reciprocate. They may be just saving their affections for the right moment, when you can reciprocate. And if this is the case, you will find a warm, joyful toddler during your special time together.

To be effective, the setting of limits must occur in a warm and secure environment. This means you will want to stay emotionally involved and keep your child engaged while you are letting him know

Once a toddler becomes organized, even arranging flowers is within his scope.

1. Admire your child's new abilities
2. Be a good follower
3. Bring your child back to organized behavior after being disorganized
4. Help your child expand the complexity of his play
5. Recognize your child's need for balance between independence and security
6. Stay emotionally involved and available while you are setting limits

which of his behaviors you find unacceptable. Even if you find yourself in a heated exchange with your toddler, it's better for your child to feel the heat rather than for him to feel you withdraw emotionally. If, for example, your child pulls books from the shelf for what seems like the hundredth time, scold him firmly rather than just clenching your jaw and silently removing him from the scene. Active and emotional involvement between parent and child helps the child make the limits a part of himself. It is also important for you to "be there" emotionally after the discipline is over. The most constructive setting of limits occurs when you are able to convey your "serious" concern appropriately—your child is able to deal with his anger as best he can, and both of you are able to regain your closeness and warmth soon after. As was discussed in the previous section, you shouldn't be afraid to raise your voice and be assertive with the child, nor should you expect the child not to voice some opposition. You will feel less helpless, frustrated, and angry if you feel you are having impact. The idea is not to "discharge" your anger but to set limits. Also, to be effective, the setting of limits must use the distance or distal modes of communication as well as the proximal ones. Gestures, sounds, and words with appropriate emotional tones will convey to Jenny that it is time to "cut it out!" A stern look followed by a "now!" will bring home the message. Obviously following up this "higher-level" dialogue with physical restraint will be necessary at times. It is a mistake, however, to use only the easier and quicker physical restraint. Your child will learn to respect your vocal overtures if they are persistent, clear, and serious, and if there is enough love and security at the foundation of your relationship.

Reviewing Your Support

Parents or other caregivers who have enjoyed a baby's warmth, taken pride in his recognition of them, and developed an effective two-way communication system may find their industrious, creative toddler difficult. Here they are, faced with an increasingly curious and independent person. They may sometimes feel that their intuition has abruptly abandoned them. To help sort out your feelings regarding the little person in your life, you need to examine each new ability of your toddler to determine whether it raises a particular problem for you. Are you uncomfortable with independence? With someone else being "the boss"? With someone else taking the initiative? Are you confused or angered by your child's constant shifting back and forth between independence and dependence? Does your child's curiosity about your body or what you do in the bathroom upset you? Think about the various ways your toddler is rapidly developing— organization, new emotional expressions, imitation, initiation, originality, independence, setting of limits—and try to tune in to whether you are supportive of his new interests and abilities.

YOUR FAMILY SITUATION

During these months when your baby is beginning to explore and become more original and focused, you have a special opportunity for admiring your baby's new abilities. But it is especially easy to overlook your baby's needs at this time because her new level of independence may make her appear less needy. However, although she gradually requires less constant physical care, emotional care needs to be maintained. She needs the security and stability of a strong emotional involvement to brave her strange new world.

Fortunately, babies usually "remind" you that you are needed. Their clinginess, night wakenings, and other familiar patterns can be a signal to you that not only do they need more love and admiration from you but also you need to examine your other relationships to see if they are interfering with your closeness to your baby. As discussed in an earlier chapter, when taking stock of your situation it is important to remember that the most obvious problems may not be the only ones causing you stress. If something is going on that causes you to withdraw from your baby or to become overprotective, it is likely that you are unaware of it. Being aware of a problem often frees you to keep it out of your relationships with your baby.

For example, Robert's mother was not aware that she felt "abandoned" by her toddler because "he didn't need me any more." Instead she started to take out her anxiety on her husband, accusing him of "not caring" and attending only to his work (which he had done for the last five years). The tension mounted between them. Robert began feeling his mother's real loss of interest in him and began waking up in the middle of the night; his mother felt needed again, but his father was tired and angry. Robert became more passive and clinging during the day. Eventually a few consultations clarified everyone's feelings. Robert's mother felt reassured about her place in Robert's life, the tension between the parents abated, and Robert got back on his developmental track, overcoming his anxieties and sleeping through the night. But their story shows how a special new ability in a child can change the family equilibrium.

PARENTAL PERSONALITY STYLES

At various points in our children's lives, most of us experience periods when our children seem especially difficult; times when we can see ourselves overreacting, or when something about our child really "gets to us." But an active toddler is able, at times, to unravel even the most patient and loving of mothers and fathers. Three new abilities in particular can be problematic: initiative, independence, and organization. Should your child be especially adept in any of these areas, you could find yourself sorely tested and even begin to react negatively toward your child.

Let's look at Brian, a seventeen-month-old who was particularly demanding and assertive. He would walk to the refrigerator, point to the Jell-O, and say, "Eat." His mother would then patiently explain that he must wait until after dinner, but he just stood there, pointing and repeating the word "eat" twenty times or more. Since he was neither out of control nor being destructive, it didn't seem fair to punish him. On the other hand, he was being extremely irritating. Brian was making life particularly challenging, and his mother did not enjoy being with him. She was equally unsettled by the amount of anger he stirred up in her.

At this point, Brian's mother decided she needed to sit down and ask herself what it was about Brian that made him so difficult. She quickly realized that he was just a bit more demanding and assertive than her other children, and it was this extra bit of assertiveness that gave her trouble (as it would most mothers). On top of this, he knew how to avoid punishment by remaining stable and organized. Looking back, the mother saw that her child had always been unusually gifted in being able to organize himself in a determined manner: he sucked hard, he doggedly practiced crawling, and now he played and made his demands known in a forceful way. Simply being aware that her child had some unique characteristics that stirred her own feelings was an important first step. This alone reduced the pressure she felt and allowed her to tackle the problem of teaching Brian to wait more patiently.

Since Brian didn't have any concept of time, saying they would eat dinner in fifteen minutes wasn't very helpful to him. So instead, his mother tried to involve him in an activity related to eating dinner and then to getting his Jell-O. She brought out some pots and pans, letting him help "cook" the dinner. This play gave dimension to the waiting time and also showed him that his mother understood what he wanted, since his activity was related to his desire. By the time he had stirred the air in four pots, it was time to clean up for dinner. Mother also used their time together to talk about the word "wait," asking Brian what he had to do before he got his Jell-O. The answer was "Wait."

Similar reactions to children who are particularly strong in certain areas can arise. Another problem with the assertive child can be worry over his hurting himself. Finding your sixteen-month-old climbing to the top of the refrigerator does not promote a peaceful feeling. Some very organized toddlers become controlling; they want to be boss all of the time. The constant struggle over who sets the rules can be exhausting and trying. Also, parents may react to an independent toddler with a legitimate sense of loss. A slight feeling of rejection is actually normal and appropriate to watching your baby grow up.

Although all of these concerns are very normal and appropriate, parents must take care not to let them interfere with the love and support their child needs. Brian's mother learned that if something is disrupting your relationship with your child, try to become aware of which characteristic it is that bothers you. Often, you'll be able to resolve the problem from there.

Envy and Competition. Ironically, sometimes a child's very success at this stage, his capacity for new organized behavior, initiation, and his own special seductive charm can stir up a parent's envy and competitiveness rather than admiration. Children of four or five are better able to handle competitive and envious feelings from their parents and caregivers than toddlers are. At a young age, as your child's new abilities for organization and initiative are just unfolding, an envious attitude may be frightening. Ask yourself if you might be teasing your child excessively or inappropriately, taunting, overstimulating and/or trying to overcontrol. Do you ever think, however fleetingly, I wish someone would take care of me like that, have feelings reminiscent of a competitive relationship with a brother or sister, or have resentful feelings? Introspection is often a good first step. Understanding your feelings can help you make your child's environment more supportive.

Even if you do not feel envious toward your child, chances are his other brothers and sisters do. They need you to help them tolerate their feelings of envy and competitiveness. Parents who are not comfortable with rivalry will not be able to show their older children how to enjoy their younger sibling's new abilities. By understanding and accepting the rivalry, parents can gradually help older children learn that collaboration has its rewards. For example, a parent can set up play situations that encourage the children to cooperate. Parents can also help older siblings take pride and pleasure in the toddler's emerging abilities by encouraging them to teach the youngster how to sort shapes, how to "draw" pictures, or roll a ball. Remember that your older children will take their clues from how you handle new challenges in the family. But even if you feel comfortable with rivalry, the siblings may still resent the newest addition. You can help them by encouraging them to talk about their competitive or negative feelings.

Overidentification. As children begin to develop their personalities, it is very tempting for parents to "overidentify" with their child and try to mold him into what they wished they had been. A mother may want her child to be very bright; she may emphasize words and books, and ignore the child's interest in building with blocks. A father may decide that his child must be a super athlete, even though the child prefers drawing and reading. It is clear that overidentification does not support the child's own originality, interests, and sense of uniqueness, but forces him to conform to an image. Some children comply with their parents' wishes and tend to develop a superficial attitude of being quite happy with the direction in which they are pushed. Others rebel. If you can step back and ask yourself whether you are emphasizing one particular area or emotional style for your child (e.g., the "perfect lady," the tough jock, the kid who is really "cool" and nonchalant) you may be able to determine if you are overidentifying with your child. If you are, think about what you are trying to experience through your child and what specific behaviors of yours show this. You don't need to stop what you're doing abruptly; just provide balance by encouraging your child's interests as well.

Overcontrol. A personality style that your child will be especially sensitive to at this stage of great initiative is the tendency to over-control his actions. For example, a father and his fourteen-month-old daughter are playing with a Busy Box. She is learning to push the buttons and levers to make different animals pop up. Rather than clapping for the child and helping her name the animal that pops up or patiently showing her how to manipulate the more complicated levers, the father finds himself ordering her to push the levers in a certain order or pushing them the "right way" himself. The game soon deteriorates into a power struggle, and the child gets upset.

An overcontrolling or intrusive attitude can be the result of fears that are stirred up by your child's new independence, as we will see in the next section. Or perhaps you just like to be in charge. Become aware of how comfortable you are when your child takes charge of a play activity while you follow. If you feel anxious or uncomfortable about giving up control, practice letting your child lead. Often, getting used to the experience will be very helpful.

Overprotection is a variant of being overcontrolling and stems from many of the same concerns with a child's new independence. We will discuss overprotection in the next section.

Being Distracted. At this stage your child brings greater organization to the family unit by creating his own bridges from one activity to another. A child who is particularly good at this sometimes outstrips his parent or family in this ability. If he is capable of shifting from a chase game to peek-a-boo to looking at picture books and is able to weave it all together into one complicated drama, he can totally confuse a parent who is preoccupied and easily distracted. Keeping track of what a child is trying to do and helping him to expand his play requires attention to the child's intent. A parent who mentally wanders in and out of the child's activity cannot be very supportive of the child.

Recognizing your own tendency to be distracted and preoccupied is not easy, but there are clues. Does your child's play seem confusing to you? Do you feel unable to help your child build bridges between activities? You may be able to focus on your child's activities more simply by paying attention. If you feel you cannot do this, you might consider involving him with other adults (such as a babysitter) for a few hours a day. In addition to having a secure relationship with you, he will also have extra support for his new skills of organization and initiative.

It is important to note that the personality characteristics we have been discussing may only be a problem if they are quite pronounced. After all, every parent has tastes and preferences, as does every child, and these should not be hidden. The key is to insure balance. No part of your child's new abilities should go unsupported. If your child is not given the opportunity to practice a new emotional ability, it will remain undeveloped. Your child's emotional interests and inclinations will endure, but at a primitive level, and they will not become a part of her advancing ability to put emotion and behavior together. In later life, your child may experience difficulty coping with an emotion, or emotions—such as aggression or anger or independence or tenderness—whose growth is unsupported.

Take a child who does not have the opportunity for aggressive play, such as banging a peg into a pegboard or playful rough-housing. He may resort to more primitive, disorganized forms of aggression—biting, spitting, or negativism. Similarly, if you forbid your child to explore a doll's body or ask questions about her own or other human bodies, the child's opportunity for greater understanding and potential for increasing ability in this area is thwarted, perhaps to result in a preoccupation with an earlier ability, such as direct physical stimulation. The principle of practice is also true for dependence and independence. The parent must help his child go from holding, to smiling and gesturing from across the room, to exploring, and then back again. This provides the opportunity for the child to practice learning how to feel secure while on her own, such as was the case with Michelle, whom we met earlier in the chapter. The child who cannot feel connected while "doing her own thing" is confronted with two equally untenable alternatives: stay close and hold on (the clinging child) or become pseudo-independent (the "I don't need anyone" child). The challenge for you is not to decide if your child should be interested in pleasure or aggression, dependence or independence, but rather to create opportunity for practicing the full range of emotional experience.

COMMON PARENTAL FEARS

At about the time their toddler begins to have the capacity to organize himself and to show initiative, certain feelings may be awakened in parents. The child's new capacities for taking charge and being independent may understandably awaken fears over separation, domination, control, intrusiveness and aggression. Some feelings support the child—admiration, confidence, and security—but others do not. Fears that co-exist with supportive feelings may play a minor role and, as we've pointed out, feeling a little rejected or concerned for your child's safety can be quite appropriate. Sometimes parents' feelings of fear become major and can undermine their toddler's development.

Fear of Rejection and/or Abandonment. Because of the toddler's new independence, one of the most common parental fears at this stage is that of being rejected and/or abandoned. Betty, for example, was a mother who, during the first year, enjoyed being close to her baby and often felt that she and her baby were "like one." This was an extremely useful feeling during the first year, but as her baby grew, she did not need Betty in quite the same way. When her increasingly explorative toddler did not want to stay in her lap and cuddle, Betty began to think, "I guess she doesn't need me." Betty reacted by withdrawing and not being available when her toddler came to her intermittently for warmth and cuddling.

The feeling of rejection experienced by parents occurs when there is anxiety about the balance between independence and dependence. As with other problems, recognizing the pattern of behavior is the first step toward a solution. We all have reactions when we think we are being rejected. What we have to do is understand our tendencies. For example, you may want to ask yourself whether you tend to reject before being rejected or try to forestall rejection by overcontrolling and inhibiting—in this case, your child's exploration.

A series of worries may also accompany the underlying fear of rejection: "The baby will hurt herself." "What will happen if she does not know where I am?" "She doesn't like to be held anymore; there must be something wrong with her." These worries, along with the basic fear of rejection, may even accentuate parental symptoms such as depression, withdrawal from the child, and sleep disturbances. At this stage, when your child is developing so many new skills, he really needs you to take pride in him and provide emotional warmth and security.

Many parents have a sense of loss at this point in their child's life. It is natural, normal, and appropriate to feel this way. Also, your feelings of loss can help you understand the loss your child feels for what he is leaving behind as he faces the unknown challenges of growth. Your empathy will ease his task and your own.

Fear of Being Controlled. Another common fear is that the toddler, now able to take initiative and be independent, will take control and "run the show." This feeling is not usually as obvious as the feeling of rejection. However, if it becomes too strong and outweighs a parent's admiration and pride for his toddler's new abilities, it can become the basis for a power struggle that can last until the child leaves home, and sometimes beyond that. Parents who are strong enough to recognize their own part in setting up power struggles can go far toward creating an environment of trust and loving support.

Abby was a woman who liked to be in control. During the first nine months of her son's life, the baby flourished in the security of her "take-charge" attitude, which was augmented by her warmth and ability to respond to the baby. Largely as a result of this solid background, at around twelve months Abby's child was ready to take charge a little, too. But Abby was fearful and constantly imposed her willpower on his. One day, when he was fourteen months old, he began lining blocks up next to each other. Most mothers would have watched patiently and tried to help carry out his idea. Abby quickly took the blocks he had lined up and piled them on top of one another.

She had decided to help him make a tower, to teach him better motor coordination. Her son reacted to his mother's intrusion by knocking her tower down and throwing the blocks. Each day, during their first few minutes of play together, Abby would be patient, allowing her son to start imaginative play. After about five minutes her anxiety would build and she would start to take charge. As if on cue her toddler would become aggressive and disorganized in his play. Abby's intrusion not only hampered her son's emerging ability to organize his activities but also helped establish a pattern of disorganized rebellious behavior.

If you suspect you might be intrusive or overcontrolling, either ask yourself or your spouse if you seem to "take over" rather than cooperate when your child is showing curiosity and taking initiative. If the answer is yes, then ask yourself additional questions, such as, "Am I afraid my child will leave me?" "Am I afraid my child will become too aggressive?" "Am I afraid my child will do something wrong?" These are the kinds of apprehensions that may be awakened by your child's autonomy, and can lead to parental overcontrolling and intrusiveness.

Fear of Your Child Getting Hurt. Being overprotective, as we've said, is a variation on being overcontrolling. In this case, however, a parent does not try to impose his or her will. Instead, fear that the child will come to harm leads the parent to hover around the child and to act panicky when the child ventures out of sight. It creates an atmosphere that says the world is an unsafe place—doom lurks behind every corner—and conveys to the child that he is unable to do anything for himself. Naturally, it interferes with his sense of initiative and experimentation. Faced with an overprotective parent, the child often becomes clingy and uncertain about taking initiative or else very negative.

In order to recognize this trait in yourself, it may be useful to ask yourself how many times you have felt panicked by your child's activities. A frequent feeling of apprehension may indicate that further introspection will be helpful. It may be reassuring to have your spouse or another adult watch your child with you a few times or to get together with other mothers and toddlers so that you can collaborate on how to ensure your child's safety without overprotecting.

Fear of Setting Limits. Another common fear that parents struggle with at this particular time of development is related to the issue of setting limits. Some parents feel they have to "tame" their child's new independence and assertiveness. They fear that if they don't, the child will become wild and unruly. Although it is certainly true that a child needs to have limits set for him so that he can later develop his own capacities for setting limits, parents must allow expression of their child's new assertiveness and curiosity.

Let's take Matthew, a high-energy eighteen-month-old who enjoys warmth and intimacy and is endowed with especially good motor skills. He runs with good coordination, rolls a ball, scribbles with crayons, and is generally well developed for his age. He likes to race around the house, pushing a little truck and occasionally hitting the furniture. His father, a passive man, tended to be preoccupied with avoiding any danger; understandably, he was not comfortable with this aggressive activity and worried that his son would go out of control. When his son was being industrious and assertive in his play, his father would interfere and make him do something peaceful, like look at a book. This interference quickly blocked Matthew's avenues for assertive behavior. When he became frustrated and tried to assert himself anyway, his father disciplined him, believing he had to set limits. It was no surprise when this very competent, industrious child began making his father's worries come true. He became rebellious, belligerent, and disorganized. He would cry and throw things. When his father yelled at him and scared him, Matthew would cry and cling to him. Matthew's behavior alternated between disorganized, aggressive play and clinging onto his parents' legs in an aggressive yet frightened way.

With an assertive, industrious child, it is best to respect the type of play he enjoys and, if he needs to be redirected, try to switch the particular activity (say, throwing balls around) to one that is less rambunctious but contains the same emphasis (perhaps a chasing game). Quiet times are important, but they should not be the only alternatives.

Other parents have the opposite problem. They are afraid to set limits. They fear ruining their children's sense of excitement or making them inhibited. Take, for example, an enthusiastic child who has a tendency to get very excited—to the point of being out of control. What starts as a game of running from room to room leads to his jumping on furniture and almost breaking it; playing with blocks leads to throwing the blocks at a window or at his brother or sister; exploring his four-year-old brother's room leads to pulling apart his brother's toys. Soon this little toddler is running, and ruining, the entire house. His parents, who don't want to inhibit him, are letting him become chaotic, disorganized, and aggressive. His older brother has nightmares of children being kidnapped.

Children need limits. It is a part of learning to become organized. But, if a parent either feels intimidated by his child or, at the other extreme, feels a need to exercise excessive control, the limits set may not support the child's growing organization. Examine your feelings about aggression and about being out of control. Think about whether you usually feel apprehensive and uncertain about disciplining the child or realize that you always seem to be angry and overwhelming. Doing this should help you see if you have any conflicts about setting limits. If so, occasionally your spouse may be able to help and supply more balance. Asking for a spouse's help is easy, and it is especially helpful in setting limits. And the more you are able to work as a team, the better it will be for every family member.

Fear of the Child's Dependence. A different kind of parental fear can arise when children do not immediately show industry, curiosity, and initiative but instead are timid and clingy. There are many reasons why children may be frightened by this phase of development. It could be that one of the past stages was not mastered. The child, for example, may have never fully fallen in love and so doesn't feel secure enough to let go. Or the child's communications of assertiveness and anger may have made the parents anxious, causing them to overcontrol the child—the child responding by becoming compliant and clingy. Or the child may sense apprehension in his parents over his emerging ability to "demand" more closeness—motioning to be picked up— and so he begins to curb it and becomes clinging instead. Some parents become frightened of or annoyed at their child's neediness and dependency. In fact, some parents react negatively to any tendency toward dependency, no matter how slight. They fear their child will never grow up or leave them alone. Parents who have these fears sometimes make the error of separating from their child too abruptly. They suddenly decide to work more; they avoid being home; they tune out when they are there. What this type of child needs is patient help to become more secure when separated from his parents.

Take young Alexander, who has been ill during much of the first

123

year of life and has reason for being more dependent and fearful than another toddler might be. His parents became anxious over his dependency and decided that he had to learn to play on his own. They forced him to stay alone in his playroom and paid no attention to his crying and fretting. This only increased Alexander's fears—after all, it told him that no matter how much he wanted or needed them, they would not come. Soon he wanted to be carried all the time, stopped talking, and had trouble sleeping. His parents finally realized the need to encourage his independence gradually. They helped him play by himself for short periods of time by staying within sight of him. They were also generous with intimacy and physical contact. For example, his mother would sit on the couch and hold Alexander while she read to him; his father would hold him as they played with blocks. They slowly encouraged his initiative and independence by giving Alexander some time on his own. They also made it clear to him that there was ample security and intimacy still available.

In many families the fear of the child's dependency is not as dramatic as our example. However, a parent's desire for his child to "be a man," "be independent," or "be tough" or the fear that he will become "too dependent" dominates and actually undermines the child's growing independence. The best way to help children become self-sufficient is not only to encourage self-sufficiency, but also to provide the emotional security and support to help them build a properly secure foundation. The fear that a child will not be able to take care of himself often leads to the very results a parent is anxiously trying to avoid. As with the other fears and feelings we've discussed, if fears of your child's dependency become so intense as to outweigh your feelings of admiration, pride, and support so needed at this stage, try to acknowledge your concerns and to tolerate your discomfort when the child shows a need to be dependent.

Misperceptions of Toddlers' Emotional Interests. In addition to the major parental fears, fear-related misperceptions may cause problems at this stage. Because a child's emotions and behaviors are becoming much more complex, parents have many more opportunities for misinterpreting and distorting their child's intentions. When a baby's behavior is simple, like crying for food or wanting to be rocked, parents usually do not distort or misinterpret this behavior unless there are unusual emotional pressures. However, with complicated behavior, parents' conflicts and anxieties often cause distortion. This can be seen in the case of the father who saw his son's assertiveness as a lack of control. And, as this father later learned, distorting originality and assertiveness into lack of control can be very upsetting to a child. In another case, one mother distorted her daughter's expressions of joy into ones of lack of control. Often her daughter became excited with a new toy, jumping and giggling when first playing with it. Her mother, a subdued unemotional person, misperceived her daughter's enthusiasm for a lack of control.

Another common problem area for parents is sexuality. Children normally begin to show a nonverbal interest in their bodies (and their parents' bodies) sometime between fifteen and twenty months. This is the beginning of your child's interest in sex. Parents' conflicted feelings often take the form of misperceptions and overreactions.

Many parents who seldom talk about bodies or sex become understandably anxious and confused when their seventeen-month-old begins to play with her genitals or the bottoms of her dolls or wants to follow her parents into the bathroom. Even though it isn't easy, try to take the longer view. Nothing is "wrong." Your child is discovering a part of his world, one that is healthy and normal, and will afford him much pleasure throughout life. You have the ability to communicate with your child and help him understand the new world he is discovering. It's important for you to be as supportive and informative as you can be without becoming too uncomfortable.

If, on the other hand, you are a parent who is extremely open about sexual matters and anxious that nothing should be hidden from your child, you may find it helpful to remain on the level of your child's interest so as not to overwhelm or overstimulate him.

The two ways in which children become preoccupied with sexual matters is: (1) if parents are anxious and tense and try to hide or ignore sexual interest; or (2) if parents are overstimulating and/or overly seductive—for example, indirectly rubbing their child's genitals during physical play.

Your child's sexual interest is one in which you should take pride, as you do in his or her other discoveries, neither overly encouraging or discouraging it. Limits or guidance are needed only if you see that your child becomes anxious or if sexuality becomes a focus that obscures your child's interest in other areas. You can, for example, explain the importance of privacy in the bathroom, or offer your child interesting alternative play if you feel that he is playing with himself too much.

There is no particular right or wrong way to deal with your child's emerging body and sexual interests and curiosities. Families often have their own cultural values that they want to communicate to their children. What is most important is that the members of the family respect their own feelings and differences, and recognize their child's need to feel natural and comfortable without becoming overstimulated or preoccupied.

Your child is trying to organize so many different emotional areas—originality, independence, pleasure, love and curiosity, assertiveness, initiative and exploration, protest and anger, setting limits for oneself, and an overall uniqueness of style. It's an enormous task for child and parent alike.

In the span of a year, your child has grown from a baby just learning the meaning of a smile to an independent, verbal, and emotionally demonstrative little human being with his own interests, aptitudes, and opinions. In the meantime, you have grown from a caregiver responsible for providing almost total physical and emotional care to a game-player, teacher, supporter and admirer, loving disciplinarian, follower, partner, and the one who knows your child's ups and downs, strengths and interests the best. You are experiencing your child's emotional awakening and growth. By virtue of your being a parent you have the privilege of sharing these beautiful—and predictable—moments of human development. And, as a parent, you have the power to help make this short time into a secure emotional and social foundation that will not only ready your child for the next milestone, learning to use emotional ideas, but which will also last your child for the rest of his life.

V | CREATING
EMOTIONAL IDEAS

—18 to 36 months

It is a cliché to state that sometime between eighteen months and three years, parents are usually confronted with the "terrible twos"—stubbornness, belligerency, and power struggles. The two-year-old who refuses to put his pajamas on, the two-and-a-half-year-old who throws his food on the floor, the three-and-a-half-year-old who will not put his toys away—all present the day-to-day challenges that occupy all of us. Equally challenging can be the curiosity and interest of your eager young child, who follows you into the bathroom and wants to know the names of body parts, or who feels it's his right to grab at you and explore your body at will.

For the most part, these kinds of challenges represent the trees rather than the forest. Once you become aware of the more general capacities your child should be developing in this age group, you will find it possible to work out effective strategies for dealing with the day-to-day dramas, however challenging.

In fact, it could be argued that the terrible twos need not be terrible at all. There's nothing in the child's emotional makeup at this stage that makes belligerency inevitable; in fact, problems mostly arise from the fact that *he* is changing, and *you* are having trouble keeping pace with him. He is developing enormous new skills for conceptualizing the world, but he still feels dependent on you; he wants to experiment with powerful new feelings of curiosity or even aggression, but he still craves the warmth and security of your embrace. As he rides this emotional seesaw it's sometimes hard to be up when he's up, down when he's down: you may still think of him (and treat him) as a baby while he's striking out independently, or you may assume his new skills betoken a maturity he isn't ready to live up to. Finding the right balance isn't easy, but if you can look beyond day-to-day power struggles and address your child's development as a whole, you're more than halfway there.

The next two chapters will help you ask questions that address these broader concerns. Looking at how well your child is developing in major areas is, in a sense, seeing the forest. Considering these areas does not mean that you should ignore a provocation from your two-and-a-half-year-old or an intrusion into your privacy from your three-year-old. Your child's actions require responses—how else will he learn that those actions matter, that he matters? When your responses are guided by an understanding of the larger developmental pattern your child is engaged in, your responses to individual incidents are likely to help your child with the broader issues he may be struggling with.

As your child progresses through his second year of life and into his third, you will be able to see his emerging ability to use ideas, to conceptualize. This ability has its origins during the second year, when your child shows an understanding of the function of an object by "talking" on the telephone or combing his hair. He also relates the idea of function to the emotional world when he begins to understand that mother is there to hug, feed or dress him, or roll a ball to him; father is there to wrestle with, read a book, or give a bath. In addition, parents and other important people are experienced as a combination of their functional attributes. They are no longer separate, visual, auditory, tactile, or smell experiences. They are now all of these experiences together, plus a person who does certain things and evokes differing emotions. Your child's ability to connect what he feels, sees, touches, or hears with its functions is an important step toward his next milestone—the ability to construct ideas and to use them to put emotions and behavior together.

Creating Ideas

In their rudimentary form, ideas are the way one's mind combines one's experiences with an object—what one has felt, seen, heard, touched—into a multisensory emotional image. An object's sensory and emotional characteristics are integrated with its functions to form a mental picture. One view is that children begin to use ideas when they can construct the image of an object after it has been out of sight for some period of time. A child has reached this stage, for example, if, after a lapse of time, the child can search for an object such as a ball that has been put behind a screen while the child was watching. In order to do this, the child must be able to create a mental picture of what was hidden—perhaps, its shape, color, texture, smell, and purpose—and then remember that the ball was put behind the screen.

In terms of the world of ideas that relate to feelings and human relationships, the level of conceptualizing has been reached when a child, for example, can construct an emotional image of a person or an interaction when that person is not present. The child is able to construct a memory of an older sibling, let's say, who has gone to school, that includes many of her sensory characteristics (how she looks, feels, smells, what she sounds like), as well as an understanding of her function and her feeling tone, including the last game of "hug the doll" or the last fight, for that matter.

As you can imagine, the ability to construct this kind of emotional image or idea provides a child with an unusually valuable coping device. When his mother is out and the child is with a sitter, he can evoke his warm loving image of his mother to comfort himself. If his father calls on the telephone and gets annoyed with the child because he keeps throwing the receiver down, he can perhaps picture his father a little while later and reconstruct for himself some of the sounds and sensations associated with talking to a "mad" father. As he learns to use this new ability, he may even pretend to be the "mad" father and yell at a toy animal, or doll.

Of equal importance is the fact that these images or symbols, as they are sometimes called, now permit a child to put ideas together in ways that allow him to plan more complex behavior and emotions. The child who is thirsty can now construct the image of his mother as the person who brings him a drink. This allows him to call for mama, and when mama comes, to say, "Juice, juice." This child has planned an action pattern based on putting two related ideas together. Initially many children may not elect to use the ideas or images at their disposal, but will instead yell, scream, or cry. Parents are then left to guess what their child wants. All the more reason for you to help your child develop the use of ideas.

One of the most obvious indicators that your child is using ideas is language development. If your child names a certain kind of food after not hearing its name for a while, for example, it shows that your child now has an idea, which he indicates through a word. If your child is upset and says, "mad," you know that he has conceptualized and labeled an emotion, thus creating an emotional idea.

The use of language as an indicator of your child's capacity for using images or symbols is well known. A less well-known indicator, and one that may be more useful, has to do with a child's capacity for make-believe or pretend play. When your child goes from realistic use of his comb or toothbrush (showing he understands the functions of these objects) to using them for "pretend play," it's another indication of his emerging use of ideas. If your child gives her doll a bottle and pretends to be its mommy, you know that your child has an active internal set of ideas that she is using in play. She is caring for the doll as she has seen someone care for babies. When your two-year-old tucks her doll into bed and tenderly kisses her cheek, you know that she has formed an idea of affection by abstracting your tone and applying it to her doll. In general, any pretend play sequence that has an emotion associated with it—the child caring for his doll or using a stick gun to go "bang, bang"—shows that he is forming emotional ideas.

A third indication that your child is using ideas is his ability to use complex patterns of gesturing. Complex gesturing is often used by children in lieu of talking, and can suggest a preplanned scheme of such complexity and clear-cut expectations that it would be hard to imagine the child is not using ideas or symbols to plan. An example is the child who gestures to Mommy to pick up and comfort another child who is crying. In addition to picking the child up, she indicates that mother should rub the child's back and pat her head. She has formed an idea of how to comfort.

Finally, some children demonstrate their use of ideas by organizing spatial patterns as in block building. Using blocks, a child may show he has an idea by simply moving a block "car" between two block "buildings" as though a road exists. Whether it is putting blocks together in a line, building fences for animals or eventually building more complicated structures such as houses, building, or later on drawing, shows the existence of a preconceived image, and suggests that the level of ideas has been reached.

Whether your child favors pretend play, language, gesturing or spatial relationships, respect his individuality even as you encourage him to express his ideas in all forms. On the emotional side, practicing pretend play, language, and gesturing may help him develop tools to identify and reason about feelings, while having fun with spatial designs may help your child develop tools not only for impersonal abstracting but for understanding how his body operates in space. On the cognitive side, practicing pretend play, language and gestures may contribute to his use of verbal symbols and reasoning in the future, while block building and drawing may contribute to the future use of spatial relationships, such as the ones involved in mathematics.

HOW CHILDREN EXPRESS IDEAS

Children express ideas in two distinct but parallel forms. The form that is more commonly recognized can be called descriptive. This simply means that your child shows his ability for having ideas by naming objects. If you ask him to name different kinds of toys, he can probably name three or four. Similarly your child may be able to look at a picture book and label what he sees. (Naming pictures can sometimes be done before the child is able to use ideas because the child is naming a visible object rather than creating the name in the absence of seeing the object. Often, however, naming objects and beginning to use ideas go together.) When you label emotions for your child, he can begin to identify these verbally too. As discussed earlier, by recalling the name of an object or emotion, he is summarizing many of its features. He knows that a ball bounces and can be thrown, that it feels soft and smooth. He knows that being happy makes him want to smile and laugh. Thus, simple labeling of an image gives your child the ability to store a vast amount of information. Commenting on how the child plays with an object—"look at how fast that ball rolls when you push it"—highlights its attributes.

The other form of expressing ideas is interactive or functional, which is somewhat more complicated but very important to recognize. To see this form, look at the way your child uses language or make-believe play in an interactive context. The child who says to you "me hungry" is using two ideas—the idea of himself and the idea of his hunger—to represent the expectation of being fed. When your child takes a stick, points it at a doll who is the pretend bad guy and says "bang, bang," it is a clear emotional interaction involving either aggression or protection. When a child says, "do-do face" to his father, giggles, and runs away, there is clear interaction. He is not just describing what he thinks of father; he is using emotional ideas expressed through language, gesture, and then behavior to lure his father into a playful chase game.

Your child's ability to express ideas in an interactive form starts at a very simple level and gradually matures. Initially, your child will simply convey some sense of intentionality, usually concerning something he wants. For example, he may request a toy through language or gesture, or may sit in your lap and indicate he wants a hug.

At the next level, your child expresses a need or desire that concerns himself plus another person, such as, "Daddy, horsey ride" or "Mommy, hug me." By doing this the child explicitly acknowledges the role of another person, rather than simply stating his demand. Here is an example of an emotional idea you might see in play: Your child is holding two dolls. One says to the other, "Me hungry." The second doll proceeds to feed the first. There are now two dolls, each with an explicit role, the needy doll and the doll taking care of those needs.

At the third level, you might think of your two-year-old child's ideas as little balloons or islands, each of which contain multisensory experiences. One short play sequence may not seem to be realistically linked to another. The caregiving scene of dolls feeding each other may give way to an aggressive shooting scene, which may then change to block building. (Although your child's more concrete behavior, such as his ability to follow instructions, will be organized at this time, his use of ideas is still fragmented.) Whatever seems to occur to him from moment to moment is expressed in his pretend play or language. Similarly, time plays little role in actual events. Whether events are separated by time or occur simultaneously, they may be linked as though they were related by cause-and-effect. One child, for example, played with a train and then "fed" a sandwich to the train. This sequence emerged when the child combined two experiences that were fun for him—having a sandwich while on a train ride. Although the connection stumps adult logic, his logic may have been, "I'm showing you what's fun for me—train rides and eating."

Children in the two-year-old range have not yet created the psychological bridges that help them link together emotional ideas. Emotional experiences that have occurred close in time, or that are related to similar wishes, or to feelings that are or appear to be similar—all these things may appear related in your child's eyes. Feeding the dolls shifts to shooting the bad guys to throwing a ball perhaps simply because these objects are located near each other.

At the fourth level, however, your child will string together a number of his emotional ideas so as to develop a more complex story, or pattern with a more organized emotional theme. In addition to feeding one doll and then another and another, your child may now have the doll perform various activities with the same emotional theme. If he is feeling exuberant, his doll may lovingly play chase with another doll, do somersaults, and then play peek-a-boo. Or perhaps many different characters—the doll, horse, bunny rabbit, and space man—are at the table being very adult and having a tea party. Activities that occur within the larger story might be decided on the spot, but they do serve to keep the story going .

The fifth level is usually not reached until thirty-six to forty-eight months, and will be described further in Chapter VI.

By eighteen months, your toddler may be at the first level of using interactive ideas described above and steadily making progress toward the next. The second level will usually occur around age two, the third around two and a half and the fourth at around three years. However, your child's specific age is not important. What is important is that toward the end of the second year, say at twenty months or so, your child shows some expression of interactive ideas and gradually develops the more complex patterns of ideas described at each level.

As your child is leaping forward in his use of ideas, you may notice that he is going backward in some other area of accomplishment. This is typical when any new ability is developed. For example, the child who is demonstrating ideas by using language, or recalling a promise made to him earlier, may also become clinging, have temper tantrums, be extra sensitive to separations, or have temporary sleep or eating disturbances. This regression occurs because, as a general rule, new advances may be a little frightening to the child; each new advance, whether learning to walk or learning to use ideas gives him a new perspective of the world. Although instability generally occurs alongside developmental accomplishments, it may be clearer during this phase because your child is taking so many giant steps forward. He can now create perspectives of the world through his ideas, and these perspectives may be comforting or scary. So if he feels shaky and babyish about separations or going to bed, don't expect too much of him. Remember that these momentary backwards slides are just that—momentary. They can be short-lived and in the service of further growth and development when handled sensitively.

Observing Your Child

As your child begins to use more complex emotional ideas, he has a widening and deepening area of emotional development to explore. At the same time, your child's increased verbal abilities makes interaction more exciting for you both. Be aware of the different emotional strengths your child can now bring to each situation. If you are, you'll be able to support your child's negotiation of the "terrible twos" more effectively.

During this stage you'll be looking for evidence of your toddler's ability to express emotion through ideas. As we've seen earlier, this ability is shown in pretend play, use of language, complex patterns of gesturing, or complex spatial play as with block building. Of course, individual differences will mean that children develop faster in one area than another; the time span over which these abilities emerge is quite long. What you will be concerned with is noticing some degree of forward momentum. Allow your child's preferences to determine how he expresses himself first. If your child is a master builder and seems to be a little slower in talking or in pretend play, encourage him in his slower areas but respect that his ability to form and use ideas is probably moving along very nicely.

CONSTRUCTING IDEAS
TO EXPRESS EMOTIONS

Does your toddler express any ideas—emotional or otherwise—through pretend play, language, gestures, or spatial play? In his play is he beginning to stay with a particular emotional play theme for longer periods of time? Over time, is he tying smaller ideas together to make a richer drama?

The poignancy of watching a two-and-a-half-year-old play Mommy is profound. The child, totally absorbed in putting her doll to bed, copies your warmth and manner—the way she smooths the covers, strokes her doll's hair, says good night. You realize not only your importance to and impact on the child, but also how she borrows from you to experience another world; through your example she leaves the world of the child and experiments with more advanced emotions. In her soft singsong voice, she praises her dolly, "Good girl," or reprimands, "Mommy mad" or calls up whatever emotion she wants to experiment with. Often, you can tell by her tone or facial expression that she is experimenting with shades of reaction. She gets only a little mad or teases the dolly. When she practices and familiarizes herself with these emotions in an environment she controls, she is then able to transfer her lessons in make-believe to the real world—where her ability to express emotional ideas is important to her development.

What should you do if your child seems to need help in learning to use emotional ideas? Let's say your child seems to have mastered all the prior tasks in emotional development but is not moving on. Jeff is a good example. He is a healthy, curious twenty-six-month-old who has not advanced past examining his toys. He enjoys moving the doors on his play garage, making the lift go up and down and watching the cars zoom down the ramp. But he hasn't begun to develop a story to go with the activity. At this age, one might expect a child to construct a two-minute play sequence where the car drives up, he puts gas in the car and perhaps pushes it through the car wash, holding as much of a conversation as his verbal skills allow. Likewise, he indicates his needs—wanting a hug or something to drink—but he hasn't begun to feed his doll or comfort it. His play contains no emotional theme.

If your child has similar play patterns as Jeff, you first want to observe whether he has, in fact, mastered the task just prior to using ideas—that is, using objects in a functional or intended manner and understanding the roles of mother and father. (If you have doubts, refer back to Chapter IV.) Let's assume he has. Your goal now is to create special playtimes that will encourage your child to use ideas. By becoming a partner in play, you can provide significant motivation for your child as well as an opportunity to practice.

During your special playtime, take an interest in whatever your child is doing and then find ways to introduce pretend play. Use what your child is doing as a transition into the world of ideas. Let's say your two-year-old child makes noise with a hammer and bell. After a period of admiring your child's play with his toys, introduce a duck puppet who uses the hammer to bang the bell. Talk for the puppet, saying, "Loud, loud." Your child may then take the duck and imitate you. Meanwhile, you can get a dog puppet and continue the play by starting a simple dialogue between the puppets, or by having the new toy give a kiss or talk on a telephone. Look how far you've already come. You have taken advantage of your child's interest in banging the bell, his delight in hearing its noise, his pleasure in using his muscles, and shown him how to do this while using a puppet to pretend. Even if your child is not interested the first time, keep trying. A different puppet or animal may catch his eye.

Once your child is interested in ideas, at least in a rudimentary form, the next steps become easier. While following your child's interests, you can bring in additional "actors" to his play and different emotional situations. If your child is holding the duck puppet and accidentally drops him, you can bring in another puppet to be Mommy to comfort the duck or suggest the child be the comforter. The child may then insist you give the duck a comforting hug and kiss too. Over

Learning to use ideas in pretend play.

time, your child's own interest will help him begin to enlarge his pretend play and his use of language. You can take him even further by encouraging him into areas of feelings where he is reluctant to go on his own.

There is no substitute for ingenuity, patience, and enthusiastic interest in your child's activities. Helping your child learn to use emotional ideas by support and encouragement is no different from helping your child learn to walk. If your child is more than the average challenge, you may even want to get some ideas from a consultant on how to introduce pretend play more effectively.

(Similar encouragement is helpful to the child who is ready to begin using language but hasn't yet made much progress. Although your child may be having trouble pronouncing words, you may recognize your own speech patterns in the rhythm of his babble. He may even be using sounds in an intentional way. These are positive signs. Your child is using his voice to make his needs known. You can help by working with your child in the traditional ways, such as naming pictures in a book or encouraging him to imitate your sounds. You can also use simple language in your pretend play.)

Let's backtrack for a moment and consider a different problem— the child who is not learning to use ideas and whose behavior is becoming difficult. As we've mentioned, emotional disruptions can be expected when ideas are beginning to form. Regressions, such as clinginess and insecurity, often occur with new advances because of the new perspective on what can be a scary world. If you are able to understand your child's needs for greater dependency and comforting, and you can indulge these needs, you will help him resolve his problems and keep them from interfering with his learning to use ideas. Contrary to popular belief, regression at this time does not mean your child is getting "spoiled" or will never return to his former independence. Everything is changing so fast for her now— she needs all her energy to cope with and understand the changes. Rest assured that, if your child has functioned in an organized and somewhat independent manner at the ages of twelve to eighteen months, the reversal that occurs as her language ability and pretend play increases will likely be temporary. Many parents have been saved unnecessary worry knowing that the need for more dependency and security at this time is part of the ebb and flow of forward growth.

However, emotional disruptions can also occur if your child has not mastered earlier tasks successfully. Trouble with earlier phases will often come to the fore when children start using ideas. The greater physical and emotional demands and abilities at this time can stress existing vulnerabilities. Demands for new abilities such as playing with peers, having a larger and potentially more aggressive body to control, and being aware of family relationships and tensions may create stress. Your child may pull away from relationships, seem hyper-irritable, or constantly cling to you.

Take Sandy, a two-year-old who was normally a clingy child but who began to cling even more while not advancing in the use of ideas. Her few words were not developing into many; her pretend play was not becoming broader or richer. In addition, she was beginning to wake up in the middle of the night and call her parents. She was also becoming more demanding and fussy about what she ate. If she did not get the food she wanted, she had a tantrum or tossed the food onto the floor.

As Sandy became more demanding and clingy, her parents became more tense and felt less like giving in. They spent most days either in concrete indulgence—holding, cuddling, passively looking at pictures—or trying to hold their child off. In a typical day a good part of the morning involved inducing Sandy to eat breakfast without initiating any tantrums, then trying to stop her from clinging long enough to clean up the house, then similar struggles with lunch followed by a few peaceful hours during naptime, after which came all the nighttime difficulties. There was little relaxed interaction and little use of our previously mentioned "distal modes of communication" (signaling through vision, hearing, and gesturing) that would help the child feel emotionally closer and secure but still be physically separate. The child did not experience any emotional communication through ideas, only through behavior.

Sandy had not suddenly turned into a spoiled brat. Rather, she had become frightened by both her growing abilities and some unfinished earlier tasks. She had not yet learned how to balance her need for security with her desire for independence. If you are a parent in this tug-of-war, you can come to your child's aid by helping her practice the earlier, unmastered tasks along with the current task. In this kind of situation, your first step is to understand the insecurity your child is feeling. Make yourself available for play at specific times during the day. In this way your child can experience closeness, not only through being held, but through eye contact or verbal interchange, and can play imaginatively with toys. Most children will release the choke hold on their parent's neck if the parent is willing to get down on the floor and play. Choose times that are convenient for you, so you won't have to feel resentful or angry. Start off the playtime by finding out what the child wants to play with. If the child can't tell you, show her toys you think she likes until something interests her. Although your goal is to help her feel more secure while practicing to use ideas, you may not want to introduce the pretend play too quickly. A child like Sandy may first need time to enjoy you as partner with no new complexities added. After a few relaxed playtimes, you can start introducing ideas, as was done earlier with the puppets. A puppet, doll, stuffed animal, or other favorite toy is usually a welcomed guest in the play.

We don't want to make this particular struggle sound too easy. You may still have to walk with your child wrapped around your leg for a while. Over time, however, as you and your child play, you will see her play out pleasurable scenes as well as ones that are scary. This is the beginning of real progress in emotional communication. Just keep it going.

If you provide play together with physical closeness for reasonable periods during the day, you will also then be able to set more effective limits when your child is overly demanding. This is partially because you will feel less guilty. You won't have to resent, avoid, or ignore your child. If she throws food on the floor because her demands were not met, you can feel more comfortable enforcing limits. (To be effective, setting limits usually requires the collaboration of both parents as well as firmness and consistency so that your child gets the idea that you mean business.) The more comfortable and secure your child feels, and the more her use of the world of ideas is being developed, the more she will want to please you, and the more likely she will be to accept the limits you set. In other words, indulgence of and attention to your child's need for dependency go hand-in-hand with effective limit-setting. You are teaching your child two things at once: (1) emotions can be expressed, but there are ways other than those she prefers at the moment; and (2) when she can not discipline herself, you will help. In this way, you *earn* the right to set limits.

Let's consider another child, Vicky, a high-energy two-and-a-half-year-old who is aggressive, impulsive, and easily distractable. She wants what she wants when she wants it. When she doesn't get her way, she throws things, stamps her feet and runs around. She also has problems with sleeping and eating. With this kind of child your basic goals are the same as with Sandy, the clingy child: to help your child practice using ideas, to provide greater security and (usually) to set firmer limits. In addition, before you can start helping your child practice to use the world of ideas, you may have to use your ingenuity to help your child focus her attention on the tasks at hand.

Vicky especially loved a game in which she and her father took turns catching each other. When Vicky was involved in this game, she seemed to be a little more relaxed and less impulsive. Her father thought Vicky might learn to enjoy pretend play if she could incorporate it into her chase game. One day her father added a slight twist to the game after he had captured Vicky's attention. He suggested that he pretend to be Big Bird, that Vicky be Little Bird, and that they fly around and try to catch each other. Vicky embraced the idea, and the two of them were suddenly operating in the world of ideas. Next time they played, her father pretended that Big Bird hurt his leg and Little Bird had to care for him, thereby adding in emotional ideas. Vicky's parents also got puppets of other characters she liked, so that she could sometimes get down on the floor and play more calmly. Gradually Vicky began to use the world of ideas in her own way, became more organized in her play, and better at self-control.

The tendency in many families with a child who is hard to control is to get totally caught up in the child's unruliness. Vicky's parents had first tried just punishing her for her willfulness and had found that she could "dig in" and be very persistent no matter what they did. They found that her unruly behavior only increased under this regime of punishment and limit setting alone. Neither was a regime that emphasized the notion of wooing and indulgence a solution. Vicky quickly raised the stakes to see what it would take to get her parents to set limits on her. The appropriate pattern must involve a balance—setting limits needs to be offset by equal amounts of emotional expression or play guided by emotional ideas. If this balance is remembered, the child will eventually be motivated to respond to limits. Obviously, the child who operates in an actively destructive manner is going to need a greater dose of setting of limits, but the key is to balance limits with engagement in ideas.

Your toddler is in the process of making a great leap forward in life. He is learning how to use ideas to guide his feelings and emotions. By developing his capacity to use ideas, he can help himself to resolve insecurities, fears (including nightmares) and other experiences which may take the form of troubling behaviors or symptoms. This is the phase that prompts parents to say, "I can almost see the wheels turning, almost see how his little mind works." If, for some reason, difficulties persist, even after you've given these suggestions a try, don't hesitate to seek a professional consultation. The same support you would give to your child's intellectual or motor development can mean healthier social and emotional development for your child.

Another reason for considering professional consultation at this stage is that "learning problems" may begin to show up now. "Learning problems" can affect using ideas by interfering with your child's ability to process information through hearing or vision. A child who hears well, for example, but cannot decipher or decode what he hears (in other words, the processing of the words is garbled) may be stubborn and defiant because he cannot understand what his parents are telling him. A child who has trouble interpreting what he sees may have trouble not only understanding the pictures he looks at but also with human gestures. Such "learning problems" often get detected only in school-age children who exhibit problems with reading or arithmetic. They should, however, be considered a possibility for a child who has continued difficulty reaching the level of ideas. A full diagnostic workup can determine whether there are problems in the way a child processes what he hears, sees, touches or otherwise experiences. If detected early, such learning problems can often be corrected more easily than later on.

RANGE OF EMOTIONAL IDEAS

Does your child express his ideas using a variety of age expected emotions in pretend play? Does he use ideas to express his emotions when interacting with you?

Between the ages of eighteen to thirty-six months, the emotions children typically experience are those related to dependency, love and security, including a sense of loss and sadness, pleasure, curiosity, assertiveness, anger and protest, setting self-limits or self-discipline and self-punishment as well as a number of fears and anxieties related to these emotional areas. (There are many ways to categorize human emotions. We have chosen these categories to help us systematically observe the emotions children use.) You can observe your child using these emotions while he is involved in make-believe play or while he is directly meeting his basic needs, such as dealing with frustration or anger. You might see your child exhibiting the following kinds of behavior to express emotions through ideas:

Dependency and security—caring for and holding a doll or stuffed toy

Pleasure—showing smiles and excitement to accompany play; indicating fondness for certain food or a special toy

Curiosity—hide-and-seek or exploring drawers or closets; search play with dolls or stuffed toys

Assertiveness—making needs known verbally; putting doll or stuffed toy in charge of activities of other toys

Protest and anger—using words such as "mad" to express anger; getting mad at an uncooperative toy

Setting self-limits—punishing a doll or stuffed toy for being naughty; responding to parental "no"

If your child does not express some of these emotions through ideas, he may express them in a more concrete manner. Anger, for example, is a challenge for most parents and children. A child who is beginning to use ideas to express anger may show this by getting mad at his doll, as suggested above. A while later, when he gets angry he may begin to express the anger verbally. A child who has not begun to express anger through ideas will not use that emotion during play and will often resort to more concrete forms of expression when he is upset, such as hitting, biting or having a tantrum.

Take the example of Jimmy, who enjoys taking care of his stuffed dog in pretend play but who has temper tantrums when frustrated. Today, his mother cannot find his green car just when he wants it. He manages to say "Car. Green," and then when it doesn't instantly appear, he turns red in the face and starts kicking, stomping, and throwing things all over the place in a full-fledged tantrum. At moments of rage like this, your teaching about ideas obviously needs to wait until you have calmed the child down. So Jimmy's mother yells a little, threatens a little, and physically stops Jimmy from kicking until he quiets down. The two then sulk in mutual annoyance for a few minutes with Jimmy going off by himself and starting to play. At this point, his mother sits next to him, becomes a partner in his play, and then gives him a hug to show that everything is all right. While she is giving him a hug, she also says, "Are you still angry?" This gives the child a chance to learn the word for the emotions he felt as well as the idea that emotions can be labeled. Gradually, his mother explains about patience and how to look for things he cannot find right away. Later on, when he wants his green car again, his mother might be able to convince him to be patient and look further. She can show him, even in hide-and-seek fashion, how to look. "Is Mr. Green Car in the closet? No, he's not here. Under the chair?" etc.

This use of ideas will probably not work each time, but he may be willing to wait and look rather than throw a tantrum at least some of the time. Your ability to tolerate intense emotion and to reconnect with your child will encourage his use of ideas to express feelings.

Remember that, when your child is seeking to vent his anger and frustration, he is probably feeling very stressed. It's important to remember that a tantrum is the result of frustration—at the inability to master a task, to communicate a desire, to understand why things are as they are. It's a kind of emotional blown fuse, and it can overwhelm a child completely, making him feel *more* frustrated and helpless than before. Don't make the mistake of meeting the child's tantrum with a tantrum of your own. If you first calm him and then reengage him in the world of ideas, you can teach your child a valuable lesson: he can be close to you even after a disruptive emotional experience. In other words, disruptions are a temporary part of life; they need not be prolonged, or permanent.

Another way to encourage using ideas to express emotion rather than using behavior is through pretend play. A first step is to use your child's behavioral way of expressing an emotion while you are playing make-believe. For example, one day our same Jimmy was taking care of his stuffed dog. His mother sat down with him, watched for a couple of minutes, and then when Jimmy seemed to come to the end of his play said, "Maybe Mr. Dog would like to play with a ball. Now where is that ball? Gee, we can't find it. Mr. Dog, what are you going to do?" She then made the dog jump around and act mad. A plastic horse, lying nearby, was next brought in as the Mommy who told the dog to behave. This type of play with the emotional behavior shows your child how to displace his feelings onto the animals. This means that he can represent his ideas symbolically. Your next step is to have the animals "talk" to each other about the specific emotion, for example, "I'm mad at you." This discussion lets your child know that feelings can be labeled. The last step is to have the animals explain why they felt mad. Explanation shows a more complicated use of ideas. Through this pretend play, a child can see how to use ideas to fulfill his basic need of expressing anger. If you sometimes accompany the child in this play, he will realize that you are comfortable with these feelings and that it is safe for him to practice representing them with ideas. Over time he will begin to imitate his expression in pretend play during his daily interactions.

In addition to learning about labeling feelings and pretend play, a third way you can encourage your child to express anger through ideas is by using words to discipline. Tell your child to stop playing with your necklace and why rather than just taking it away. Obviously, you will have to use physical force when necessary, but even these occasions can be accompanied by verbal commands. Your goal is to elevate your child from the level of physical force.

We're going to digress slightly now and talk a little about the mixed attitudes in our culture toward aggression. Some people feel that if a parent helps his child express and explore his angry feelings, the child will take it as a sign that his parents approve of anger and aggression and will tend to express these emotions more and more. However, we think that using ideas permits children to express wishes and feelings at a "higher" mental level. Ideas become a way of handling or figuring out feelings rather than doing or acting out the feelings. An angry thirteen- or fourteen-month-old can either control his anger, cry, or kick. On the other hand, a twenty-eight-month-old can take a baby doll, pretend it is baby sister, and express his anger at the doll, instead of dumping baby sister out of her infant seat. This added flexibility is an important advance. However, it is important for you to search your own attitudes and emotional reactions to aggression. If you find yourself overly stimulated or excited by aggressive play than by other kinds of play, your child may certainly pick up your attitude. If you genuinely support your child's inclinations to practice using ideas, however, it is likely to help your child develop more flexible coping strategies.

Getting back to the range of feelings your child can express, let's take an example to illustrate this point. Little Robin was a bright and industrious three-year-old who seemed to know just how to get under her parents' skin. They were beginning to have problems with her, especially at mealtimes. She would refuse to come to the table and insist on playing with her dolls instead. Robin's parents would become annoyed, upset, and then angry, all to no avail. Then, just as they were about to explode, Robin would appear and grudgingly eat. Dinnertime got to be so unpleasant that Robin's father took to staying late at his office. The family's life was deteriorating in general, and both parents were perplexed and frustrated, particularly since Robin seemed to be doing so well outside the home. In nursery school she was making friends and playing cooperatively. She was warm and engaging, assertive and curious, verbal and had a sophisticated ability for complicated pretend play. Robin's parents couldn't figure out what was going on. They decided to consult a professional.

During a consultation with the therapist, he noted that, while both parents were excellent at pretend play involving ideas and positive emotions, both parents avoided play that centered around aggression and assertive behavior. Dolls kissing and hugging were fine, but cars crashing into one another or dolls shooting each other with makeshift guns immediately halted play and led to an angry lecture on violence followed by a snack to make Robin "feel better." Robin's parents were trying, in the only way they knew, to transmit their own strong feelings about aggression and violence to their daughter. But they weren't doing it effectively.

As a result, Robin was learning that direct expression of her assertive and aggressive feelings was not permitted, and expression of her feelings through ideas was not permitted either. Since Robin had these feelings (as everyone does) they had to go somewhere. Robin was becoming a master of subtlety, indirectly expressing her aggressive feelings by frustrating her parents at every opportunity. As Robin's parents became more willing to tolerate her pretend play of fighting and anger, she no longer needed to act on these feelings by torturing her parents. Instead, she would pretend one doll was angry with another and say, "You may not watch TV." Robin's mother even got to the point of playing "child" to Robin's "Mommy," and would let her daughter reprimand her for misbehaving. Once Robin's considerable energy and imagination were permitted to deal with her negative feelings, she came up with a number of masterful ways to deal with them.

By getting help, Robin's parents were able to see the forest instead of the trees—that is, focus on the range of their child's emotional experience. They were then showed how to deal constructively with an isolated problem. They came to realize that pretend play fosters thought in place of action, and the best way for Robin to learn to deal with her natural aggressive urges was to use her considerable imagination as part of her relationship with her parents.

Let's look at another example of using ideas to fulfill basic needs, this time with a child who needs security and closeness. Though your child still needs physical nurturing such as hugging and cuddling, he can meet some of his dependency and security needs through his new capacity to use emotional ideas. In this scene, you are in the kitchen cooking as your child comes in, wanting to be held. Having spent time with him a little earlier, you now need to cook dinner. This is a good, uncontrived opportunity to teach your child a new way to experience security and closeness. When your child reaches out and starts whining, explain that you are cooking and will hold him later. Suggest that he be your helper, then take out some pots and pans and let your child sit near you on the floor. Encourage him to pretend to cook on his own make-believe stove.

Organizing this activity might seem like a taxing job. It might seem easier just to order your child back into the playroom. However, you are teaching your child a very important lesson. He is learning that he can experience closeness, intimacy and security by using his ideas in pretend play—that he can feel close to you by imitating you, or sharing your concerns, rather than by clinging to you. He does not have to experience security and closeness only by being held and cuddled; he now has an alternative.

As part of this activity, you can also use our old friend, distal communication modes—signaling different emotions across space by talking, looking, and gesturing—a capacity you have already helped your child develop during an earlier stage. Using this type of communication can establish a warm and secure atmosphere. So, the scene becomes child beside you, imitating your cooking; you glancing down, being expressive, talking to him, asking how his beef stew is coming. Through this partnership, your child is encouraged to use the higher level of ideas in the service of meeting his more basic needs.

An emotion that can become much more prominent during this stage is fear. Although it may be noticeable during other stages (with, for instance, separation anxiety), the fears a child experiences are often a sign of the child's ability to use ideas. He invents his own meaning of an event or even something as simple as the sound of a vacuum cleaner. Having a nightmare, for example, suggests that the child is experimenting with frightful ideas in his sleep; being fearful of shadows or, as he gets older, of robbers coming in to "steal away my baby sister" are signs of the child's level of sophistication of ideas as well as perhaps some of his own hidden wishes. He cannot have nightmares—or fears about the vacuum cleaner—until he is ready to associate ideas and feelings with an object, and can imagine that object being where it is not.

Fears are as much a part of life as are satisfactions, pleasures, and accomplishments. Much as you might wish to protect your child from them, you cannot deny their existence. Of course your child's should be looked at as part of his total functioning. Their presence in his emotional makeup should be accompanied by progressive development in his abilities to experience *all* emotions, from intimacy and pleasure to assertiveness and curiosity, as well as by a growing capacity for friendships. Where fears exist as part of this broader pattern, they should be sympathetically addressed. The child should be made to feel that it is all right to have fears and that you are eager to hear about them. Don't belittle your child's anxiety by telling him, "You're not afraid of *that!*" He or she should be reassured that fears, like dreams, are make-believe, and that you will be there to protect them and make sure that everything is okay. Where abrupt family changes such as divorce, separation, a change in sleeping arrangements, or an illness in the family seems to precipitate unusual fears, you should be aware of the potential impact on the child. Providing extra opportunities for closeness and communication, including pretend play and talking about emotions and security, can help the child through the transition. In this manner, the child sees that the world is safe, comforting, and not as frightening as his fears suggest. If your child is so frightened that he is not involved in important age-appropriate activities such as going to school, or exploring his house or neighborhood, then his fears are interfering with his interests and inclinations. If this behavior continues for more than a few days, you may want to seek a professional consultation.

It should be stressed that when you explain feelings to children you will not always get a response. But that doesn't mean they aren't listening and absorbing your message. A short example can illustrate this. Two and a half year old Jenny was doing well with her toilet training, when her regular babysitter took a vacation for a week. By the middle of the week, power struggles were developing over going to the potty. One afternoon Jenny refused to go to the potty and take her nap, instead insisting on buckling her sandals. Her mother tried to reason with her about obeying but got a deaf ear in return. Finally her mother said, "I know that you miss Betty and that you are mad you can't see her. But you still have to go to the potty and take your nap." With no sign of acknowledgment, Jenny spent another minute trying to buckle her shoes and then stood up and went into the bathroom. She did not give a direct emotional response to her mother's suggestion—such as saying "miss, Betty" or "Betty away"—but showed she acknowledged her mother's awareness of her feelings by being cooperative. Many times, when a child is being negative and stubborn, she is reacting to her emotions. If you are able to put the emotion into an "idea" either through words or pretend play, the child may be better able to deal with the feelings. However, don't overdo this type of detective work and overwhelm your child with your ability to "read her feelings." You're a parent, not an encounter-group leader.

You can help your child experience his emotions through ideas in any area: pleasure, assertiveness, curiosity, and setting self-limits as well as the ones we've covered. Chances are, you have a very willing learner who will delight in crossing the bridges you build from the concrete world to the world of ideas. As time goes on, you also have more tools and materials with which to build your bridge. Remember, if you can allow any and all emotions to surface in interactions, pretend play and talk, help your child use his ideas to fulfill basic needs and demonstrate how to use ideas to label and figure out feelings, you have gone a long way to support your child in one of his most human abilities.

USING IDEAS WHEN STRESSED

Is your child able to use ideas to communicate his emotions when mildly ill, when angry, or after a brief separation from you? Can he recover from a stressful situation and interact using emotional ideas? Can he use ideas to express emotions which concern a more permanent stress?

In the previous stage, we talked about toddlers learning to compose themselves after being upset. Now the task is to help them not only return to an equilibrium but also be able to exchange emotional ideas about the stress. Again, once the intense emotion has subsided, ideally, you and the child should reestablish some contact and comfort. This may mean holding and cuddling after a disagreement is over, as well as establishing closeness through emotional ideas and discussions of the disruptive event. Expect your child's capacity to recover from stress and use emotional ideas to be quite uneven, particularly in the early part of the third year (twenty-four to twenty-six months or so), when it is still new. Gradually, however, your child should begin to learn to reengage emotionally with a little help from you. If you do not see this capacity begin to emerge, you will want to continue to be very available after the stress to encourage your child to be involved with you.

Here is an example of how one can help reestablish contact and to cope with separation. Two-and-a-half-year-old Leslie misses her mother and begins to cry and be stubborn. If at this point her babysitter elects to send her off into a corner to be by herself, she learns that her emotional expression leads to being alone. She still misses her mother and has no better way to cope with it. On the other hand, let's see what happens if the babysitter helps her cope with her emotions. First, she soothes Leslie with holding, talking softly, and stroking her head. She even briefly distracts her with a toy. When Leslie has calmed down, she offers her a book on what different people do and talks about where her mother might be (for example, saying mother might be at work and then showing her pictures of people in an office, suggesting things the people might be doing). Here, the sitter does not try to have Leslie forget that she misses her mommy but tries to help her cope with her feelings. Leslie has learned a number of things at once: she can calm down after feeling upset, she can use ideas to help her feel better, after being angry she can still be close to her babysitter, and, while it is not as good as having her mommy at home, she can think about her mommy and be helped by her babysitter through various means. She may decide that thinking about her mommy is painful and choose distraction rather than focusing on mommy. This is also all right. The pictures related to her mother create a brief transition that allows her to think about her mommy, then permits her to forget about her mommy for a time.

By the time a child is two and a half, she can with your help often practice and prepare herself for being left. Her preparation involves repeating the separation experience in pretend play. A typical example is the child who doesn't want to stay at nursery school without a parent. Let's say her parents do all the right things before school starts. They visit the school a few times and let her play there; they talk about going to school and staying with the teacher; they read books about school; and the first couple of days, they stay for part of the class, easing her into the situation. All this and the child is still distraught at their leaving. That evening father and daughter are down on the floor playing when the little girl starts talking about going shopping and leaving the father at home. She begins to practice being the one to leave. She informs her father that she is going to the store, that he is to be a big boy and not cry, and that she will be back soon for him. She steps into the next room briefly and then returns, announcing, "I back now. You big boy?" Her father assures her that he was a big boy, but that he did miss her. On hearing this, she promptly says, "Again," and begins the play over again, repeating it several more times.

The next day in school, she initially protests when left, but stops— after two loud squawks. The rest of the morning she is relaxed and playful. The evenings of the following two weeks were filled with many separation plays and gradually, through her practicing, she settled into a relaxed, happy experience at school.

Unfortunately some stresses that befall a child are not temporary. Needless to say, an enormous stress is death. It has long been thought that children do not have a concept of death similar to that of adults until seven to nine years of age (when they understand death as something irreversible). Although death and related subjects such as loss are probably about the hardest issues for children to comprehend, this perception is not completely true. Many four- and five-year-olds do understand that, when people die, they are not coming back and that, while they may "live in heaven," it is fundamentally different from their being here to touch or to speak to.

When there is a death in the family, one often wonders how much to tell the child, what will frighten the child, or what will be helpful to the child. Often questions arise such as whether children should be brought to funerals. Here there are no easy answers, and individual family and cultural patterns must be taken into account.

As a general rule, whether the child is two and a half or five years old, you should listen for his concerns and questions, not providing too much information and overloading the child, but providing the facts in a supportive manner. You will need to gauge the child's ability to understand what has happened and try to explain factually what has occurred in a language the child can understand. A two-and-a-half-year-old may well be able to understand that Grandpa will not be coming back because he was sick and died. Even though the child does not understand what dying means, he begins to associate that word with someone being old and sick and no longer being there with him.

Both immediately and for the next days and weeks to come, you should also pay attention to any questions, allusions, or pretend play (such as children being hurt or left) which relate to the child's experience with the lost person. The child may, through any of these modes, show his own concerns. These concerns often focus on whether he or his parents are going to die. By both listening carefully and putting these concerns into words, you can reassure the child. He should be made to feel that you hear these concerns and that you understand them.

Two of the most common difficulties families encounter around issues of death (or other permanent losses such as divorce) concern your own feelings of depression or anxiety. If you assume the child feels the same way you do, you may overexplain to the child or transfer feelings of sadness and despair to the child that the child does not have, thereby confusing him. On the other hand, if you feel that these issues are best not talked about, you may try to protect the child from any knowledge of the event. Regardless of the amount of protection, the child knows at some level that a change has occurred but is alone with his confused, sometimes troubling thoughts.

What is important for you to realize is that more than what you tell the child or whether you bring the child to the funeral (the latter decision can be based mostly on the family's preferences and cultural patterns), the essential element to communicate is that the death occurred. Your level of comfort with the children and your ability to provide security and extra tender loving care during this period of change is what is felt most by the child. In addition, should the child lose a parent or other very close person the need for extra security, and understanding is obviously even more important. If it seems appropriate, because of the overwhelming nature of such an event a family should be comfortable in seeking professional consultation to help with the transition.

Another permanent stress most children encounter is the birth of a sibling. The reaction of the older child to the baby involves a mixture of feelings—love, curiosity, and admiration as well as rivalry and envy. When the baby begins to be mobile, assert her will, and, most important, intrude into the other children's playthings, the other children begin to experience rivalry in its most direct form. At this point, protecting one's territory may become a major issue and the battles begin—it's natural that the older child wishes to protect his possessions, both emotional ones, such as mother's love as well as concrete ones such as toys.

Some degree of rivalry is sure to occur and is a sign of a healthy and vigorous family. The older the elder sibling is, the more likely it is that this sense of the new baby as being "other" will be stronger, and his definition of the family as *not* including another baby will be more clearly formulated. But, of course, much depends on how the parents handle it. The challenge for most families is how to create a balance between cooperative, loving feelings and rivalrous, even envious feelings. Here a couple of principles may be useful. The first is to try to maximize the older child's contact with mother and father after the baby's birth. For example, when the mother has a Caesarean section and only sees the older child for a quick visit while she is in the hospital, the child may resent the baby for keeping her mother away. Since many hospitals now have more liberal visiting rules or even a special family visiting room, older children can be brought to see their mother by the second day post-delivery and then visit every day. Their father's following the visit with a special activity, such as going to a favorite park, can put a more positive light on their separation from mother. The children's having extra support at this time, such as the visit of a relative they like, can also help them feel that this time is special—that even though they are missing their mommy, there are compensations. Often the new baby can in fact be perceived as an addition to the family if the older siblings are not too stressed.

Another principle is to try to involve the older children in cooperative ventures from the very beginning. Although girls seem to take more readily to the role of playing Mommy, boys can also identify in this way. For example, the older sibling can hold the diaper while you are changing the baby. The child can sometimes help hold the bottle while the baby is being fed. Or, if you are breast-feeding, there is no reason why you should not be close to the older sibling, maybe explaining how the baby is sucking. When the baby stops sucking and looks up, nothing will intrigue a young child more than to see his baby brother or sister smile at him, just as he does at mommy. That interaction helps him feel involved and part of the family. It often invokes in little children the same feelings it invokes in adults— one of extreme love. In fact, in families where involvement between the older siblings and the baby occurs, they often begin competing not so much with the baby, but with their mommy and daddy for holding or playing with the baby. This is, in part, because they too are caught up in the urgency and compelling nature of the new baby's inviting smile and seductive glances.

To lessen the intensity of sibling rivalry, you should make sure you give individual time to each of the children. This helps keep them less resentful and competitive with each other. Likewise, you also want to help them cooperate with each other. Sometimes, when it seems you see nothing but fighting between children, you can break this cycle by developing games where their playing together as a team and trying to outsmart you leads to everyone getting a prize.

When all is said and done, however, competitive feelings are a part of life and children should have a sense that they are acceptable. Competitive behavior however will often require certain limits, particularly not hurting each other. Vigorous competition can be supported and talked about in the family. In this way, you can convey a sense that this area of experience is of equal importance to love and tenderness. On an individual basis, the principle is to help the child organize all his emotional experiences—love, tenderness, as well as competition and rivalry—as feelings that are expressed in the form of ideas.

DEVELOPING UNIQUENESS

Is your child beginning to show a style that suggests his personal uniqueness? Does your child's personality have some continuity? In other words, can you say of him, "He's usually happy, active, mischievous, or shy," for example?

Between ages two and three, your child will begin to use his new ability with ideas in his own, individual manner. Perhaps your child will like to do things that involve activity: running, playing chase games, or playing hide-and-seek. Others will prefer to play in one small area or have verbal exchanges rather than physical ones. At the beginning your child will experiment and try out all kinds of new roles for himself, and this is natural. But, after a while, you will see some unique characteristics emerge that give a sense of stability to your child's personality, particularly as he gets closer to age four.

You can foster your child's confidence in his uniqueness by taking pride in his individuality. If he's going to be a powerful superman, then that's what you admire about him. If he's going to be the master block builder, a budding water colorist, a cautious, let's-figure-it-out-first type, or a let's-jump-in-and-get-to-it type, recognize it and take pride in it. You may still encourage balance in the ways discussed earlier, but not without recognition of uniqueness. For example, if Tara is misbehaving, her parents could say, in an impersonal manner, "We don't misbehave in this family," or they could say, "*Tara*, please stop waving that stick. It's dangerous," which is obviously a much more personal communication. (Often the words "we" versus "*Tara*" are not as important as the tone or eye contact.) It's also important to make the child's responsibility clear in any situation which requires the use of discipline. If Tara does not stop waving the stick, for example, her mother might say, "You did not stop when I asked you to. Now I will have to take the stick away from you." The general principle is to be personal, convey a sense that your child has responsibility for his action, and appreciate the unique and personal way she chooses to behave or misbehave.

Supporting your child's uniqueness takes on even more importance at the next stage, when your child begins to master more complex forms of cause and effect; however, it warrants one further word here. It is very important to accept your child's individuality, his preferences for one style of play rather than another, his enjoyment of one activity over another, but at the same time, it is also important to make limits clear. Setting limits gives your child something to define himself against. If you are able to set limits without being overly intrusive or controlling, you'll be providing him with a firm boundary against which he can test his own ideas.

USING ALL SENSES FOR
THE ELABORATION OF IDEAS

Does your child use all of his senses as well as his fine and gross motor abilities to understand emotion and communicate his ideas?

By using all of his senses your child will have an integrated view of himself and an appreciation of his impact on his world. When one sense is weak, a child may miss out on important subtleties. A child with auditory discrimination problems may not sense verbal feeling tone; a child with visual-spatial discrimination lags may not read facial expressions or body language well. In both cases, the other person's emotional message may be misinterpreted and the child's reaction inappropriate and confusing to both him and you. This may be particularly relevant for a child who has been slow to develop his ability for self-regulation or for coordinating motor skills, such as walking, talking, and using a crayon. He may face a greater challenge coordinating his senses and figuring out his and others' feelings. If it is difficult for him to coordinate two actions, it may also be difficult to coordinate two sensations and feelings. With a child with this challenge you may observe that he finds it difficult to recognize and react to social subtlety or complexity. It is not obvious to the child, for example, that when he gets angry at someone, that person may very well get angry in return. Or perhaps he kisses all the children at school whether they want to be kissed or not. He doesn't coordinate their cues with his behavior. In such situations you can help your child to learn to label and elaborate his sensations and feelings as well as to be patient and reflect on the other person's intent. You can also do this in your own interaction with your child or through pretend play. When helping him practice, try to have extra empathy as well as set firm limits. Often children with sensory or motor lags receive remedial help which does not focus sufficiently on their special social and emotional challenges. Many of the suggestions made earlier and in the next chapter apply to children with sensory or motor lags. You must be prepared, however, to provide extra *practice*. You should also be aware that children with sensory or motor lags often take longer to get the information in, whether it's emotional information or numbers or letters. Once they get their information in, their ability to figure things out may be excellent, even a bit special because of the challenge in getting the information in the first place. Therefore extra help in learning to accurately perceive, especially potentially confusing emotional signals, is important.

DEVELOPING FLEXIBILITY

By the end of this stage, is your child beginning to cooperate graciously, or are you constantly struggling to enforce your will?

This is the age that can truly try parent's patience. All children seem to find at least one or two areas to dig in and insist on their own way. For some it may be what they wear or eat; for some it may be never being ready to leave a friend's house; for others, bedtimes may be the battleground. Some of this negative, stubborn behavior is normal and healthy. Between two and three (and usually beyond), children are testing their assertiveness and independence. They are expressing their desire to control their world, or as one three-year-old said, "I want to be the boss, at least sometimes." This desire to be the boss seems to be one of the most natural and early inclinations. But the question is, what happens when the power struggle becomes the predominate mode of interaction as opposed to simply an incident of assertiveness, of a desire for control over one's world or of a play for some autonomy?

Power struggles often arise because three factors needed for the child's healthy development are imbalanced. First, children of all ages need to receive nurturance and love. They simply must have enough holding, cuddling, warm interaction, relaxed playtime together, understanding, and empathy at times they are able to respond to. Next, children need to have opportunities to express their natural inclination to be the "boss," to have some control over their world, to express their independence. Finally, all children from eight months through the rest of childhood, need some limit-setting, whether it is the eleven-month-old who is not allowed to grab his older sister's toy, the twenty-month-old who must learn to come to dinner, the two-year-old who must go to sleep, or the three-year-old who must clean up his toys. All children need to learn how to follow limits and eventually internalize those limits. (Children have the ability to begin observing limits as early as the end of the first year or middle of the second year of life.)

Often when one or more of these three factors of nurturance, autonomy, and limit-setting are absent, power struggles result. Let's

Organized games show the use of ideas guiding complex behavior.

look at the parent who, for a variety of reasons, is unable to satisfy the child's nurturing and security needs. The child may decide on what a distinguished colleague calls, "love by irritation." Not getting closeness and warmth through cooperative endeavors, the child gets them by rubbing against the parents the wrong way.

Let us look at another situation in which the father or mother interferes with the child's autonomy and expression. The child may provoke power struggles in other areas. Take the nineteen-month-old who was learning to play with his new music box. He could jerkily wind it up and eventually was able to get the musical sounds. But mother wanted him to turn the handle to her rhythm. She didn't like the way he was turning it. She was afraid he would "break it," and so began interfering with how he played with it. Pretty soon control over the music box transferred to a power struggle over eating, sleeping, and almost everything else that his mother asked him to do. It was as though he said, "If she won't let me be the boss some of the time with my own toys, then I'll have to try to be the boss other times."

Parents often miss the critical point that children need some control over their own lives. If you can allow this control in some areas, your child will be much more willing to be cooperative in others. The key question for you to ask is, "Am I giving my child the opportunity to be the boss over some areas that are reasonable for a child of his age? Am I exploiting this opportunity to the fullest?" If you are, then you can be very firm in other areas. If the answer to this question is no, and you do tend to control him or intrude your will in almost all areas, then you may have the answer to why the child is not cooperating with his eating habits, cleaning up his toys, going to sleep, or getting dressed. The child may make a stink about these issues anyway, but he is more likely to respond to limit setting and reason if he feels his autonomy is being respected in some areas.

Providing certain areas in which the child is the boss can be tricky. If you try to dictate the specific areas too closely, you are, in fact, being the boss, even though you are saying otherwise. You need to give the child some broad areas and within those the child can make *his own* decisions. Which broad areas you choose—from what the child has for snacks, to what kind of toys he wants to play with or to what kind of clothes he wants to wear—should be based on the family's own values, traditions, and cultural patterns.

The third critical factor in your child's emotional equilibrium, setting limits, is equally important. Some children respond to a lack of limits by feeling insecure. With no checks on their own aggressiveness, they get frightened. In order to create these checks and balances, they sometimes precipitate power struggles. In that way they are sure that the "policeman or policewoman" in their lives will get back. Unfortunately, however, they usually choose inopportune times. (Children seem to be intuitively gifted that way.) If you enforce limits in areas important to you—respecting property, responding to authority, considering others' feelings—power struggles over trivial issues such as which socks to wear (dirty versus clean, matching colors, and so forth) usually subside. You also need to seize opportune times for limit-setting—in particular, when you are home with the child and have ample time both to explain the limits to the child and enforce them rather than in a restaurant.

Sometimes your power struggle with your child mirrors one you're having with your spouse. If each of you has a different idea about what is appropriate for the child, the child can respond to your subtle conflicts with power struggles of his own. Even when parents think they are keeping their own differences of opinion private from the child, there are, unfortunately, very few secrets in families. You both need not agree on everything, but it is important to work through some of your differences and accept compromises with one another, especially if the child's behavior is reflecting your disagreement. Enforcing limits in areas of emotional concern to you but in conflict with the age-appropriate interests of your child, such as curiosity about the body or experimenting with new motor skills (tumbling, jumping, or rough-housing) will usually prove unsuccessful.

A power struggle over any issue is, by definition, irritating. But most parents agree that struggles over toilet training are the worst. A few tips on toilet training may help make the process less traumatic.

Toilet training has two obvious components to it—the emotional and the mechanical. Mechanically speaking, you want to start training a child when he has sufficient motor control not to require undue attempts either to anticipate on your part or to regiment the child to go at certain times of the day whether or not there is the impulse. Usually the child has this motor control somewhere between twenty-two and thirty months. (Further advice on the mechanics is available from a number of other books.) The emotional aspects of toilet training broadly concern the child's willingness to regulate his own muscles in the service of pleasing his parents. (Subsequently, he wants to please himself as well.) Shame and guilt should not really enter the picture, and toilet training must be seen in the context of the overall love relationship between parent and child.

As children progress further into what is called "the terrible twos"—or the "wondrous twos," as indicated earlier—they can use "ideas" to be the boss and exert their will. One way to keep them from applying their willfulness negatively to toilet training is to train them after they are physically able to control their muscles but before they practice manipulating ideas and locking you into a number of power struggles. In other words, try to train them while they are excited

Helping Your Child . . .

1. CONSTRUCT IDEAS

— make sure your child understands the functional role of objects, people, and feelings
— create special play times and take an interest in your child's activity
— use your child's favored activities to introduce pretend play
— if your child shows temporary regression, provide extra security
— if your child has problems with earlier tasks, integrate earlier and later ones
— with a clingy child, create opportunities for him to feel more secure through pretend play, distal modes of communication and being held; set more effective limits
— with a hyperexcitable child, attract his attention
— provide security, help him use distal modes, set limits
— if your child appears to have a learning problem, seek consultation

2. ENCOURAGE A RANGE OF EMOTION

— help your child form ideas or thoughts with actions and feelings
— introduce feelings which he expresses behaviorally into pretend play, i.e., if he can't talk about anger, show him how the puppets get angry
— help your child use feelings to meet basic needs by discussing the feelings, i.e., if he feels insecure, talk about how it feels to have you go out and leave him

3. USE EMOTIONAL IDEAS WHEN STRESSED

— establish contact after a disruption, i.e., "I'm sorry I shouted at you. I want to give you a hug"
— help child to reengage using emotional ideas, i.e., "You know I get mad at you when you dump your toy basket. Why do you want to do it?"

4. DEVELOP UNIQUENESS

— respect individuality
— convey a sense of intentionality about responsibility, i.e., "You've spilled your milk. You have to help clean it up"
— be personal, i.e., "I liked the way you sang that song, Joey"

5. USE ALL SENSES TO ELABORATE IDEAS

— encourage the use of senses or motor functions not already incorporated in interactional learning situations

with their new abilities—on the upturn—and before they really decide to take you on. The other way to minimize the power struggle is to watch the balance of nurturance, autonomy, and setting limits described above. Often when a child is unwilling to be trained, he is letting you know that the balance is not right.

Should a child not get trained until four or even older, it can undermine his sense of internal regulation and self esteem. Even though he will not be trained because it is not what he wants to do, he also feels uneasy when he can't regulate a body function or he sees that his peers do. Although embarrassed by wearing diapers, he is conflicted about wanting to have his parents do things for him and wanting to grow up.

In summary, power struggles, however much they may seem like an issue of the moment, are often the result of an imbalance between three basic needs of children—nurturance, security, and love; opportunities to be the "boss" expressed through initiative, control, and independence; and opportunities to respond to and learn to internalize limits. Looking at each of these areas and trying to put them into balance with each other often helps correct tendencies toward chronic power struggles.

Creating a Supportive Environment

Your child needs your help in order to make the jump from concrete behavior to the freedom of ideas. We all know adults who haven't managed that leap. They tend to handle their emotions through actions or through physical sensations alone. They do not know what they feel. They have no alternative ways of finding satisfaction or achieving their goals. Here is an area where emotional needs can be satisfied by using the mind. This is your child's introduction to a whole new world of challenges and satisfactions as he begins to exercise his mind, body, and emotions as one.

The easiest way to encourage your child to use emotional ideas is to be available and take part in his world of activity, both real and pretend. Being available does not mean that you must play with him on demand. It is good for children to play by themselves and to learn to accept delays and frustration. However, there should be some times during the day when you can spend attentive half hours or so with him.

Encouraging your child to use ideas at the descriptive level is relatively easy. Reading books with your child, helping him name the objects he sees, talking about pictures in relationship to his own toys and experiences and, of course, learning about emotional ideas should continue throughout the day as you interact together.

Language can also be used to encourage the use of ideas at the interactive level. Rather than simply describing an action, an interactive use of language suggests a desire. For example, a child can see a boy riding a bike and state, "Boy riding bike" (simply descriptive) or he can say, "Bike, I ride." Ideas on the interactive level have a goal in mind that is purposeful and involves social interaction suggesting emotions, needs, or desires.

When you use language, you'll want to focus on ideas that have emotional value to your child. If your child says, for example, "Me, cake," whether you respond with, "Yes, you may have the cake," "No, you'll have to wait until after dinner," or "Which cake would you like?" your child's communication with ideas is supported. Responding with, "The cake is good, isn't it?" is descriptive, but it neither addresses the child's request nor is interactive. As long as you respond in kind, using ideas to express agreement, disagreement, another alternative, or elaboration, you will encourage his use of interactive ideas.

Many children who are interested in pretend play often practice using their ideas on their own. This practice is helpful to them as long as you are a partner in the play, either actively or as a supportive presence, part of the time. To be based in reality, pretend play needs to be interactive some of the time; otherwise, the child may become lost in his fantasy. Having you as a partner gives to the fantasy a base of reality. You are there providing real feedback and using real emotions. You are also there to establish any necessary rules, such as no kicking, biting, or breaking of toys. Setting up rules gives the child real boundaries upon which to play out his fantasy. The relationship with you and the implied rules, in a sense, are the reality foundation, the stage on which many pretend dramas may be played out with security.

Play partnership allows you not only to show interest and approval but also to help your child stretch his imagination and expand his use of emotional ideas. When he plays a game involving one doll feeding another, for example, take the role of the baby by saying, "Oh, that's good milk, I want more." Your little son or daughter may gleefully give more, to which you can say, "Oh, all full now." Having brought some closure to that interaction you may then wait to see what your child does next. He may naturally go on to a new theme which you can be involved in, or if he has trouble starting something, you can suggest that the dolly go do something different.

When your child is involved in aggressive play, help broaden the story by suggesting, perhaps, that the bad guy is escaping and your child has to find him. Or be a real sport and offer to be your child's horse to chase the bad guy. But be wary of taking control of the play situation. Some children may need extra support in areas they are unable to develop and play out on their own, but try to avoid running the show. For example, Peter's mother may notice that Peter repeatedly plays shooting games with his toy soldiers. Though she is tempted to suggest the soldiers kiss and make up, she knows Peter may feel that his own inclinations and interests were being undermined. In reaction to this lack of respect, he could find it difficult to be comfortable with his own interests and desires.

In her attempt to broaden Peter's play, his mother first tries to determine whether there are circumstances that support his preoccupation with aggression. (A parent might have an apparently aggressive profession, such as a soldier or policeman, or an aggressive hobby, like hunting. Or, there may be a lot of fighting and anger in the family or rough-housing with the child.) Peter's mother finds a few possibilities and decides to gently introduce the idea that Peter's soldiers sometimes get hungry and need to sit down and eat. In this way, Peter's imaginary play gradually encompasses eating along with shooting. Eventually, Peter's soldiers are able to go home to their parents and give them kisses. Peter's mother could, in a maternal, uncontrolling manner, introduce the themes of affection, intimacy, and nurturing into his play. By broadening his play in this way Peter can build on his existing interests and not undermine his own sense of himself.

On occasion, your child may demonstrate assertively whether he wants you to take an active or passive role. If you begin to help your child do something, he may take your hand away and say, "No." In this case, you can be satisfied in the role of admiring audience. Your child's desire to be the director of his play is not a rejection of you. He is merely showing his comfort in developing his own pretend play.

It is especially important at this stage for you to make sure that your actual behavior helps the formation of emotional ideas as well as your make-believe play with your child. A mother, for example, may show her daughter how to be comforting when her dolly hurts herself, but approach her daughter's actual woes impatiently. Among other things, the mixed emotional signals a child receives undermine her ability to understand newly emerging emotions and ideas. Your actual interaction carries the brunt of the emotional weight. Pretending can't make up for lack of actual emotional interaction. Pretending provides an indirect route for trying out and learning about new emotional ideas.

Finally, at this age you will want to begin to help your child differentiate between fact and fantasy. For example, two-and-a-half-year-old Richard arrived home from nursery school with good news. "I'm a girl," he stated. Mother diplomatically said, "Oh, you feel like a little girl? What is it like?" He mentioned that little girls wore dresses, the names of one or two girl playmates, and then, pointing, said, "Emily has a new toy." Although it became clear from further "discussion" that Richard was envious of Emily's new toy, his mother was still not exactly sure why he was interested in being a girl. She said to him, "Gee, I guess it's nice to be everything; a little boy, a little girl, and anything else, too." This remark sparked his pretending to be a cowboy and then a pony. At the end of his pretend play his mother pointed out to him what a nice and loving little boy he was.

If Richard's mother had simply changed the subject, she would not have provided Richard with an opportunity to elaborate his feelings and ideas, nor to have his misconceptions addressed. In this instance, his mother encouraged the elaboration of her child's ideas while at the same time helping him appreciate the reality of the situation. Saying that he is a boy and how nice he is helps Richard appreciate the special facts of reality without undermining his emerging capacity for experiencing complex wishes.

All of the principles we have described so far serve a common purpose in addition to the specific goals described: they help your child practice using ideas. Any new skill needs practice and certainly something as startling as the use of ideas needs a good deal of practice—practice in the areas in which your child finds the most satisfaction, practice in getting his needs met, practice with "real" and "pretend."

Creating a Supportive Environment

1. Be available to interact and play with your child

2. Encourage your child to use ideas at the descriptive level, i.e., "Can you tell me what color your shirt is?"

3. Encourage your child to use ideas at the functional interactive level, through either language or pretend play, i.e., "I bet you can give that dolly a hug"

4. Become a partner in the pretend play, but do not take control

5. Introduce themes that your child avoids in a way that does not undermine his own sense of self

6. Make sure your interactions with your child in daily situations help your child elaborate his new emotional ideas just as in pretend play

Reviewing Your Support

Because of the complexity of your child's development at this stage, you may face not only small anxieties or doubts but also more troublesome reactions to your child's emotional development. It's very important to assess carefully each possibility that has a potential for interfering with the emotionally rich exchange of emotional ideas between you and your child.

YOUR FAMILY SITUATION

Marital problems can occur at any stage in your baby's growth. We mention them at this stage for a specific reason, however. This is a time of great emotional blossoming and understanding, a time when emotions and ideas meld and blend, and your child needs great freedom to practice using them. If you and your spouse are in emotional hot water, one of the most common ways of dealing with it is to cool things down. This means that emotions are smoothed over, ignored, denied, stifled. Concrete concerns replace emotional connections. It is important for you at this time to become aware of such a pattern. Your child's interest in dependency, bodies and sexuality, competition, now at the ideational level and gradually with the language will surely threaten a family that already can't deal with these emotional themes and has begun to deny them.

PARENTAL PERSONALITY STYLES

There are two main reasons why a child may not display certain emotions through ideas. One is because the child does not have an inclination in a particular area. The other is because the parents are not encouraging or are subtly discouraging their child from forming and expressing them. Essentially, if you have never had much practice using ideas to express emotion, it can be difficult to do so with your child. When your child begins to practice using ideas by describing feelings or interactions, you may feel on uncertain ground.

Perhaps you are unable to talk about angry or intimate feelings or support your child's curiosity in pretend play when he wants to undress and explore a doll. This is not to say that you do not use ideas to carry out daily work or to think and plan. However, when it comes to emotional interactions in which strong needs are being expressed, you may not be able to respond in kind.

Take the situation where an angry three-year-old child says, "I hate you. I wish you would die," in reaction to her not being allowed to have ice cream because she didn't finish dinner. The intensity of your reaction to this statement—whether mild or strong—is not important. What matters is that you verbalize your reaction rather than just punish the child. Let's say her father doesn't like the child to talk that way. He can explain firmly that it makes him feel bad when his daughter says this, that he knows she loves him; that you can be very mad and still love a person. He can try to get her to talk about her feelings. If he feels so inclined, he can also punish her, maybe, saying that because she was naughty, she can't have any ice cream for two more days. An angry father who is not accustomed to talking about feelings probably would just punish the child. The child does not have an opportunity to practice using ideas to express emotion, rather just behavior, and consequently may have more difficulty in learning to do so.

Lack of practice may not be the only reason a child is not encouraged to express emotions through ideas. People sometimes find certain emotions to be frightening, either in a general sense or in a specific area.

Let's look at a specific case. Bobby, a twenty-seven-month-old boy, had been doing beautifully, when he suddenly became very interested

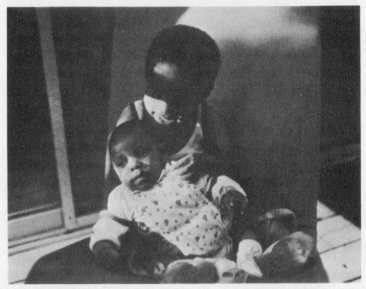

The birth of a sibling can be a way to learn the mature force of empathy and love.

in taking off all of his doll's clothes and looking for the "penis." He himself liked to run around the house naked, sticking his chest out. His father, who had been very close to him, now began vacillating between being overly punitive and emotionally withdrawn. His father spanked him whenever he discovered him without his clothes and also began spanking him for any little mishap, such as spilling milk or messing up his toys. His father also withdrew from their normal intimacies, such as stories before bed, hugs, and cuddles. Instead, his father began finding meetings and activities to occupy his evenings, leaving Bobby's mother to be the story reader and comforter at bedtime. Needless to say, Bobby found this shift quite confusing and may have even felt his body interests were "bad" or aggressive. Usually a well-controlled child, he began biting and hitting his ten-month-old brother. (Antagonistic behavior often occurs when the younger child begins to be mobile and becomes a competitive threat.)

He also began fighting with other children in his play group and was becoming generally impulsive and angry. His smile, his giggles, his sense of joy seemed to decrease, and more and more, he took on the characteristics of a stubborn two-year-old.

When his parents decided to seek consultation, his father was helped to understand his particular fear: using ideas and fantasy play in connection with the human body. He had always been uncomfortable discussing feelings and ideas about his body and became scared and anxious when his son showed an interest that was normal and appropriate for his age. In a supportive setting father was able to talk about some of his anxious feelings about his body. Interestingly, emotional ideas are often more frightening for a parent with conflicts than emotional behavior. He was also able to recapture the closeness he missed with his son.

Gradually, from the help he received, father was able to help Bobby "play out" his interest in bodies. When Bobby pretended to have monster arms, father helped him with the drama; when Bobby wanted to know the name for his genitals, father provided the information factually; when Bobby wanted to run around naked before a bath, his father allowed him his joy. Bobby's interest in his body became only one interest in many. He was once again his cooperative and curious self, and the family regained its equilibrium.

That you may be able to show an emotion does not mean you are necessarily comfortable with it on an abstract, emotional level. Some people, as with Bobby's father, are able to demonstrate feelings through behavior but are afraid to think about them. The parent who punishes his child but cannot incorporate the feelings of anger into imaginary play is such an example. (In this area in particular, some parent's difficulty is the reverse; they are great talkers but not doers. This is not a desirable outcome either.) One explanation for this dichotomy is that some people grow up with the notion that thinking about anger, for example, is bad or will bring forth punishment. The thought is worse than, or at least as bad as, the act. As adults they may feel so conflicted that they either simply avoid these feelings, become concrete or become overly controlling. It is as though angry behavior (or sexual or curious behavior) does not make an angry person, but angry thoughts do. Thought is equated with the self whereas action is disassociated with the self.

The best way for you to find out if using emotional ideas is frightening to you or if you never learned how in the first place, is to expose yourself to this challenge. By forcing yourself each day to take advantage of the opportuntiy for pretend play and verbal interchanges with your child, you can see how you react. Do you feel anxious inside, have sudden urges to interrupt play, or just feel confused and "out of it?" Would you rather hit, feed, or take your child to the bathroom than "talk to him" about what he really feels? Identifying which emotional expressions bother you enables you to put energy into your troublesome areas, and cut off your normal "escape routes."

Another tactic is to explore whether you are able to daydream about the emotional area in question—anything from dependency and security to anger and protest—or discuss it with friends or spouse. In this way, you can pinpoint whether the problem lies only in your relationship with your toddler, or goes beyond.

If you find that you do avoid certain emotions you can still be supportive of your child by ensuring that both you and your spouse set aside time for pretend play and conversations involving emotions. Having both of you participate is important because people often emphasize different emotions, themes, or types of play. Having both parents as well as older siblings or grandparents available can fill in the emotional gaps and be very enriching since each one adds a different little goodie to the menu. Your child then gets a chance to use ideas and imagination in a variety of areas. Of course you do not want to overwhelm your child, but certainly playing with mother, father, an older sibling, or a regular babysitter at different times would not be an overly difficult meal for your child to digest, particularly in the two- to three-and-a-half-year-old range.

A family's inability to support their child's new capacities can result not only in his having a difficult time developing that capacity, but also in a rupture of family relationships which can lead to a disruption of earlier accomplishments. For example, a child who is frustrated because his parents can't respond to his emotional ideas may become impulsive. His mother and father may then begin fighting over how to control little Johnny better. So if introspection, examination, practice, and family discussions don't produce a result that satisfies you, you may benefit from a professional consultation. With knowledge of which emotional ideas cause you discomfort, you benefit your child by supporting his healthy development, and you, challenged by the developmental thrust of your child, benefit from fuller self-understanding and emotional interactions.

Your child will use ideas to guide and organize his emotional life. As his use of ideas develops, you will see him begin to express his emotions through ideas rather than through behavior, you will see him create his own experiences through the use of his budding imagination and also interpret his new worldly experiences by combining them with memories and understanding of past events. The wheels are turning; you'll be able to picture your child's mind brimful of ideas, theories, the wildest logic and most wonderful sentiments— as well as the most awful ones! Once he reaches the level of ideas and thinking, it is as though your child has a tremendous new telescope through which to take in and orchestrate experiences of an entirely new dimension. Engage your child and his wondrous new capacities, and you'll both make some discoveries about each other and the world.

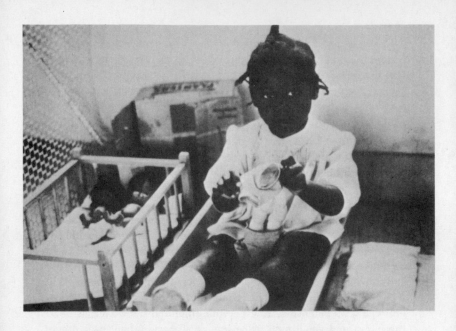

VI | EMOTIONAL THINKING: THE BASIS FOR FANTASY, REALITY, AND SELF-ESTEEM

— 30 to 48 months

Seeing your young child's ability to use ideas in an emotional context can be so absorbing that you might not think anything else of importance could happen—at least for a while. But, hard on the heels of learning to form ideas and use feelings comes your child's next milestone, emotional thinking, that is, the ability to manipulate these ideas. Emotional thinking is your child's ability to go beyond elaborating ideas in the various emotional realms where the child has one doll comfort another or say "hug!" to his mother. He will now begin to organize and manipulate his ideas into a cause-and-effect under-standing of his own emotions and the world that begins to take reality into account: his emotions in play and language become more orga-nized and have greater continuity (so that the doll falls down and is comforted by Mommy, has playtime with her doll friends, and then is cuddled and read a story by Mommy as the doll gets ready for her nap); his pretend play can be both fanciful, such as scary ghosts flying around and closely corresponds to real situations as with cooking "rock" soup; and, he not only plans his actions, but also considers alternatives. His ability to combine many ideas and feelings together logically allows him to create new experiences for himself. In other words, just as your child learned to combine blocks to make an original house, now he can combine emotional ideas. He may create new feelings of shame and, eventually, guilt based on his own feelings about his "bad" wishes and behavior.

He is developing a new sense of what is "me" and "you." With this he gradually is able to grasp the idea of expectations and standards that are a part of "not me," but which will become a part of himself. And with his new sense of what is "me" and "you," he may also show more compassionate love, here and there. He now emerges with the "cause-and-effect" logic at the level of emotional ideas that he de-veloped earlier at the level of behavior.

At two or two and a half, for example, Amy makes up a game as she goes along. She puts a hat on her doll, takes a nearby crayon and makes freckles on the doll's face. then sees a drum and has the doll happily play a song. The sequences occur because an item is available. Amy, as yet, has no well-planned internal scheme.

As Amy goes from three years old to four, the story elements conform more to reality. When four-year-old Amy has "friends" over for dessert, she first calls to invite them, then she carefully sets the table. Small talk is heard as dessert is served and compliments to the chef are enthusiastic. Everyone uses his best manners and is polite. Although it is still possible for an astronaut to join the party, Amy has shown that she has a strong internal picture of how the party should be conducted. Similarly an appreciation of the cause-and-effect of feelings emerges—Amy may comment, during her play, "when I don't get my way, and get mad" or that the doll whose mommy left feels scared.

Your child's emerging capacity for emotional thinking evolves over time. It does not strike magically at the age of three or four but progresses by degrees. At two years your child's emotional ideas about his feelings are like little balloons, not necessarily connected to one another and not connected necessarily to principles of logic or reality. But by three and four, his "balloons" begin to arrange themselves into various patterns, such as what is self and nonself, what are impulses and their consequences, or what are loving feelings and angry ones.

This process of connecting and organizing feelings will continue to develop. The three-year-old can appreciate that his angry feelings and behavior may lead to punishment or to angry looks from his daddy. This is an important step on the way to moral consciousness—the realization that his actions (and emotions) can have emotional consequences for others.

Appreciating How the World Works

The question is, how does your child begin to develop logical links between his "balloons" of emotional experience? How does he begin to understand that he is the sum of his happy feelings, sad feelings, and other feeling selves, and that he reacts with a certain emotion depending on the situation?

One way to think about this process is as follows. As your child matures and experiences his emotional world in different situations, he becomes capable of seeing and learning about similar and different qualities in emotional experiences. With appropriate opportunities for interaction, he may gradually begin to realize that each emotion he experiences or expresses causes an emotional response or effect. Just as he began to recognize cause-and-effect in terms of his behaviors, when he was six to twelve months old, your three-year-old now learns cause-and-effect in terms of his emotional ideas. If he says to you, "I hate you," and you look hurt, sad or get angry, your child comes to appreciate that the words "I hate you" have an effect. Your child's image and feeling inside become connected to an end result, that is, your reaction. Similarly, if he says "I love you," and you smile and give him a hug and a kiss, your child sees that his "balloon" of experience which he has labeled love leads to a loving response in return. After a while, with appropriate experiences, the little balloons that contain his own feelings begin to connect up into one larger pattern. In the same way, the balloons containing the experiences your child associates with you begin to connect together. Earlier, for example, your child's own experience of anger might have mingled with his perception of your anger, making it hard for him to distinguish his own anger from yours. He did not have the capacity to connect and organize his *own* feelings, and so separate them from yours. Now, however, a difference is emerging between emotions that are his own and those that are a reaction to him.

The ability to distinguish between ideas and feelings from the self and those from others is partly based on growth in the still-developing brain of your young child. He is literally developing new connections between the neurons or fibers within his brain that in part enable him to make complex distinctions. This growth creates your child's foundation for his increasing physical, intellectual and emotional abilities. However, experience is also necessary to foster development in these areas, especially with regard to his ability to separate his own emotions from those of other people.

Let's take a child, for example, who, at age four can do a puzzle that calls for a high degree of organization and understanding of cause-and-effect. In terms of the inanimate world, this child is quite bright. At the same time, however, the same level of understanding may not be evident in his relationship to the human world. Perhaps once, when this child says, "Love you, Mommy," his mother responds with a smile. The next time he says this, his mother (thinking he's trying to manipulate her when in fact he is not) ignores him, and the third time mother goes into a tirade because he has just smeared peanut butter and jelly all over the living room sofa, or she's just had a fight with his father. From this confusing mixture of reactions, the child may not develop a coherent idea of love, its consequences and effects. He may be able to do a complex puzzle, but he may not be able to understand what to most people is a simpler relationship: giving love equals receiving love. Instead, he learns that his loving feeling leads to an unpredictable response. Consequently, the "balloons" that define his loving feelings may not be clearly interrelated.

The same process may occur for other types of understanding that are necessary to appreciate how the world works. One example involves the ability to categorize what is alive and what is not. A two-year-old in his own way recognizes the difference between a toy cat and a real cat, but at times will play with the toy cat as though it were real. In his mind the child cannot fully and clearly categorize the "pretend" animal for the real one, even though he is learning to make these groupings. He, for example, is already more comfortable with a pretend bear than with a real bear at the zoo, and in his own way knows the difference. As he moves toward three, however, the child begins to more fully organize and categorize the qualities of what constitutes the animate and inanimate world (such as touch, smell, movement, sound) so as to separate the experiences related to one from the experiences related to the other.

Another understanding that should now be developed is your child's sense of time. He is learning to organize events grouped not only on their qualities but also on their time frame. The experiences that happened yesterday are in one group, and the experiences that happen today are in another. Your child will also begin to group spatial relationships and, slightly later, the experiences he hopes for tomorrow.

A major emotional advance of your child, then, is his ability to group emotional ideas at a higher level of organization. Now he plays at make-believe, but he also appreciates more fully what is real. He is learning which feelings and wishes are part of himself and which ones are part of another, and, most important, how his wishes and feelings have impact and cause consequences.

Your Child's Personality Functions

You will discover, as your child develops the ability to group experiences into cohesive units, that—with his new understanding of an emotional self-versus-others—he now has greater ability to test reality, to control his impulses, to stabilize his moods, to integrate his thoughts, feelings, and actions, and to plan ahead and focus his concentration. These personality functions are essential for participating in school, developing friendships, and later for working and establishing a family. Let's look at them one by one.

Reality Testing. This allows your child to separate reality from make-believe and is essential for dealing with life's challenges. Reality testing helps him distinguish between his feelings and those of others; between subjective thoughts and objective facts; between what is inside him and what is outside. When a child does not successfully make these distinctions, day-to-day experiences that require "objective" assessments of the world may lead to unpredictable behavior and "illogical" thoughts and feelings. For example, a child may think others are angry with him when he is actually angry with them. The understanding of self-versus-others is the foundation of reality testing because the feelings and thoughts of the "self" must be separated from what is not the "self" in order to distinguish between what is subjective and what is objective.

Regulating and Controlling Impulses. This is another important function of the personality. Your child needs to understand cause-and-effect for this. If a child does not understand the relationship between what he does and what will happen either in the world of ideas or behavior, he has no reason to control his impulses. If he does not understand that his behavior causes his mommy to get angry or that his bad language leads to his daddy's annoyance, why should he control his hitting or not use foul language? Only the appreciation that he, himself, can cause reactions from others gives him a basis for impulse control (Of course, if you have a typical three- or four-year-old, he'll choose *not* to use this delightful ability as much as he'll choose *to* use it.)

Mood Stability. Your child's ability to maintain an even mood may, in part, result from his capacity to sort out and group different emotional experiences and feelings. Many of us wonder at the two-year-old's ability to go from a temper tantrum to sadness to joy and even great activity before we've even brushed our teeth. By age three-and-a-half to four, and certainly by the age of four to five, you'll see greater stability of moods; that is, your child may be in a "good mood," or sad and disappointed, for half the day, perhaps, in part, because, with his increased mental abilities and wider experiences he can now appreciate some of the relationships between and therefore group smaller units of experience, feelings and thoughts, into larger patterns. Your child's ability to categorize feelings, wishes and ideas may also allow him to categorize many transient emotions into a pattern which is an overall "mood," and to refrain from being preoccupied by minor unhappy sensations when feeling happy, or pleasurable sensations when feeling sad. This is the age when it begins to be difficult to distract your child with a toy or a trip when he seems determined to be grumpy.

Combining Thoughts and Emotion in a Way That Makes Sense. This is another basic personality function. It is not unusual, for example, for a two-and-a-half-year-old to giggle over a sad event, or say, "I hate you" with the broadest, lovingest smile on his face. In other words, the connection between an idea and the emotion associated with it is not clear. Gradually, however, your child will learn, through trial and error and over wide experience, to connect certain thoughts and emotions into units of experience. By the time he is between the ages of four and five, you will see much more connection between what your child says and what he shows in terms of feelings. Your child will be able to communicate his feelings better and interact in a more complex fashion interpersonally, though you can expect this integration to break down when he is under emotional stress.

Focused Concentration and Future Planning. These are skills that are essential for learning in school. Both the ability to understand the difference between self and others, and the ability to understand the concepts of present and future will in part help your child to plan how he or she wants to be at some future time. Knowing the consequences of your actions, in a sense, allows you to do "A" in order to accomplish "B," even as "A" takes time. Your child will gradually be able to tolerate frustration, persevere at a task, and anticipate accomplishment. Picture the child who has no concept of self-and-other or no understanding of the relationship between ideas, actions, and their consequences. If the child's thoughts and behavior have no consequences, then it takes no sense to plan. Why be "good" to receive praise or respect if you are not able to connect the feelings and behaviors of "being good" with their consequences, the sense of being respected or praised? If each experience is an isolated balloon, there is no ability to connect an experience now with its consequence in the future and focus on a larger task which must be planned in terms of final accomplishment. How difficult it would be for a child to delay immediate gratification or to work at simple arithmetic or learning letters without a sense of some end result.

Through emotional thinking, energetic three-year-olds become proper tea-party guests.

Emotional Memory and Repression

Many children astound, and sometimes embarrass, their parents when, quite early on, they are able to recall the names of people, places, and things from the past. It may have occurred to you to ask what part memory plays in your child's ability to organize emotional ideas. We're going to take this opportunity to digress slightly and speculate on this interesting topic.

Some discussions of childhood memory maintain that there are two kinds of "repression" which cause the absence of memory. Primary repression occurs when children of an early age simply do not retain the information about events of an earlier age as they develop. At a somewhat later stage secondary repression occurs when children push back into their unconscious earlier experiences that invoke feelings which are unpleasant or disruptive to their current functioning. (The active jealousy felt at age three toward the birth of a brother or sister is forgotten by four and a half or five.) But, consider a slightly different theory of emotional memory, which may prove to have explanatory value.

The mechanism for forgetting emotional events may be related to the state of mind in which the child experiences the event. Research has been done concerning how memory functions under different states of consciousness or under drugs and medications. Sometimes, learning that takes place during one state of consciousness, during hypnosis, for example, can only be remembered when the person is in that state of consciousness. The same is often true for activities learned while people are under medication. A series of names learned when taking drug "A" may be better remembered when the person is back on drug "A."

Keeping this in mind, let us now think of the different levels of emotional development—the world of organized behavior, the world of emotional ideas, and the world of more logical emotional thinking— as three different states of mind. When a child operates in the first state or behavioral world (nine to eighteen months), before he uses emotional concepts and ideas, he remembers and can repeat certain behaviors. Similarly, once the child becomes aware of emotions and starts using emotional ideas in the second stage (eighteen to thirty months) in pretend play and in language, the child can reproduce these ideas and recall emotional events. He does not forget that he wants his candy or that it was promised to him later, although he may not understand the time sequence and demand the candy two minutes after he was told he would have to wait three hours.

However, during the next stage there is a change. We have observed clinically that, as a child moves from using emotional ideas in an illogical or unconnected manner to using ideas more logically (thirty to forty-eight months), he begins to forget what occurred in the state before logic dominated his thinking. He does not remember sleeping in his crib, he does not remember bringing his baby sister from the hospital, or his reactions to her, he does not remember wearing diapers. He does, however, remember new events—such as holidays and birthdays on which he received presents—he learned under the organization of logical emotional thinking. It is as though the emotional memories in these three different states of mind—behavioral, illogical emotional thinking, and logical emotional thinking—are walled off from one another. That the memories, in fact, still exist can be seen when they are sometimes recovered during hypnosis or psychoanalysis. Perhaps, then, one's ability to remember emotional events is related to the states of mind during each developmental stage, as well as to the emotional coloration of each event.

If you test your own memory, you probably remember events from your late childhood and adolescent years, but not much before the age of five, except in a spotty way. Do early talkers (that is, individuals who have shown evidence of early emotional thinking) have greater access to earlier memories than people who talked later? Does the proverbial "absent-minded professor" exist in a more abstract, mental state, so that he has limited access to memories from less abstract mental states? There is still much to be learned about the role of emotional memory in your child's ability to organize his ideas, but over time he will come to understand that the little bits and pieces of personal experience that he put together at random are all part of a larger, more logically connected reality in which everyone participates.

Observing Your Child

If your child is going to develop a healthy personality with the capacity to remain intact and grow, she must learn how to test reality, regulate her impulses, stabilize her moods, integrate her feelings and actions, focus her concentration, and plan. These functions do not necessarily just occur. They are an outgrowth of both your child's mastering earlier milestones and of your support for her greater organization of emotional experiences. With these basics your child will be able to develop these aspects of her personality as fully as possible.

Observing whether your child is accomplishing this latest milestone is not as straightforward as observing earlier tasks. Because your child's personality functions, which indicate her increasing emotional organization, are new, they may fluctuate a good deal—you may see them, then you won't. Consequently, more reliable indications of her reaching this milestone are behaviors which combine many of these new functions (such as understanding cause-and-effect at the level of personal relationships) as well as some of those which show directly that she is combining emotional experiences logically (such as separating fantasy from reality).

SHOWING CAUSE-AND-EFFECT INTERACTIONS

Is your child gradually able to string a number of ideas into organized, logical patterns, either verbally or through play? Is she beginning to show a greater balance between make-believe and logical reality? Is your child beginning to show cause-and-effect interpersonally?

To understand cause-and-effect interactions, a child at this stage should be drawing on several new abilities simultaneously. She distinguishes between her feelings and actions and those of the other person (reality testing); she appreciates that her action will cause a reaction (impulse control); and she understands that the whole interaction can have larger consequences (focused concentration and planning).

You can see her understanding of cause-and-effect in her pretend play, which shows how she can link causal units into a complex and somewhat realistic pattern (for example, at her toy kitten picnic they all make a mess, then are punished with no dessert and finally are good, get their dessert, pack up and go home); in her verbal exchanges, which show an appreciation of consequences (for example, your daughter has just thrown a ball you told her not to, and your favorite lamp is now in pieces. She says, "It was an accident, Mommy, please don't take my cartoons away!"); and in her expectations, which can indicate an understanding of delay (when your three-year-old says "I want an apple," and you reply "Wait for dinner," your child responds "too long").

With a three-year-old whose thoughts, words and actions rarely seem to follow one another, you will find it hard to know what she is communicating from moment to moment. Carefully observe the sequencing of her emotional ideas, however she communicates. You may need to help her practice linking cause-and-effect when it comes to ideas and emotions. If she is not forming bridges between her different emotional experiences, she will not develop an integrated self.

Another way to help your child practice linking cause-and-effect interactions is through pretend play. Let us consider a simple example. Your child's doll is "climbing" a tree and falls. You can say, "Oh, he must be hurt. Maybe he needs a doctor." From your reaction, your child sees that falling leads to injury and requires a doctor. And that when in need, help is not far away. This extension of the scene lends a cause-and-effect quality to the world of emotional ideas.

Before discussing specific techniques to help your child expand his emotional logic, remember—as noted in the last chapter—that your "playing" with your child is itself an experience grounded in reality. Even spontaneous play has implied reality rules. Your child isn't allowed to bite you, break up the house, or hurt himself. Since the playing involves you, there is also a real human relationship with direct feelings. Your child senses your empathy, warmth, love, and, at times, your frustration, anger, and need to set limits. The rules for "playing" and the emotional relationship with you provides an emotional reality which is the foundation for flights of fantasy. In this way, "pretend" is grounded in reality. In addition, the pretend play itself has its own logic or reality which can be practiced and expanded.

The easiest way to help your child practice linking cause-and-effect interactions is by paying attention to her conversation and providing her with logical responses. For example, Judy, three-and-a-half, is watching television while her mother cooks dinner. After a few minutes she goes into the kitchen and asks "What can I do?" Mother might respond by saying, "I'm busy. Go back and watch TV. Dinner will be ready in ten minutes." Judy might be annoyed, but, nonetheless, her communication has been responded to logically. Mother could also respond by saying, "Okay, Judy. Why don't you put the napkins on the table?" Again her request is understood and, in this instance, her mother shows an awareness and acceptance of either Judy's desire for closeness or a wish to participate.

On the other hand, the mother might hear the same request and feel overwhelmed by her daughter. She might choose to ignore her. She might even think to herself, "I'm not going to let that little kid nag me any more." Judy, who does not know of mother's private fantasy, gets no support for her communicating wishes through ideas and becomes confused by the impact of her wishes. With repeated instances she may begin to withdraw, become impulsive or sullen. In order to make sure your response is in keeping with your child's communication, you need simply to concentrate on what your child is saying. If you ignore her or change the subject, your child gets no reality feedback. An older, more sophisticated child may see that a parent changes the subject out of anxiety; but three- or four-year-olds may just get confused and even feel that communicating wishes or feelings through ideas is either bad, dangerous, or disorganizing.

There are basically two techniques you can use to help your child elaborate a play sequence in a purposeful and cause-and-effect manner. Starting with the scene your child has already created, you can suggest, as the mother did in our earlier example, introducing more characters. This addition changes the subplot within the same context. Another way to help is to stay with the theme but shift the context. If the child above decided that her doll was not, in fact, hurt, her mother can suggest the doll might want to go home and tell her mother about the near miss, or go to the circus to see how the pros climb to high places without falling.

Your goal is to help your child maintain his play theme while encouraging him to go the step beyond where he or she is at the moment. This support gives your child experience with logically connected sequences, which, although make-believe, resemble how the real world works. You should see your child, over time, spontaneously apply cause-and-effect interactions from the real world to his play. He will have dolls loving each other, getting angry at each other, having adventures with each other, and all will experience more realistic consequences of their actions.

While your child is still learning to use cause-and-effect with ideas, you will see shifts between the earlier, more illogical play and play that adheres to reality. Don't feel that every play situation must be logical and reality-oriented. Even seemingly illogical play can serve a purpose at this age. For example, the child who has monsters eating his dolls, then pretends a storm has begun, and then begins taking one of his dolls apart, may be concerned that things will fall apart and be dangerous. Most probably, you will not be able to discern this theme, nor should you. Your child, however, needs to feel free to "play out" these kinds of emotional ideas in a secure environment without undue anxiety or concern. Since he is not quite able to express these ideas logically, he is expressing them in the only way he knows how. What you should look for at this stage that is different from the two-year-old stage is a balance between illogical make-believe play and the beginnings of, and eventually the consolidation of, reality-oriented play. If your child's play shifts back and forth between illogic and logic in the same play session, or at two different times during play, encourage him in whichever mode is dominant at the time. However, overall, encourage your child's communication through play, language, and interaction to be more reality-oriented and to contain logically connected sequences.

As with pretend play, some children show a preference for first applying cause-and-effect relationships to spatial configurations, such as building block towers or houses, making corrals for horses, space-ships, and so forth. If this is true of your child, look for his capacity for building to increase in complexity: units will connect into a more logical and integrated whole. For example, by age three your child might put one square on top of another square with a smaller square on top and call it a rocket ship, or, he may put two enclosures next to each other as though he's building a house with two rooms.

Your child's ultimate goal is to understand and apply cause-and-effect relationships in his personal interactions. However brilliantly he may be doing puzzles, building houses, or even interacting in pretend dramas, becoming involved in emotional interchanges with people means he is applying cause-and-effect thinking across a range of experience. For example he is learning to know about what feelings and behaviors are associated with happy interactions, angry ones, power struggles, mild teasing, and major provocations. It's just a step from thinking, If I pile this block on this block I'll have a house, to, If I hug Daddy, he will be happy, or If I throw my milk on the floor, Mommy will be mad. At this stage, as in earlier stages, it is most important to make sure your child feels secure with people. You can follow the principles for wooing your child, substituting activities that are appropriate for his age in place of holding and cuddling. Using his already developed thinking abilities, for example, try to involve your child in working cooperatively on a block design. As you work you can put an arm around him occasionally or show enthusiasm for his construction. If there is a game your child especially likes to play, become a partner, perhaps passively at first, then more actively as he warms up. Finding the right playmates can also help. A child with similar interests can mean the difference between boredom and interest. But remember, if your efforts do not work and you are concerned about his becoming withdrawn, a professional consultation can probably help you determine what the problem is.

USING IDEAS ACROSS
THE EMOTIONAL SPECTRUM

Does your child use all emotional themes at various times in his personal relationships and play? Do the themes follow a logical sequence of cause-and-effect? In play, can your child shift from one emotion to another, yet integrate them into a theme? Do his emotional themes during play remain intact even when the emotions become more intense?

Throughout the last three stages your child's range of emotion has been an important element in his development. Now there is an added dimension—a range of interconnected, cause-and-effect emotional patterns in both interactions and play: the naughty doll gets punished; the doll who has a nice surprise becomes happy; the doll who gets hurt is cared for.

When children are able to evidence logical emotional patterns, they employ many of the personality functions described earlier. For example, a four-year-old pretends she is "Mommy." She comes home from shopping, goes over to "baby," hugs and kisses her, and asks her how she is doing. She then holds baby in her lap and looks at a picture book with her. After that they cook dinner together. This sequence is planned, maintains an even mood and integrates emotions and ideas. When children have conflicts with a particular emotion, they are often unable to portray that emotion in an organized sequence. They may either become illogical and disorganized when the emotion surfaces, or they may avoid the emotion in play so as not to become confused.

For example, three-and-a-half-year-old Philip is playing with two dolls who hug each other. Immediately he pretends to be a bear and starts racing cars around the room. After a minute or two this activity becomes a little wild. Philip starts flinging the cars around.

Philip's mother was puzzled at first by his behavior, but learned to be on the lookout for it. Recognizing that she was seeing the absence of cause-and-effect emotional play, she knew she could help if she could get Philip to stay with the emotion he started by adding logical sequences onto the play. The next time he started to play with the two dolls, his mother joined in. Philip had the two dolls hug, then decided he was a bear. His mother asked whether or not the bear also had somebody that he liked to hug. Philip hugged his kangaroo, then went after his racing cars. "Gee, I wonder what happened after you two hugged?" his mother asked. She was surprised to see that Philip did indeed have a sequence in mind, but it was a scary one. He showed her how the two dolls, and the bear and the kangaroo began to fight. Philip's mother empathized, saying "Oh, they must be mad at each other." It was Philip's turn to look surprised. His mother was giving him the message that it was okay to go from loving to fighting.

Gradually, Philip became more interested in the themes of closeness and began using ideas in his play which expressed love and tenderness. To his mother's delight, he also began expressing more warmth toward her and also toward his father. Using words and emotional ideas helped Philip over his concerns.

Often when a child becomes disorganized around or avoids an emotion, it's because the emotion scares him. If you pay attention to how your family deals with a particular emotion, it may provide clues as to why your child is not comfortable.

In Philip's case, his lack of cause-and-effect emotional patterns stemmed from an earlier pattern that he and his mother had initiated. When Philip was an infant, his mother had been overly controlling whenever she tried to be tender. And when Philip became negative and rebellious, she withdrew, making him more angry. Marital problems had contributed to his mother's pattern. These difficulties were now resolved and she was more comfortable being tender. But Philip needed extra support to disengage from the earlier patterns.

If, as in another example, your child happens to shy away from assertive or aggressive play, he may not be comfortable with aggression and may not put his anger into words and ideas to communicate his feelings. He may, instead, have temper tantrums and pound things with his fists. To help your child with his conflict, you can say during play, "Gee, what happens when that little doll gets mad because the mommy doll won't give him a snack before dinner?" If your child changes the subject, try saying, "I'll bet that little doll gets mad and says, 'I want some candy.' " If your child is frightened by the verbal

Even a grown-up firefighter needs help from his mother from time to time.

expression of anger, he may giggle at your suggestions or may just watch you carefully as you elaborate this theme.

The child who withdraws or becomes disorganized in order to avoid an emotion, such as the one above, calls attention to himself. The child who avoids emotional areas but is, on the surface, very outgoing and competent may be easily overlooked. If a child does well with his friends, for example, a concern for his lack of intimacy at home is ignored or rationalized. But this child is also using avoidance, just not as visibly. Though you would not guess it, some children who appear to be "shy" may have greater flexibility and variety in their emotional lives than some who appear more confident and successful in school and with peers.

Chances are your child will show a preference for one or another thematic area—for aggressiveness, love, curiosity, whatever. He does not need to have a perfect balance between all emotional areas. What is important is that you encourage your child toward logical follow-up in the areas he finds difficult. As we discussed in the previous section, you can do this either by carrying the emotion forward to the next sequence (the bear hugging another animal), or by carrying through in terms of what would follow logically. Gradually introducing difficult themes helps your child learn that he can put difficult feelings into emotional ideas and thereby practice new patterns of interaction with greater security.

Remember, however, that although pretend play is important, it is still the means to an end, not the end in itself. Pretend play is like a window. Through it you can see the range of ideas and emotions with which both you and your child are comfortable. But comfort in pretend play does not always guarantee skill in using emotional ideas in the real heat of the battle. Do not make the mistake of thinking a contrived, pretend drama can substitute for real interpersonal comfort in dealing with important emotional issues. You will have to watch both pretend play and actual interactions to determine whether your child's skills are "crossing over." Pretend play can be a good practice ground for exploring new emotional areas your child may find a little scary, but always pay special attention to the real interactions you are having with your child. As with Philip, if an emotional area is too scary even for pretend play, it will almost certainly be difficult in real interactions.

Some children are able to show a full range of emotions and use them in logical sequences when the emotions are not intense. However, should you notice that, when feelings of pleasure, assertion, or curiosity reach a certain point, your child tends to become frenetic or withdrawn, he can probably use your help dealing with intense emotion. The extremes—children who seem to be distracted or withdrawn across all emotional levels—are rare. More often your observation will reveal particular situations which affect your child.

You can give the most help to your child by becoming aware of which emotions at what level of intensity precipitate his tendency to become either withdrawn or disorganized. You can then be alert to times when you need to reduce the intensity of an emotion and provide more structure and use of ideas. For example, a little girl plays with her trucks. As the action builds, she is unable to contain her excitement and suddenly begins to throw the trucks around.

Seeing this, her mother can comment that the trucks are out of control and suggest they stop for a red light. Or she could "notice" that one truck has a speed pedal that is stuck and ask for help correcting it.

This restructuring follows your child's interests but allows you to introduce ideas and talk about how the excitement makes her feel. Gradually your encouragement to talk about the feelings helps your child learn to put actions and feelings into words. In this way, a greater tolerance and comprehension of the troublesome emotion can evolve.

One emotion that some claim can be observed in eight- and nine-month-olds and that may surface as an emotional idea during this stage is sadness. It is often a sign of emotional maturity involving caring and loss and is quite close to the feeling of sadness in adults. It may be evoked by the loss of a favorite toy or disappointment about a change in plans as well as the more catastrophic events such as the death of a loved grandparent. You may also see this emotion surface in a worrisome way as part of a general character trait, which usually stems from your child's not liking himself or feeling he is not liked by others. Sadness should be judged against the backdrop of your child's overall attainment of his emotional, developmental milestones. Your four-year-old who is sad and feels that no one likes him for a few days, but is able to experience a full range of emotions in an interpersonal, cause-and-effect world by using ideas, may only be struggling with a particular developmental challenge. Perhaps he feels separation from his mother or father, a temporary sadness which he may work out for himself or a response to a family crisis. This is the normal and appropriate expression of sadness for a four-year-old— after all you can't feel this sadness unless you value and love someone or something. The child who continually feels ugly, who feels that no one likes him, and who also avoids using emotional ideas in major areas such as assertiveness may have a more difficult problem. Don't hesitate to use professional help to overcome a problem like this.

To help your child deal with sadness, encourage him to talk to you and watch the kinds of emotions and ideas he uses in pretend play. Thoughts and feelings that he may not be able to communicate directly, he may be able to say indirectly through play. You can also review your own behavior so you know you are providing security and warmth, appreciation of your child's new skills and challenges and effective limit setting. Any unusual stresses in your family should also be considered.

As you encourage your child to carry emotions to their logical conclusion, you'll also want to encourage the integration of emotional opposites—activity and passivity, love and hate, gaining something and losing something. (Your child integrated these opposites at the functional level when he was organizing his behavior. Now his goal is to integrate them at the level of emotional thinking.) Your child is now ready to shift gears from being passive and contemplative to being active and aggressive; shift from being angry and aggressive to being loving and warm, within a reasonable time frame. There is no longer a separate loving self and hating self. By four-and-a-half, your child should begin to understand that he, as one person, can have different feelings toward another person.

If your child knows he can have two opposite feelings for the same person, he is then able both to separate different emotional experiences and create a larger grouping of emotional ideas. Parents who are comfortable with various emotional polarities help their children develop this ability. If your child is fundamentally secure with his anger at you, he will gradually be able to integrate this reaction with his loving feelings. You can help by engaging in all emotional areas. In this way he knows you will not leave him or withdraw from him when he is angry. In addition to being available for your child to practice a range of experiences, you'll also need to be sure that he is not being overwhelmed by your interest in his emotional life. If you constantly overreact to your child's emotions, by, for instance, making a transient feeling of loss or sadness a major calamity or by intruding and not respecting privacy ("what are you feeling now . . . and now . . . and now"), he will learn only that emotions are overwhelming.

If a child does not form emotional ideas in certain areas, his reactions to these emotional areas remain at an earlier, behavioral level of development. At earlier levels intense feelings may seem mysterious, confusing, and even frightening. If the child cannot name this feeling that grips him, or know what causes it, or whom it's directed at, his confusion is understandable. The confusion may lead to a child's primitive behavioral reaction becoming even more intense. Avoidance increases as the cycle continues. You can keep your child from getting caught in this cycle by becoming aware of the areas he avoids, and gently fostering their development. A child always has emotions. The question is, does he learn to elevate his emotions to emotional ideas which can then be used for emotional thinking.

UNDERSTANDING COMPLEX EMOTIONAL RELATIONSHIPS

Is your child beginning to distinguish different levels of emotion? Is he beginning to judge different situations? Is he fine tuning his reality testing?

Your child's nascent ability to appreciate complex relationships between ideas helps him fine tune all of his emotions and feelings. Your child will begin to distinguish between being a little bit angry, moderately angry, very angry, and fiery mad as well as begin to realize that each of these different gradations and shadings can lead to different consequences. Once your child realizes that different levels of feeling lead to different outcomes he can begin to refine his experience of a specific feeling. Take, for example, the special love your child feels for you in comparison with the love he feels for friends. His new ability shows that he now groups experience in terms of qualitative differences. (As an aside, the ability to appreciate different degrees of emotion is similar to the later developmental ability of lining up sticks according to height, width or thickness. It is also interesting that, while children show a quite complex emotional understanding at an early age—beyond their intellectual understanding of the physical world—the reverse seems to be true in early adolescence when their intellectual capacities reach a fairly high level. In adolescence, children seem to apply their abilities more to the impersonal, non-emotional world, such as mathematics or science, than to their emotional lives.)

Being able to classify experiences more precisely and recognize shades of emotion also enables your child to reason more flexibly about his experiences. Therefore, your child knows he can act differently within his family than he can with a friend or at school. He can say to you, "I'm mad at you," and know that within the family, anger is acceptable. He also knows the same comment to a friend might mean that his friend may not want to see him for a while.

You'll be able to see your child's ability to distinguish shadings of emotion and to group his experiences accordingly in his language and play. For example, he will talk about the family as a unit, clearly showing an understanding of family versus nonfamily members. Or he might talk about feeling "a little love," "love you all the way," suggesting the capacity for shadings and gradations. He may also realize during the day that witches are not real, though at night he may still be frightened by them. In his play you may see a greater ability to differentiate between fact and fantasy. He may be able to appreciate cartoons while realizing that they are not an accurate portrayal of the world. Or he might say, "I'm the Incredible Hulk"— and smile at you conspiratorially or shrug and say, "just pretend." With his new understanding your child gets to keep his fantasy world, but maintain a balance between it and reality.

Some children have islands of fantasy—for instance, this is the stage at which a pretend friend may appear. A pretend friend will probably enrich your child's fantasy life without interfering with his development. His "friend" can provide your child comfort or perhaps, be fingered as the culprit when the milk is spilled. Only when his "friend" interferes with your child's development should you be concerned. Should your child choose, for example, to play with his "friend" at school rather than other children or always to make him the culprit without any sense of responsibility, you would want to find out what was making him withdraw or shirk all responsibility. You can also let him know when it is appropriate for him to be with his "friend"—at home, or when he's falling asleep, for example. Gradually his level of comprehension that his "friend" is pretend increases.

Another tendency to watch for as you observe your child's ability to distinguish shadings of emotion is the child who only attends to concrete tasks, such as doing puzzles, drawing letters, or talking about things he did during the day with no excursions into fantasy. This child may have an underlying worry about maintaining his ability to organize his emotional ideas. He shies away from fantasy for fear that he will get lost there. If your child avoids all fantasy, first look for stresses that may be making him uncomfortable; then very gradually introduce fantasy into his play and conversation. While he is climbing on a jungle-gym, for example, suggest he pretend to be Tarzan. If your suggestions make him anxious, drop the subject and gently pursue the idea of pretend another day. Fantasy, or "pretend" provides

"A family drama."

the opportunity for a child to experience all his emotional proclivities—which, after all, is part of what makes him distinctly human.

Your child's emerging awareness of subtlety and ability to refine groups of experience is a milestone at the foundation of his ability to be more empathetic and less egocentric. In essence, your child now has different selves—the old self that experiences the world ("I want everything and everything has to be perfect") and the new self that observes his own behavior. There is a part of him that can now say, "Gee, I'm being greedy," or, "What I said is not nice." This ability for self-reflection allows your four- to five-year-old to do what he couldn't at age three, show more advanced forms of empathy. But this is only the beginning of a long road. Your child's empathy continues to increase gradually throughout late adolescence and into adulthood. It is one of those abilities that, though it starts early in life may or may not develop to any great extent. Some people, as we all know, stay very egocentric with little ability to step outside themselves. Others are able to create a group of internal experiences, which help them become less egocentric and more empathic. Glimpses of your four- or five-year-old being empathic through ideas are a promising indication of your child's growing ability for emotional thinking.

You can help your child develop the ability to see complex relationships between ideas by focusing on content, that is, by explaining where certain kinds of behavior are appropriate and where they are not. For example, teasing is okay at home but not at school, jumping on the couch may be okay at home but not at Aunt Sally's house.

Your child's abilities in all of these areas become much more developed between the ages of five and ten. Their early emergence, however, is a sign of his ability to consolidate the basic functions of his personality; reality testing, impulse regulation, integration of emotions, mood stabilization, and focused concentration. As your child struggles to refine his experience and understand subtlety, he is gaining a better sense of how he and the world work, how he can understand problems and seek solutions to them.

TRIANGULAR RELATIONSHIPS

Does your child react to both parents? Is he able to use one of you to soften the reaction from the other? Does his play involve three-person systems?

Your child's ability to see shadings and gradations of emotional feeling allows him also to see complexity in relationships. He can now expand his two-person system to a three-person system in which child, mother, and father are the points of a triangle. In the two-person system, your child's interactions focused on getting a certain need met; getting a drink or being loved by either his mother or father. He was unaware of intrigues, rivalries, and subtlety. If he wanted his mother all to himself, he might literally push his father out the door with no regard for his feelings. In a three-person system, however, a child sees relationships between three independent entities. Now if a child wants his mother to himself and his father is there, his father may be seen as a rival who is capable of becoming angry and perhaps punishing the child. Now that your child has reached the stage where he can grasp the cause-and-effect relationship between his feelings (and actions), he can look at the implications of his actions and examine his feelings for all involved. You may also be able to see your child's shift to triangular interactions in his pretend play. An intrigue between three people might arise—two dolls playing a trick on the third doll or keeping a secret from someone else. In nursery school, relationships begin to exclude someone.

Since much of our lives are made up of intrigues involving triangles, learning to deal with the three-person system is quite important. The three-person system can apply to groups as well as individuals—in international politics, for example, the alliances may shift but a triangle still remains.

The question is, how does a three-person system benefit your child more than a two-person system? Basically, it's because having three people in a system gives your child greater flexibility. It buffers the intensity of feelings and provides him with alternative outcomes. Now that your child understands subtlety, feelings do not have to overwhelm him. His internal world becomes more stable. Let's take a girl who is angry at her mother. Rather than fearing her anger will cause her mother to abandon her she can either look to her father to take her mother's place, or think of her father as someone who will keep mother from acting irrationally. The triangle is an efficient system of emotional checks and balances, allowing your child to work out complicated relationships between feelings.

Your four-year-old will probably be ready to move into the three-person system, but she may not make the move unless you support it. It is crucial at this stage for the three of you—mother, father and child—to interact with each other. (If you are one of the many single parents in our society, there are ways of coping with this particular stage of development. You may want to skip the next few pages, then return to them after reading the section headed *For Single Parents,* beginning on page 199.) For example, if mother and son are very close, father, feeling rejected, may begin to spend less and less time at home—which just perpetuates a lopsided relationship. To correct this situation, the father must instead woo his child into a relationship with him. Though at first his child may not respond to his overtures (perhaps fearing he will lose his relationship with mother), father's continued availability will eventually win; it may be difficult for father to disregard his inclination to flee, but his child's rejection of him is the signal that he is needed more than ever.

In such situations fathers often have difficulty having the patience to make time available on their child's terms. Whether a child wants to watch TV, play "boring games," or reread the same story again and again, the father must remember that his child may need a long warmup period (as much as a couple of months), and that he needs to be wooed into a closer relationship. During this period, the activities are less important than the child's feeling that his father is available to him on his own terms. A father's patience, availability, and help will aid in making his child feel safe and secure, and will eventually lead to a more "equal" relationship.

Naturally, if it is a mother who needs to establish a closer relationship with her child, the same rules apply. If your child can feel warm and loving as well as assertive and competitive with both of you, he has a grand opportunity to see how this complicated three-person system operates.

Your child's need for both of you is especially true in certain emotional circumstances. Let's look at helping your child deal with anger. When either parent feels free to discipline, your child experiences feelings of anger and aggression with each of her relationships. Thus, her father, for example, is not an overwhelmingly frightening figure because she knows what happens when her father gets angry at her. If only the mother sets limits and the daughter has no experience with father's anger, the father might be too frightening for the child to incorporate into her three-person system.

Let us take another situation in which four-year-old Ruth is struggling with her separation feelings toward her mother. She often becomes involved in power struggles with mother, but it is clear she is of two minds: she wants to be close and secure one moment and wants to provoke and domineer the next. (The reason for this vacillation is that children at this age still perceive the mother as an overwhelming figure in comparison to themselves.) When Ruth gets angry, she quickly panics and, needing security, clings to her mother.

Here, her father can make himself available as a source of love, nurturance and dependency, and provide the comfort and security which allows Ruth to be more comfortable with her anger at mother. She may say "Mommy is being too bossy," and go to sit in her father's lap. This helps her to hold on to her anger long enough to feel comfortable with it. Once Ruth is comfortable she can then intuitively examine her feeling: she can see that anger doesn't lead either to her destruction or to mother's. Soon she can see that, although her mother is bossy, she is also funny, loving, playful, and really not so bad at all. Thus, Ruth is able to work out a more realistic relationship with and perception of her mother. It is not impossible that, without her father's support, she would work out her separation problems anyway, but it certainly would be more difficult.

Focusing on the negative features of a loved one is a very common way for children to become more independent. By "undervaluing" you for a time, the way a teenager does, your child is trying to become less dependent on you. Ideally, your child's focus on the negative is only transient and, with greater independence, she can return to a more balanced picture of you.

You can expand your love and support one step further by becoming, at times, your child's ally. With your child's basic need for security in mind, both of you can be flexible so that in any given situation, he feels support. From mother and child playfully beating father in a game, to one parent siding with the child in a difference of opinion, your emotional tone can convey empathy and sympathy that will make it easier for your child to explore the subtleties of a three-way relationship.

Usually, a child already has a primary alliance with and dependency on her mother and needs to become more independent of her (even if the mother works). Therefore, although each parent can have a separate alliance with their child, as well as their primary alliance to each other, the father-child alliance can be particularly helpful. If father and child together can withstand the mother's anger or bossiness, the child can then return to loving a mother who is no longer overwhelming and frightening. By reducing the power struggle, the child is able to internalize the sense of security mother provides. A mother-child union against the father can also help the child to see that alliances can be formed in many different ways and that she can experiment and form different ones.

You, as parents, must not lose sight of the fact that your alliances must be made with the basic understanding that mother and father are the primary alliance. Your alliance promotes a secure and stable home life and helps your child continue her development. Your child needs to realize that, no matter how hard she tries to get one or another of you to be her primary ally, mother and father have the more fundamental alliance, which is really a family alliance. If the balance of power in your family triangle shifts to parent and child against the other parent, a child can easily become frightened of breaking up the parental relationship. If the father overplays his alliance with his young daughter, for example, she might become frightened that she will actually overwhelm her mother, on whom she must still depend. She may behave in an arrogant and pseudo-competent manner even though she is quite scared. A fixed parent-child alliance is almost never in the interest of the child except under unusual circumstances, say, if one parent is suffering extreme emotional problems and the child and other parent have to join together to help take care of the disturbed parent.

For Single Parents. A single-parent family can support excellent growth, development and emotional care just as a two-parent family can. It is the ingredients that are provided that count, not whether they are being provided by one or two people. Some special issues, however, are certainly more easily handled in a two-parent family.

Fostering triangular relationships is obviously one of them. If there are brothers and sisters at home, a close friend, a teacher, or your new love interest, you will see your child use what is available to create triangles. Our only suggestion is to help your child expand his relationship patterns so that he does have other adult figures to be close to. Given the opportunity, your child will inevitably learn to experiment with triangular relationships. It is only one of the important aspects of his emotional and cognitive development that you, as a single parent, will have to be particularly conscious of supporting.

As you can see, your child's ultimate sense of personal security will begin to consolidate as he becomes able to interact freely in a three-person system. Your child learns to group experiences involving himself and others, practice with shadings and gradations of feeling, and experience a fuller range of emotions than might otherwise be possible. His budding independence and ability to see his mother in a more mature manner may give mother a pang or two, but it means that everything is working together to enable your child to cope with the ever-increasing complexity of his emotional world.

EMOTIONAL STABILITY

Can your child tolerate being separated from you? Can he resume his relationships and activities after intense anger? Does he become overstimulated by nudity or overly preoccupied with his body?

The emotions that most frequently cause a child to regress are separation and loss, aggression and anger, and interest in the body. Because they are particularly difficult emotions for your child to handle at this stage of development, let's examine them individually.

Separation and Loss. As we've mentioned, your three- to four-year-old child still needs to balance his need for independence with his need for security from mother, father, and other loved ones. The mixture of feelings associated with separation—from missing and loss to anger or being excluded—are all natural and normal feelings you can expect your child to have.

In general, your child's interest in independence gets a boost through conversation, pretend play and physical activities with others his own age. Also of considerable help is his ability to have separate, organized sets of images of himself and his mother, father and other loved ones which incorporate both the emotional tone and specific interactions between that person and your child. Though he has had this capacity, as you will recall, as early as at eighteen months, his capacity is now much greater. He can now evoke his picture of you for as long as he needs it to make him feel better. Even more importantly, your child is capable of holding onto and using this image in spite of intense emotions (such as being angry at being left behind). He now has a symbolic "security blanket" of emotional memories.

The degree to which your child can retain this picture is often related to the feeling of security and closeness between parents and child. A child who is unsure of his relationship with mother for one reason or another has more difficulty making mother's qualities abstract and combining them into an internal image. When he becomes angry or scared at being left, he is unable to put the parts together to construct an image. Without an image to give him stability, he becomes unable to cope.

Let us say your child becomes very upset at being left—even if you are only going to a movie. When you go out, he grabs your legs and screams. This is no mild provocation or goodbye ritual; it becomes a temper tantrum. In the short term, your best effort may be spent helping your child calm down and giving him a little more time to feel comfortable with the babysitter. Before you go out you and the babysitter might do something together with your child, like look at a book. (It is always important for your child to be familiar with the sitter and have time to warm up to him or her.) The next day, when your child is feeling more secure, try to talk to him about how he feels when his mommy and daddy go out and leave him behind. If you raise the issue when the waters are less turbulent, he may be able to easily share why separation is so difficult. (Don't avoid this step for fear of another storm!) You may also follow your child's lead if he decides to play out scenes of separation: dolls may cry as parents go off and abandon them. You may witness this scene followed by houses falling apart because of thunder, fire or other catastrophe. Your child may be trying to show you what he fears might happen if you leave him. Warm empathy to his concerns are almost always helpful. You may find that he is more angry about being excluded than left.

Your tolerance of your child's expression of feeling is necessary for a long-term resolution to the problem. When you empathize by saying that you know it is hard to be left, that he must miss you, he then has the opportunity to put his feelings into words even if he is angry. He also has the opportunity to experience important elements for his image of you—those of understanding and caring. In addition, by understanding his feeling of loss, your child begins to see that, although he may feel bad, nothing disastrous will happen in your absence.

That your child can tolerate sadness, feelings of loss, and longing is an important lesson for him to learn. (See Chapter V for discussion of more permanent loss.) Once these emotional ideas help him comprehend his experiences, separation will be far less catastrophic for him. Rather than thinking the house will fall down, he can think about his parents at the movie, or about being left out. If he is able to talk about missing you, being "left out," and wanting to go along, the issue shifts to a different level. He no longer feels that a global catastrophe has taken place, but instead that he has been excluded from something he would enjoy. This isn't pleasant—but neither is it cataclysmic.

Aggression and Anger.   Another feeling that can keep your child from reaching the milestone of emotional thinking is intense anger. When your child's anger becomes acute it's natural that it may frighten you as well as your child. His emotions can become so frightening that he loses his ability to hold onto an organized mental image of himself as well as one of you. As we've seen, if your child feels that his anger can really go out of control, he may assume that it can destroy him and the people he loves. On the other hand, if he finds that he can control and regulate his anger, he gains confidence in his ability, and your ability, to handle such intense feelings. They are no longer "life threatening" to him.

In order to deal with your child's very angry feelings, you'll need to balance empathy and compassion with firm limit-setting. If yours is a family, like so many, which tends to err on one side or the other, remember that balance is pivotal. If your very impulsive child's lack of control frightens him, you will want to provide a great deal of both compassion and systematic setting of limits. If your child has relatively good internal capacities to regulate his strong emotions but tends to withdraw, you may need to emphasize empathy and compassion rather than limit-setting. If he feels that you are afraid of his feeling, he must then feel frightened, too. If he senses you are confident that his anger can be controlled, he can begin to absorb this confidence himself and use it to regulate his feelings.

How do you convey this type of confidence to your child? One important way is our old "eyeball-to-eyeball" technique. This means staying with your child when he is extremely angry and setting limits in such a way that he is first able to regain control of himself. Depending on your child this may mean wooing him; speaking in a firm voice; or perhaps distracting him. Communicating your engagement and emotional involvement is what is important here. Raising your voice, insisting that he stop hitting his two-year-old sister, looking at him sternly as you tell him he can't see his favorite TV show, and listening as he complains about the punishment can provide this sense of emotional engagement.

Once your child has regained control, don't stop the interaction. It is important for you to maintain contact after the incident, and here is why. If you and your child withdraw from each other, a secret war may begin. Your child, still seething angrily, accuses you of delib-erately tripping him when he brushes by. You, also still seething, blame him for accidentally spilling his milk. If this kind of "illogic" continues, your child will believe that intense feelings lead to illogical and disorganized patterns of thinking.

Let's take a brief look at a few of the less helpful reactions that many of us have used at one time or another. Many parents send their child to his room when he is having a temper tantrum. Doing this may give a child the sense that his anger will always lead to separation. Under these circumstances he may find his anger even more frightening than it was initially. Although it is occasionally helpful for a child to go into another room to calm down, it must not be done in such a way that the child feels you want nothing to do with his anger.

Another typical parental reaction is to say, "I'm not going to let that little kid push me around!" Though the parent may begin by talking to the child about what happened, a power struggle usually follows. But at least this parent is more likely to be emotionally involved with his child. However, a parent who can avoid the extremes of abandonment or a power struggle when setting limits is most likely to convey that his anger can be tolerated by both you and him. Obviously, no parent should feel that he must walk a perfect tightrope all the time—parents are emotional beings, too. Becoming a "robot-parent"—functioning without showing feelings—is the worst type of interaction for your child.

There is another interesting development concerning aggression that takes place at about this time. By age four, your child may be quite sophisticated about expressing aggression and may become "passive aggressive." This means that when your child is angry he will spill water on the rug, break something, or manage to step on your toe, all seemingly by accident. You'll have to give your child a point or two for ingenuity, but you'll also want to set limits effectively. If you deal confidently with your child as he tries to outsmart you, for example, by saying that you think his spilling his milk on your favorite rug was his way of getting even with you, he will appreciate that you are not so dumb after all. You will also be helping him to internalize limits in subtle areas of aggressive behavior. And besides, if the two of you can carry off this interplay in a good-natured manner, your child will be testing his wit and cleverness against yours—important practice for his later life.

Interest in the Body. Interest in pleasure, and particularly in pleasures that can be brought about by the body, is another emotional interest especially pertinent to your child at this point. Between ages three to four and a half, your child will show an even greater appreciation for the sexual differences between boys and girls. You will find him inspecting his genital areas, finding pleasure in touching various parts of the body and expressing curiosity about your body.

Your child's emerging interest in his body and in pleasure can strengthen his sense of himself and his sense of others. When your child sees himself, in part, as a sexual self (in the childlike sense that he knows the differences between boys and girls and experiments with touching his body) his understanding of the real world is enhanced. He has a deeper, richer picture of what a person really is.

Your goal in this instance is to encourage your child to have a healthy respect for his sexual curiosity while at the same time avoiding situations that overstimulate him. Your ability to stay on the right side of this fine line requires an appreciation of your child's interest and his desire to experiment, balanced with careful limit setting.

Your family's attitudes about nudity and sexuality will naturally be geared to your own comfort or discomfort. The range of acceptable attitudes is wide, because we've seemed to realize that the major issue is not so much what the child does or does not see, but how the child feels about it. Bodies in themselves need not be overstimulating to a child. What you *feel* about nudity—not nudity itself—may be what leads to overstimulation. A parent who is sexually frustrated, for example, may walk around naked, unconsciously enjoying his child's excitement. On the other hand, the parent who is anxious about nudity may cover up all the time. In these cases, it isn't the parent's behavior that is critical, but rather the emotional vibrations the child is receiving. (However, parents who are very comfortable with nudity must still be alert to the possibility of overwhelming their child.) You can be comfortable with your inclinations and give your child a sense that you are confident about what limits ought to be set.

Because your child may not be able to limit his own interests and want to overreach himself, you must establish bounds. If, on seeing you nude, your child becomes overly excited—maybe being very aggressive or withdrawn, keep him out of the bathroom. In such a

Understanding allows Mommy to begin introducing the new addition to the family with warmth and closeness.

case, when your child wants to get into your bed, or when you are undressing and your child wants to watch, make clear in a calm way that you require privacy, too.

Your sense of confidence, which may derive from lots of thinking and discussion with your spouse and friends, will help your child realize that in this matter, as with anger, you can help him to control and regulate his feelings, no matter how intense they may seem. Respecting your child's curiosity while helping him set effective limits helps him to have a fuller yet stable understanding of himself and the world.

SPECIAL BEHAVIOR PATTERNS

Is your child experiencing problems such as nightmares, impulsive or negative behavior, stomach aches, or easy distractability?

At various times, most children experience difficulties with friends at school, parents, babysitters, or have specific fears. These difficulties often lead to troublesome behavior which, in turn, causes parents to become confused and upset. To discover the problem, your first step is to set some time aside to gently explore areas with which your child may be concerned. Be willing to be a good listener, to understand how your child perceives the problem, then help her find solutions. But remember, your tone of patience and empathy and your child's sense of being understood may be more important than practical advice. If you are able to specify your child's difficulty, you can probably help her deal with it. But in most cases, even if you can't discover the source of the problem, you can be of help indirectly. We suggest each parent spend thirty to forty-five minutes alone with her either every day or every other day so that she has the sense that the time is all "hers." Your child should also be able to dictate how the time is spent. Ample toys such as dolls, action figures, and play-houses will be needed. During this time your child will have the opportunity to indirectly convey what is on her mind.

It's a good idea to follow her lead in talk and play. Prepare yourself also to tolerate her doing or saying nothing for as long as fifteen or twenty minutes. Even when you are trying to be helpful, your child might need "proof" that you are truly available before she "unloads" what is on her mind. Eventually she may lead "discussions" and, over time, bring out her worries. If you are both available to your child, she may be able to work out her concerns or fears on her own.

You can also be a willing partner in these discussions by trying to help your child sequence her ideas logically and extend what she is talking about. It may take you some time to get to the point of discovering that such interaction is necessary to your child's health and emotional development, as happened in the case of Sam.

Sam was an angry and negative child. His father was a businessman who traveled extensively, leaving Sam and his mother alone for a week or so at a time. His mother had never adjusted to his father's absences and was angry herself. She vacillated in her treatment of Sam between being somewhat withdrawn and overly controlling. She dealt adequately with the tasks at hand of feeding, clothing, and caring for Sam's other physical needs, but paid no attention to his feelings or emotional development. This was partly due to the fact that she wasn't even experiencing her own emotions, in order not to feel angry at Sam's father.

Sam missed his father but couldn't express this to his mother since she didn't want to listen. So Sam became a bundle of trouble. Gradually his mother began to realize that her son was upset, and tried to discover the cause. Since Sam was only three and a half, he couldn't really express to her the turmoil he felt inside. His mother began to take the time to play with him, letting him take the play wherever he wanted to. Repeatedly, Sam played a game which involved his leaving for school, his father leaving on a trip, his mother leaving for work, his friends coming and going. The main experience of his play was clearly separation. After playing with his mother every day for some time, Sam was able to communicate his concerns directly, and became much less negative. As Sam and his mother learned to communicate, his mother was able to tell him about how she and his daddy loved him and how his daddy missed him. They counted the days together and imagined where daddy was between telephone calls. The next time his father returned from a trip, Sam was able to tell him that he both missed him and was angry at him for being away.

The support that Sam was able to get from his mother in sorting out and defining his feelings came in the form of relaxed, permissive play.

The goal of their time together was not for Sam's mother to play

Helping Your Child . . .

1. SHOW CAUSE-AND-EFFECT INTERACTIONS

— help your child practice relating cause-and-effect interactions
 · through language, respond logically to your child's communication; do not ignore communication or change subject
 · through pretend play, help him go one step further in his story, either by adding more characters to the scene, or shifting the concept of the characters
— help the child who is more interested in spatial configurations to use emotional ideas with people
 · become a building partner and provide both physical and emotional warmth during your play times; invite other children over to play
— if your child is not involved in emotional, cause-and-effect exchanges, use the involvement in his pretend play to woo him into these exchanges
 · again, become his partner and gently introduce emotional themes into the play

2. USE IDEAS ACROSS THE FULL EMOTIONAL SPECTRUM

— gently introduce an emotion he avoids into your child's play
— add on logical sequences when your child's difficulty with an emotion causes him to make an abrupt shift in the story
— pay attention to how your family handles any emotion your child seems to be uncomfortable with
— when the intensity of an emotion causes your child to become excitable or withdrawn, be alert to when the intensity is too much; provide more structure at this time so as to reengage him; encourage him to talk about his feelings; help him put actions into words
— with a child who seems particularly sad, encourage him to talk about feelings; watch if his play communicates any problems indirectly; consider any family stresses that may exist
— encourage your child to integrate opposite, emotional feelings toward one person

3. UNDERSTAND COMPLEX RELATIONSHIPS

— with the child who overindulges in fantasy, try to identify family stress, ensure you are providing enough security and setting effective limits, give the context for when the fantasy is appropriate
— with the child who overindulges the reality orientation, look for family stress and lack of emotional support, gradually introduce the idea of fantasy into conversation and play
— use language in more subtle contexts to convey a sense of gradation

"shrink" and make interpretations to Sam. She never said, "Oh, I know why you are so naughty. It's because you're angry at your daddy." Rather she was simply available as a warm and empathic person who helped her child elaborate what was on his mind and created an opportunity for her child to feel secure with her. Feeling the helpfulness of his parent and the warmth and secu-

4. ENCOURAGE THE TRIANGULAR RELATIONSHIP

— encourage your child to have a balanced relationship with both parents
— form uncontrived temporary alliances with your child, while maintaining primary alliance to spouse
— do not undermine your spouse

5. FOSTER EMOTIONAL STABILITY

— separation and loss
  · foster your child's independence by involving him with peers
  · when child is unwilling to separate, help him calm down and feel comfortable wherever he is staying; later on, help him talk about his feelings; emphathize with his reaction; help him see the reality of the absence as opposed to some frightening fantasy
— aggression and anger
  · balance empathy and compassion with very firm limit setting
  · do not let your child's aggression frighten you
  · go "eyeball-to-eyeball" with your child when he is angry: help him regain control; set firm limits
  · reengage your child after the explosion
— interest in the body
  · if your child overreaches his tolerance, parents should establish bounds by emphasizing their need for privacy
  · be comfortable with your own standards
  · respect your child's curiosity

6. CHANGE SPECIAL BEHAVIOR PATTERNS

— be involved alone with your child for 30 to 45 minutes each day or every other day
— allow your child to dictate how time is spent; provide play setting
— follow your child's lead in conversation or play
— try to help your child sequence emotional ideas logically
— be warm, empathic, and a good listener

rity of the relationship allowed Sam to use his own resources to work out his problems with separation and being abandoned. His mother served as a soothing force which helped Sam heal his own wounds. Once more cooperative, Sam was able to team up with his mother and together they could handle his father's trips more easily.

Creating a Supportive Environment

Basic to helping your child use emotional thinking is your support of his understanding of the relationships between various ideas and various feelings. In order to support the cause-and-effect relationships between ideas and between feelings, you must respond in a cause-and-effect way, empathically, in a timely manner, with subtlety, with an appreciation of fantasy and reality and with the appropriate setting of limits.

Respond in a Cause-and-Effect Way. You and others in your family must read the child's communications accurately and respond in a manner that shows a *cause-and-effect connection.* If your child says, "I feel mad," you should respond by addressing the issue, maybe finding out why, rather than suggesting the child will feel less mad if she plays outside. There are a wide variety of responses at your disposal to show your child that you understand what she is saying. Although it may be preferable to respond empathetically, you can be negative (as we all are sometimes) as long as the response is logically connected and not confusing.

Respond with Empathy. An *empathic response* requires you to be honest with yourself. Children can feel the difference between a superficial response and one that is really felt. A negative example will illustrate the subtle confusion which can result from a "false front."

Janey asks her mother to come out with her and pick flowers in the garden. Her mother smiles and says, "Yes," but her smile is tense. She's actually annoyed that Janey wants to pick flowers from her garden, but she is afraid that saying "no" will inhibit her child's zest and curiosity. Her mother, seemingly light-hearted, accompanies her daughter, talking about how lovely the flowers are and how much fun it is to pick them. Just under the surface, however, she is both tense and angry. Janey senses this. Though she feels supported in the logic of her ideas, she also feels that there is some illogic between her own spontaneity and excitement over picking flowers and mother's tension and anger. Fifteen minutes later, when her mother yells at her for dropping some food on the floor, Janey is even more confused; she has no way of knowing that her mother was, and still is, annoyed about picking the flowers.

Being empathic does not mean that your child's every request should be satisfied. It does mean, however, that even when saying no, you can consider your child's feelings. If you really do not want your Janey to pick the flowers, there is no reason to agree. However, you might suggest an alternate activity, like drawing or making flowers.

Respond in a Timely Manner. A *timely response* to your child's complex communications is important for cause-and-effect learning. The parent who is reading the newspaper and waits a full two minutes before explaining to his child why he cannot take him to the park is not giving timely feedback. The child may become both discouraged in his use of language and ideas as well as impatient. On a more subtle level, the parent who does not give a spontaneous or immediate response because of anxiety or confusion about what his child is asking may cause him to have a sense of "time warp" or confusion.

Don't confuse an immediate response with immediate gratification. Learning to wait is a key lesson for your child to master at this stage. He must learn to wait, be patient and to tolerate frustration. You'll be happy to know that he does not need immediate gratification of each request, continuous conversation or unflagging involvement in his pretend play. As long as you actively support his abilities some of the time, your child's new capacities for using ideas will emerge.

When your child needs to wait, be explicit with him and say, "You will have to wait now," or, "I'll be able to do that with you later." Whether you respond to your child's request by complying or by telling him that he must wait, you are giving a logical response that will help him develop a sense that his ideas lead to other ideas. In fact, when his request is rejected, he is learning that his ideas will sometimes lead to a response which will inhibit his intended action.

Teaching your child the lesson of waiting requires balance, respect for family and cultural traditions and respect for your child's natural curiosity and ingenuity. Use real situations in order to teach it. When you are relaxed and playful, get down on the floor with your child and enjoy the fun. But when you are busy and your child is being a "pest," use the opportunity to set limits. Only if you find that most of the time you are too busy and tense to enjoy participating in your child's play or if you find that most of the time you comply with his wishes for fear of "inhibiting" him do you need to consider a change of pattern.

Parents are led to believe that they must be consistent, that is, always respond to the same issue in the same way. Consistency is good up to a point, but your child also needs to understand *context and subtlety*.

Let's follow Caroline, four-and-a-half, around for a while. She has been testing limits of late. Her mother asks her not to touch the walls with her paint-smeared hands. Caroline sticks out her tongue and gives her mother a Bronx cheer. Her mother responds to her daughter's complex ideational communication with an equally complex ideational communication—she punishes her. Later that day her mother, Caroline, and her baby brother are at the grocery store. Her mother tells Caroline to stop racing up and down the crowded aisles. Caroline gives Mom another Bronx cheer. Although her mother is tempted, for the sake of both consistency and her temper, to punish Caroline as she did at home, she envisions the scene that will result: Caroline crying, screaming and running away, her baby brother bawling in his carriage. Her mother's alternative is to say, "If you don't listen to me, Caroline, you will be punished when you get home." The little charmer sticks out her tongue and continues to behave provocatively. Her mother informs her that her punishment-to-come has just escalated. When they get home her mother, true to her word, punishes Caroline for her behavior in the grocery store. Caroline not only remembers why she was punished, but may even think twice before repeating her performance.

The point we are making in the example above is that a totally consistent approach to reward and punishment, while perfectly understandable itself, does not help a child appreciate subtlety, differences and, most importantly, context. Children begin learning context in early infancy and much of adult life is governed by context: what is appropriate in one setting is not appropriate in another; the way something is said may be more important than what is said. For your child to understand that he must behave one way at home and another in public, that different rules may apply to different people, are important lessons in his life. He may learn that in certain situations he has "leverage," but that if he uses it too much, he will pay later on. Tradeoffs like this teach your child to appreciate the way the world

Imaginative three- and four-year-olds can identify emotionally with the feelings of the characters.

actually works. Cause-and-effect may still be consistent, just more subtle.

If you have more than one child, at some point you will face the complaint that you are not treating your children equally. In other words, you will be charged with inconsistency—usually in the form of favoritism. You might try to treat your children exactly the same, but this is inevitably a losing battle. Instead, you can take the opportunity to teach them both about subtlety and context. Explain early on that they are different. Of course, like all learning experiences, the learning should be gradual and balanced. For example, a three-year-old girl whose two-year-old brother is having a birthday party might be given a present or two, with the understanding that her brother is getting more. The blow is softened and she may also understand context a little better. The older the child, the less necessary to soften the "blow," but remember that your child's understanding of various degrees of provocativeness, anger, warmth, and love are all learned to a great extent from the responses he gets from you.

None of the foregoing is conventional wisdom: much traditional child-rearing advice warns against violating consistency. Don't *ever* pick your child up if she cries and refuses to settle down to sleep, says this school, because once you violate the rule she will expect to be picked up whenever she has a nightmare or just doesn't want to go to bed. But your good sense, and your responsiveness to your child and to her emotional signals, will tell you that when she is sobbing with terror during a thunderstorm you simply must pick her up and comfort her. Listen to the voice that tells you when you should ignore the rules; don't let consistency interfere with your—and your child's—appreciation of context.

Separate Fantasy from Reality. Supporting cause-and-effect relationships also means helping your child to distinguish fantasy from reality and to realize that there are various levels of both. For example, if your four-year-old runs around the house shouting "I'm Superman" and starts jumping off the couch, you might be concerned that he will hurt himself, should he really think he can fly. You might wonder aloud whether he thinks that he is really Superman or whether he is just pretending. He may reluctantly acknowledge that "it is just pretend." You might then say, "Okay, Superman, don't hurt yourself." You are helping your child who may have temporarily been "carried away," without undermining his gusto or enthusiasm.

Fantasies in the form of fears may be more difficult to put in perspective. Perhaps your son just saw a TV program on alligators and is now afraid to walk in the grass or won't go to bed because of "witches." There is no substitute for patience. With you at his side, take the child into the disturbing situation one step at a time, explaining and showing him reality. Examine the grass, hand in hand, being two alligator hunters; bring him back to bed and have the light on, checking under the bed and in closets for any witches. A comforting back rub and explanation about some dreams being scary and others being nice will help to reassure your child.

You will often help your child make these clarifications intuitively. You might have difficulty, however, if your child's fantasy happens to fit a fantasy of your own. Let's say you are very concerned about robbers and sometimes have nightmares about them. When your child tells you of a similar dream, it may be hard for you to communicate convincingly that it was only a dream. Even if you say the right words, your anxiety level and tendency to jump at shadows may suggest to your child that you too believe burglars are a real and pressing concern. In this situation, you need to come to grips with your own fears. Have your spouse reassure both you and your child by examining the reality of the situation.

Set Limits. Setting limits is an important part of understanding and responding to your child in a way that fosters his logical use of ideas. Setting limits is usually connected to your child's provocative expressions of anger. His breaking your china, hitting his sister, or kicking you is meant to upset you. Once recognized, appropriate setting of limits is a very realistic communication back to your child. It lets him know what is appropriate to do and what is not. In some respects, it is clearer than almost any other kind of communication. A sharp "no," or "wait" followed by a punishment where appropriate is very purposeful, and helps your child see that his emotional ideas have consequences.

Setting limits will also help your child feel secure. Between the ages of two-and-a-half and three-and-a-half, children are unsure of their own ability to set limits. If your child is hungry and wants to eat candy just before dinner, he does not yet know he can control that desire. He wants what he wants when he wants it. If you enforce a firm limit your child gains confidence that he, in fact, can wait. He learns that he can bear yearning for the candy and still enjoy it later. Having experiences of this kind can teach your child that a strong yearning is not an overwhelming experience; he will not fall apart if it isn't satisfied. But don't think that this learning happens by itself. It's just like any other lesson and requires lots of practice.

Learning self-restraint has far more fundamental results than your child's realizing he can control his wish for candy. Your being able to constrain and tolerate the intensity of his feelings helps him feel more secure about his ability for self-regulation and self-control. His very sense of self becomes more organized. He realizes he does not have to hit his brother, bite his mother, or destroy a friend because he cannot have his way. Imagine how upsetting it must be for your child to feel that he cannot control his anger and that he may actually hurt you, on whom he is dependent for nurturance and security. Being able to control himself gets him out of a tremendous bind. The more secure your child feels, the less he worries about his own or other people's survival and the more he can use his developing capacities for seeing the emotional and interpersonal relationships between different ideas.

Reviewing Your Support

At this milestone of emotional thinking, your child's goal is to use emotional ideas in logical sequences. Supporting your child's optimal development of this ability will require that you once again take an honest look at where your strengths and vulnerabilities lie. Spend some time on the following questions: Do you want your child to stay the "baby" in your family? Does your child communicate ideas that make you feel anxious? Do your child's communications confuse you? Are you comfortable dealing with your child's intense feelings? Does your child have traits that you admire? Are you comfortable in a three-person system? Does your child's new ability to behave more logically inspire your admiration and allow you to interact with ease?

YOUR FAMILY SITUATION

As we've mentioned, at this stage children are especially sensitive to parents' undermining each other. This does not mean that you are always expected to be in complete agreement or have no conflicts. But it does mean that a continuous atmosphere of tension and lack of support can create anxieties in your child which can lead to behavior problems. There may be issues such as a preoccupation with work or stress from another family situation that are causing conflicts, or there can be tension arising from the stress of being a parent. If parents, for example, are in competition with each other and constantly struggle over who makes the decisions about their child's discipline, schooling, activities, clothes, or friends, their child will be likely to draw the appropriate conclusion that his parents cannot handle the situation and that no one is really in control. For a small child who is just beginning to understand the world and the way it works, this can be a frightening experience.

PARENTAL PERSONALITY STYLES

Achieving the ability to think emotionally is a major milestone in any child's life, and it is not something easily mastered. Some fairly typical parental behavior patterns can undermine the child's ability to use ideas in a cause-and-effect way and to shift between the worlds of fantasy and reality. They include not responding logically and appropriately, being fearful of confrontation, not respecting the child's individuality, and not being available for a three-person system.

Illogical or Inappropriate Responses. As we have said, if your child is to learn that ideas can be organized according to logical sequences, he obviously needs to have his communications accurately read and responded to. At one time or another, however, most of us will distort or misinterpret what our child is doing. This often happens when we "project" our own feelings onto our child. Overprotection is a common reason for a parent to project his fears onto a child. Heather, who is running a low-grade fever, hurts herself slightly and cries a little. Her mother, who is a bit of a hypochondriac, conveys her fear that a major catastrophe may have occurred. Heather's mild concern in contrast to her mother's greater upset confuses Heather's interpretation of the event—was the fall only mild or was it a major injury?

Sometimes, problems with responding logically and appropriately may be related to a specific area. One mother was very supportive and empathic except when her little boy wanted to pretend that a stick was a gun. Rather than saying, "Put that down. I won't permit you to have make-believe guns here," or, on the other hand, tolerating his play, the mother would try to trick her son by saying, "That stick looks like a thermometer. You must be sick and want me to take your temperature." She thought her distortion was clever because it would discourage her child from playing with guns by associating them with physical illness. This was much too sophisticated for her son to figure out, however; he became confused and had illogical connections. This type of distortion, if repeated, could cause a child eventually to connect illness with healthy competitive and aggressive strivings.

If a parent continues to distort his child's meanings, it is possible that the parent is using his child to gain satisfaction of his own unconscious desires. This can lead to chronic problems with the child's sense of himself and with the meanings he attributes to himself and others. Consider, for example, the very cautious and careful father who sees his daughter shooting a water pistol at one of her dolls. Let's assume that this father has a hidden fantasy of being an aggressive "macho man." Seeing his daughter with the water gun, he becomes alarmed at her display of the aggression he actually fears in himself. He tells her harshly that guns, even water guns, are not good. Later in the day, however, he recounts a newspaper story of a robbery with obvious pleasure. The next day he sees his daughter acting aggressively with one of her friends and says, "Stop it." But the grin on his face indicates his approval, even though his words are to the contrary.

This father, while protesting against his daughter's aggression, is actually covertly (and unconsciously) supporting it. He projects his private fantasy onto his daughter by characterizing her playful aggression as menacing; and supports this part of her character by indirectly letting her know that he enjoys it. His behavior may have consequences in adolescence. Parents are sometimes involved in their child's delinquent behavior—on one level they protest and on another level they take secret pleasure in their children's antisocial behavior. They are glad that the teenager is not letting the school system push him around or they say that they were like that when they were young.

Whatever causes the "communications gap" between you and your child—projection, anxiety about a certain emotion, confusion of reality and fantasy—your realization of the problem can help you "tune in" more effectively. Sheer effort and awareness may be sufficient for you. If not, it may be very useful for you and your spouse to talk about the tendencies you see in each other. Sometimes when one of you is unable to see a problem and the other can, one can support and help the other react more logically to your child's communications. Supporting each other and helping each other feel more secure will help you feel less anxiety within the family which, in turn, will lessen the tendency to distort meanings.

Mutual help and support may be the exception rather than the rule in families in which there is difficulty understanding a child's communications. Parents who do not operate as a team but instead get into an adversarial relationship with each other feel more insecure and cause them to distort or misinterpret meanings even more. If these distortions compromise the child's use of cause-and-effect interactions and, therefore, his development of emotional ideas, his ability to tell real from unreal may lag. As a consequence, he may have mood swings, tendencies toward impulsivity, difficulty in concentrating and focusing attention, and/or difficulties with putting together feelings and thoughts. If you see these trends in your child and your family, do some serious self-reflection and work so that your child can get back on his developmental track. Consultation and therapeutic work with the entire family at an early phase can go a long way toward preventing more serious difficulties later on.

Intrusion or Withdrawal. As with earlier stages of emotional development, the tendency for a parent to be either intrusive or withdrawn can cause difficulty. At this stage either tendency can affect the child's ability to connect ideas logically. Intrusiveness is often a defense against anxious feelings. If your child's interest in the human body makes you anxious, you may suddenly find yourself either trying to take control of his play or withdrawing by hiding behind the newspaper. In order to alter your tendencies of intrusiveness or withdrawal, you must obviously be aware of them first. By recalling time you have spent with your child over a two-week period, you may get insight into particular emotions or interests that made you uneasy. Although your awareness may not be able to resolve your discomfort, you can at least guard against withdrawing or intruding whenever the emotion or interest arises.

Preoccupation. Another pattern that you and your family should be alert to is the tendency to become preoccupied. You may not distort meaning but instead undermine your child's ability to maintain his focus. If you are preoccupied and inattentive when your child wants to look for a doll's special dress to go to a party, you might then see a ball next to the doll and suggest that the doll wants to play kick ball. This confuses your child's master plan and might cause her to lapse into the more fragmented style of a younger child. Similar fragmentation occurs when your little boy begins to tell you that one of his racing cars beat another, and you respond by talking about getting ready for bed. Your response doesn't distort your child's meaning particularly, but it takes him on a tangent unrelated to his immediate concerns and communications. Even if you are intentionally changing the focus of the child's play because you don't want to go along, you can state your feelings and *then* try to distract the child to another activity.

The tendency to become preoccupied and to not respond in a meaningful way to your child should be corrected, if at all possible. Sometimes simply focusing extra concentration on what your child is doing and being aware that an appropriate response is important may be sufficient. Should you find your preoccupation difficult to reduce, you may benefit from some consultation and guidance.

Anxiety about Confrontations. When a parent finds intense feelings to be distressing, he or she may become illogical at a potential point of confrontation. A four-year-old says, "I will *not* clean up my toys. No way!" The parent, backing away, suggests he invite a friend to play. This exchange does nothing to reinforce the child's logical sequencing of emotional ideas.

If you tend to avoid confrontation or to avoid your child after an intense emotional episode, try to change your pattern. By becoming aware that intense feelings make you uncomfortable, you can work on conveying to your child that you are the *boss*. How you do it is up to you, the important thing is to do it. Whether you sit and explain or demonstrate by your tone of voice that you mean business, remember to trust yourself—whatever you are most comfortable with is usually the best for you.

In addition to conveying to your child that you are the boss, it is extremely important to reconnect with your child after a blowup and help him understand what happened and why. Communicating this understanding requires the highest level of your involvement, especially if you have a tendency to withdraw or to berate your child after a confrontation. It may be easier for you if you can determine why you do withdraw, but even if you cannot, you can still make an extra effort to regroup after an explosion, explain in a logical way why you were angry and then warmly offer a way to reconnect.

Inability to Appreciate Uniqueness. Respect for your child's uniqueness, which we discussed in Chapter IV and V, is an important element in your child's growing ability to be logical and reality-oriented. Some families unwittingly undermine a child's uniqueness by overemphasizing similarity or conformity. "Ted is just like me," or "We do things by the book in this household." Your child needs, at least in some areas, admiration and respect for his individuality. At this age, as at earlier ages, your child's sense that you take pride in him and respect something special about him is pivotal. His willingness to conform to your wishes and give up some of his own inclinations depends on it. Life is full of tradeoffs. In order to make them, your child needs admiration.

In order to give him what he needs, begin by asking yourself, "Are there things about my child that I admire and that are very special to him?" Almost all children have special features that truly deserve admiration. Finding these even small ones, is an important beginning. If you truly do admire him, he will sense your attitude. If you cannot, you may be too involved in competing or over-identifying to have seen his uniqueness. An awareness of your patterns can be very helpful to your child during this stage of his development.

Difficulty with a Three-Person System. We have already mentioned the obvious importance of both mother and father being available to their child in order to support the shift between a two-person system and a three-person system. This isn't all that is necessary, however. Parents must make sure they do not fall into an undermining pattern. For example, a triangular relationship may initially be formed—that is, your child considers the interrelationships between himself and both of you—but he does not feel the support of the three-person system because you and your spouse undermine each other. In other words, if your child is angry at his mother, his father cannot act as a buffer for your child's feelings because his father is also angry at his mother, though under the surface, perhaps. Your child feels that two of you together could truly devastate the third and becomes frightened. He feels he needs to protect one against the other and cannot afford to get too angry at either one or the family may not stay intact. In this situation, your child may return to the simpler two-person system of relating and remain at a level where he sees the world in global, all-or-nothing terms, because the subtlety of triangles is just too frightening.

It is necessary, therefore, that during this phase, you be especially alert to the way you and your spouse are getting along. If you are involved in mutual anger, competition, and lack of warmth and support, your child is likely to feel the tension. In response he may try to deal with it "quietly," by compromising his ability to use emotions to figure things out, or he may call attention to himself with sleep disturbances, impulsive behavior, or a host of other problems. Even though you may feel too angry to want to make an effort at improving your relationship, you should try to talk with your spouse.

Another deterrent to movement into a three-person system occurs when one parent is anxious about it. If your child begins, quite naturally, forming alliances with one of you and then the other, or playing one of you off against the other, your own difficulties with triangular relationships in your upbringing may cause you to become anxious and to withdraw precipitously. Let's look at two short examples.

Billy was entering a stage in which he longed to have his mother for himself. He would hit his father on the arm and then hug his mother slyly and provocatively, illustrating a mock takeover. His father, however, often took Billy's action quite literally; he would walk into his study and work for the rest of the evening. His behavior left Billy frightened on two counts: he feared he had been too successful in his attempt to take his mother for himself and, more important, he feared he had lost his father, whom he still loved and wanted in his life.

Brenda's case was similar. She liked tumbling and climbing and competitive activities with her father. Her mother, feeling very neglected, suddenly decided to focus all her attention on Brenda's younger sister because "she needs me." Needless to say, Brenda quickly became panicked at "losing" her mother.

Under either of the above circumstances a child may pull back to a more concrete, two-person world. Your child should not have the burden of reassuring you that his competitive feelings will not kill you or that his temporary need to be with one of you does not mean he is really abandoning the other. He is only a child, who loves you and needs you and is merely accepting the healthy challenge of learning to operate in a three-person system, however well he is doing it.

You and your spouse can weather the temporary disappointments and anxieties generated by your child's development as a competent person by staying in close emotional touch with each other. Even if you find yourself unaccustomed to talking about emotional issues in your family, if you can get through the first couple of weeks, both you and your partner will probably find your talks reassuring and strengthening to your relationship. If after a number of weeks, however, your discussions seem to make matters worse, or a problem stays the same, then you may want to call on a professional. Chances are that professional help can make your discussion times with each other more useful.

One of the most basic—and most successful—ways in which you can combat a family pattern that makes it difficult for your child to develop a triangular relationship successfully is for each of you to spend time alone with your child. Billy's father now spends time with him on a consistent basis. Brenda's mother, who was hurt that her daughter preferred her father, reestablished close and intimate contact with her daughter by becoming interested in tumbling herself and then moving Brenda into her own interest in cooking. Although Brenda still routinely plays with her "mommy doll" by giving her "injections" and then kills the doll off in the most imaginative ways, now her mother doesn't take the pretending so literally and accepts her daughter's rich fantasy life. The mother's new interest in athletics allows them to compete with each other while still being involved with one another.

COMMON PARENTAL FEARS

Major parental fears at this stage of development are often in reaction to a child's greater ability for independent functioning and logical thinking and for a heightened interest in the world. Although we've touched on them throughout this chapter, let's now take a closer look.

Fear of Your Child's Independence. Now that your child can plan, anticipate, and think fairly logically, your fear of emotional separation may come to the fore. Mothers frequently talk about how difficult it is when their child goes off to nursery school, prefers to play with the kids on the block or, equally important, asserts his own will in an organized, logical manner.

When a parent feels anxious about his child becoming more independent, he may try to "hold on" by controlling his child. This period may seem similar to an earlier "independent" phase, from twelve to fourteen months or so, when you and your child struggled for power. Now, however, your child has the added power of his emotional ideas and logic. Your four-year-old girl may say, "I don't want to wear pants. They make me look like a bag," after you have just bought her five pairs of pants for school. Or your little boy may scream in protest if you try to put a warmer shirt over his Spiderman T-shirt. Your reactions must balance an interest and understanding in their pride in appearance with parental leadership—"enough is enough." As you probably well know, some of this behavior is inevitable, but it will become much more difficult to resolve if you are frightened and want to keep your child dependent by trying to control without respect and admiration. Your child still needs you and will for a long time to come. Only the way you are needed changes and, if you are able to swing with it, your healthy relationship with your child will continue far into the future.

Fear of Your Child's Logical Thinking. Your child's new ability for logical thinking may leave you feeling you've had an overdose of reality. Many of us who like our reality with a touch of distortion may be made anxious and downright fearful of our child's new ability for cold logic. Should your daughter say to you, "What are those bumps on your face? They look ugly," she may be accurately portraying your skin condition. Aside from being surprised by your daughter's capacity for this level of logical description, you may find that you become quite uneasy, particularly if you fantasize being a "flawless beauty." You can easily imagine—and have probably experienced—many areas in which your child's capacity for speaking the "truth" in a logical and perceptive way can intrude on tendencies to live in a make-believe world. Your child's ability for greater assertiveness and competitiveness (which can also raise conflicts in mothers and fathers) also enhances his logical, realistic abilities.

Of course, since your child is also learning feelings of empathy, which we mentioned before, you can begin to explain the concept of tact. "When you said Grandma was fat, her feelings were hurt," or, "Even if you feel that way, you don't have to say it out loud," can be explained and illustrated. Gentle steering in the direction of discretion is not aimed at fostering hypocrisy, but rather is aimed at encouraging a human being to show sensitivity to the feelings of others.

Fear of Your Child's Interest in the World. You may have specific fears about the interests and inclinations of your child. He now understands sexual differences to some degree. He is more interested in illness, what happens to people in hospitals, and even death, though he does not understand it. Any one of these specific concerns about the body, damage, illness, power, or love can touch off your own fears. Although you may have been able to ignore your child's pre-verbal or illogical interests in a certain anxiety-provoking area, now you cannot. She wants to know "How are babies made? Will my breasts be big or small?" Your child can converse in a manner much closer to adult discourse and can pick up subtlety and innuendo. She can cause your anxiety to surface, and she will be sensitive to it.

The key to your dealing with these three types of fears—of greater separation and independence, of greater logic, and of the organized expression of anxiety-provoking emotions—is to *tolerate* the anxieties your child creates, to *grow* as your child grows and to be *flexible* enough to work on your inhibitions, anxieties, and conflicts. As with all problems simply recognizing it can be a big first step. Form an alliance with your spouse, using each other for security and sugges-tions. Take advantage of professional consultation to help you over the rougher spots. Your child may still be small, but he is a person in his own right, beginning a life-cycle that may lead him far from home. Your love, support, and best efforts can help insure his healthy growth and give him a strong foundation on which to build his life.

As your child practices and experiments with new feelings and ideas, you, as parents, have to walk the fine line between supporting his growth, independence, and experimentation and remaining sen-sitive to his needs for basic nurturing and security. This is not an easy line to walk, and there is no perfect way to do it. The best that you can do to encourage your child's security is to be comfortable with being warm and nurturing, to set effective limits, and, above all, to engage your child in the use of cause-and-effect emotional ideas. He can then use higher-level conceptual abilities to understand and cope with his emotions to form an organized sense of self, to differ-entiate between real and pretend, and to figure out the subtleties of complex interpersonal patterns. As a result, you and your child can have an increasingly deep, sophisticated, and satisfying relationship— a relationship that will form the basis of his abilities to become in-dependent and to internalize the sense of security he gets from you and make it his own.

Conclusion

We've been able to take a long look at your baby and child's first feelings in life. By the time he has reached the age of four or five, a tremendous amount of emotional development has taken place. Though your infant's first milestone of calmness and attentiveness may seem worlds away from your sophisticated child's enormous emotional and intellectual abilities, two tendencies guide his journey growth and development. The first is the tendency for regulation and harmony— that is, your baby's desire to feel organized and relaxed. Depending on your child, this can mean very different things. Your child, for example, may feel most relaxed and in control when he is engaged in intense physical activity, listening to music, or getting ready to fall asleep. But whatever your child prefers, his "first feelings" of inner peace sustain and nurture his emotional growth, and help him become a stable person.

Your child also will tend to seek out experiences in line with her emerging developmental abilities and to practice her new capacities. You've seen your infant's hunger for new sights and sounds as she develops her vision and hearing. Or, as she begins to recognize you and the special characteristics you have, she "falls in love" with you— she's practicing her capacity to develop special preferences and develop loving relationships. Don't forget that, just as your child practices her motor skills until she achieves mastery, so she stretches her emotional capacities through practice as well. She will continually try to reaffirm her experiences, which is why it is so important for you to be there to support and guide her.

Parents marvel that each new day brings new achievements, new interests, and capacities that their children pursue with a relentlessness that is remarkable. Each new development ushers in new experiences of the world. The perspective of your crawling baby is changed dramatically once she can walk—the child who has learned to form emotional ideas and think—her own experience—has stepped into another dimension.

In order for your child to develop to his full capacity, the two tendencies—regulation and harmony, and exploration of new experience and practice—must be working to encourage each other. When they do not, as sometimes happens, then it is your task to step in and do what you can to help. There are many examples throughout this book to show you how this might be done. You'll remember the infant who was sensitive to certain types of stimulation. High-pitched voices were an irritant to him. His interest in hearing new sounds was competing with his ability to stay under control. By lowering the sound while still offering other sounds and sights, touch and movement, his parents helped him stay simultaneously regulated and interested in the world.

At an older age, regulation and harmony may operate in opposition to exploration and practice in another way. The two- to three-year-old who learns to evoke a mental image of her mother is able to comfort and regulate herself with this image in mother's absence. However, the same ability to create mental images may also cause her to have nightmares, which obviously upset her comfort and regulation. The nightmares, on the other hand, may represent the child's healthy tendency to practice a new experience. Your task in this instance is to help your child strike a balance between exposure to experiences and ideas that serve to regulate her and those which may unsettle her.

With your love, guidance, and awareness, your child will achieve each emotional milestone in an environment that neither over- nor under-challenges his capacities. Though you and your child will undoubtedly have to endure some "growing pains" as milestones are reached, you'll learn to gauge your child's tendencies either to rush in until he's over his head or hang back until he's prompted, and can adjust your responses according to his needs.

Your job as a parent often requires hard work and tough decisions. At each stage in his development there are questions you must ask about your child, yourself, your family, and your circumstances. It's never easy to see your child falter, to become aware of difficulties in your own personality, those of your family, or interactions within your family and work systems. You are the one who has to be strong enough to acknowledge problems and work to overcome them, or seek help in overcoming them—your baby can't.

What we have tried to do in *First Feelings* is provide milestones to mark as you watch the emotional development of your Sally, Jeremy, Billy, or Beth. We have described what happens during each stage of development, as well as some of the common difficulties encountered and ways to deal with them. Your support of your child's age-appropriate experiences in a way that helps him feel a sense of full emotional engagement, mastery and control is one of the most essential ingredients for what we all treasure as parents: a secure, mutually enriching, loving, and exciting family life.

Appendix

CHARTING YOUR BABY'S
EMOTIONAL MILESTONES

This chart highlights some of your baby's unique abilities in each stage of development. It helps you to know and enjoy the steps involved in your baby's learning about his emotional world. This includes such basic tasks as learning to see the world as regulating, interesting, and loving as well as more advanced tasks of using ideas to integrate dependency needs with being assertive, curious, and autonomous. While watching for particular steps, remember that babies also enjoy many other things. Even though you want to encourage your baby to smile at you or respond to you, your baby also needs time to relax, look around, or just suck on his fist, if he wants to. When a baby enjoys his new abilities only some of the time, he can be showing both his mastery of them and his selectivity. So, although over time you should expect your baby to be more babbly when you talk to her or initiate greater interaction, don't expect her to do so all the time. She enjoys variety, too.

As more of your baby's new abilities unfold, the earliest accomplishments continue to be refined. Therefore, always fill out the chart from the beginning, even if the child is not a newborn. Thinking over the earlier months will sometimes help you appreciate your baby more fully and see the exciting changes. Your noting that a few expected steps are not occurring will help you identify areas for constructive practice and understanding. If further practice and understanding do not lead to progress or if many of the expected steps are not occurring, a professional consultation may be indicated.

Charting Your Baby's Emotional Milestones

I / SELF-REGULATION AND INTEREST IN THE WORLD —*Birth to 3 months*

Increasingly (but still only sometimes):	YES	NO
– able to calm down	☐	☐
– sleeps regularly	☐	☐
– brightens to sights (by alerting and focusing on object)	☐	☐
– brightens to sounds (by alerting and focusing on your voice)	☐	☐
– enjoys touch	☐	☐
– enjoys movement in space (up and down, side to side)	☐	☐

II / FALLING IN LOVE —*2 to 7 months*

When wooed, increasingly (but still only sometimes):	YES	NO
– looks at you with a special, joyful smile	☐	☐
– gazes at you with great interest	☐	☐
– joyfully smiles at you in response to your vocalizations	☐	☐
– joyfully smiles at you in response to your interesting facial expressions	☐	☐
– vocalizes back as you vocalize	☐	☐

III / DEVELOPING INTENTIONAL COMMUNICATION —*3 to 10 months*

Increasingly (but still only sometimes) responds to:	YES	NO
– your gestures with gestures in return (you hand her a rattle and she takes it)	☐	☐
– your vocalizations with vocalizations	☐	☐
– your emotional expressions with an emotional response (a smile begets a smile)	☐	☐
– pleasure or joy with pleasure	☐	☐
– encouragement to explore with curiosity (reaches for interesting toy)	☐	☐
Increasingly (but still only sometimes) initiates:		
– interactions (expectantly looks for you to respond)	☐	☐
– joy and pleasure (woos you spontaneously)	☐	☐
– comforting (reaches up to be held)	☐	☐
– exploration and assertiveness (explores your face or examines a new toy)	☐	☐

IV / THE EMERGENCE OF AN ORGANIZED SENSE OF SELF
—9 to 18 months

Increasingly (but still only sometimes):	YES	NO
– initiates a complex behavior pattern such as going to refrigerator and pointing to desired food, playing a chase game, rolling a ball back and forth with you	☐	☐
– uses complex behavior in order to establish closeness (pulls on your leg and reaches up to be picked up)	☐	☐
– uses complex behavior to explore and be assertive (reaches for toys, finds you in another room)	☐	☐
– plays in a focused, organized manner on own	☐	☐
– examines toys or other objects to see how they work	☐	☐
– responds to limits that you set with your voice or gestures	☐	☐
– recovers from anger after a few minutes	☐	☐
– able to use objects like a comb or telephone in semirealistic manner	☐	☐
– seems to know how to get you to react (which actions make you laugh, which make you mad)	☐	☐

V / CREATING EMOTIONAL IDEAS —*18 to 36 months*

Increasingly (but still only sometimes):	YES	NO
– engages in pretend play with others (puts doll to sleep, feeds doll, has cars or trucks race)	☐	☐
– engages in pretend play alone	☐	☐
– makes spatial designs with blocks or other materials (builds a tower, lines up blocks)	☐	☐
– uses words or complex social gestures (pointing, sounds, gestures) to express needs or feelings ("me, mad" or "no, bed")	☐	☐
– uses words or gestures to communicate desire for closeness (saying "hug" or gesturing to sit on your lap)	☐	☐
– uses words or gestures to explore, be assertive and/or curious ("come here" and then explores toy with you)	☐	☐
– able to recover from anger or temper tantrum and be cooperative and organized (after 5 or 10 minutes)	☐	☐

Later in stage and throughout next, increasingly (but still only some-times):

– uses your help and some toys to play out pretend drama dealing with closeness, nurturing, or care (taking care of favorite stuffed animal) □ □

– uses your help and some toys to play out pretend drama dealing with assertiveness, curiosity, and exploration (monsters chasing, cars racing, examining doll's bodies) □ □

– pretend play becomes more complex, so that one pretend sequence leads to another (instead of repetition, where the doll goes to bed, gets up, goes to bed, etc., the doll goes to bed, gets up, and then gets dressed, or the cars race, crash, and then go to get fixed) □ □

– spatial designs become more complex and have interrelated parts, so that a block house has rooms or maybe furniture, a drawing of a face has some of its parts □ □

VI / EMOTIONAL THINKING: THE BASIS FOR FANTASY, REALITY, AND SELF ESTEEM —30 to 48 months

Increasingly (but still only sometimes):	YES	NO
– knows what is real and what isn't	□	□
– follows rules	□	□
– remains calm and focused	□	□
– feels optimistic and confident	□	□
– realizes how behavior, thoughts, and feelings can be related to consequences (if behaves nicely, makes you pleased; if naughty, gets punished; if tries hard, learns to do something)	□	□
– realizes relationship between feelings, behavior, and consequences in terms of being close to another person (knows what to do or say to get a hug, or a back rub)	□	□
– realizes relationship between feelings, behavior, and consequences in terms of assertiveness, curiosity, and exploration (knows how to exert will power through verbal, emotional communication to get what he wants)	□	□
– realizes relationship between feelings, behavior, and consequences in terms of anger (much of time can respond to limits)	□	□
– interacts in socially appropriate way with adults	□	□
– interacts in socially appropriate way with peers	□	□

Bibliography

We have described how the infant organizes experience through a series of emotional stages, each one characterized by unique features and new levels of complexity. This bibliography provides selected readings on aspects of the infant's and child's unique ability to engage in an organized emotional experience. The readings are of general and historic interest and relate to the special capacities that characterize the stages of emotional development presented earlier. Because these articles are of a technical nature, they may be particularly useful to parents and caregivers with strong backgrounds related to the emotional and intellectual development of children. Students and professionals who wish to study further the ideas presented in the book may also find these references of value. A more detailed bibliography is available upon request from the authors.

General

Ainsworth, M., Blehar, M., Waters, E., and Wall, S. *Patterns of Attachment*. Hillsdale, N.J.: Erlbaum, 1978.

Bower, G. H. "Mood and Memory," *American Psychologist*, 36:129–148, 1981.

Brody, S. *Patterns of Mothering*. New York: International Press, 1956.

Brody, S., and Axelrod, S. "Anxiety, Socialization and Ego Formation in Infancy," *International Journal of Psycho-Analysis*, 47:218–229, 1966.

Chander, C. A., Lourie, R. S., and Peters, A. D. *Challenge for the 70's: The Report of the Joint Commission of Child Mental Health*, L. L. Dittman (ed.). New York: Atherton Press, 1968; Harper & Row, 1969.

Doxiadis, S. (ed.). *The Child in the World of Tomorrow*, Athens, Greece, 1979.

Emde, R., Gaensbauser, T., and Harmon, R. "Emotional Expression in Infancy: A Biobehavioral Study," *Psychological Issues, Monograph Series*, Vol. 10, Monograph #37. New York: International Universities Press, 1976.

Erikson, E. *Childhood and Society*. New York: Norton, 1950.

Erikson, E. *Toys and Reasons: Stages in the Ritualization of Experience*. New York: Norton, 1977.

Escalona, S. K. *The Roots of Individuality: Normal Patterns of Development in Infancy.* Chicago: Aldine, 1968.

Fraiberg, S. *Every Child's Birthright: In Defense of Mothering.* New York: Basic Books, 1977.

Fraiberg, S. *Infant Mental Health.* New York: Basic Books, 1981.

Fraiberg, S. *The Magic Years: Understanding and Handling the Problems of Early Childhood.* New York: Scribner's, 1959.

Freud, A. *Normality and Pathology in Childhood. The Writings of Anna Freud, Vol. 6.* New York: International Universities Press, 1965.

Green, M., and Solnit, A. "A Vulnerable Child Syndrome, Part III; Care of the Dying Child," *Pediatrics,* 34:58, 1964.

Greenacre, P. *Emotional Growth.* New York: International Universities Press, 1971.

Greenspan, S. *The Clinical Interview of the Child.* New York: McGraw-Hill, 1981.

Greenspan, S. I., and Pollock, G. H. (eds.). *The Course of Life: Psychoanalytic Contributions Toward Understanding Personality Development, Vol. I; Infancy and Early Childhood.* Washington, D.C., DHHS Pub. No. (ADM) 80-999, U.S. Government Printing Office, 1980.

Greenspan, S., Weider, S., Lieberman, A., Nover, R., Lourie, R., and Robinson, M. "Infants in Multi-Risk Families: Case Studies of Preventive Intervention," *Clinical Infant Reports,* No. 3. New York: International Universities Press, 1985.

Greenspan, S. I. "Intelligence and Adaptation: An Integration of Psychoanalytic and Piagetian Developmental Psychology," *Psychological Issues,* Monograph 47/48. New York: International Universities Press, 1979.

Greenspan, S. "Psychopathology and Adaptation in Infancy and Early Childhood: Principles of Clinical Diagnosis and Preventive Intervention," *Clinical Infant Reports,* New York: International Universities Press, 1981.

Greenspan, S., and Lieberman, A. "Infants, Mothers, and Their Interaction: A Quantitative Clinical Approach to Developmental Assessment." In Greenspan, S., and Pollack, G., (eds.), *The Course of Life, Vol. I, Infancy and Childhood,* Washington, D.C., DHHS Pub. No. (ADM) 80-999, U.S. Government Printing Office, 1980.

Greenspan, S., and Lourie, R. "Developmental Structuralist Approach for the Classification of Adaptive and Pathological Personality Organization: Applications to Infancy and Early Childhood," *American Journal of Psychiatry,* 138:6, 1981.

Greenspan, S., and Porges, S. "Psychopathology in Infancy and Early Childhood: Clinical Perspectives on the Organization of Sensory and Affective Thematic Experience," *Child Development,* 55:49–70, 1984.

Hesse, P., and Cicchetti, D. "Perspectives on an Integrated Theory of Emotional Development." In Cicchetti, D., and Hesse, P. (eds.), *Emotional Development,* San Francisco: Jossey-Bass, 1983.

Izard, C., Kagan, J., and Zajonc, R. *Emotions, Cognition, and Behavior.* New York: Cambridge University Press, 1984.

Izard, C. E. *Human Emotions.* New York: Plenum, 1977.

Jacobson, E. *The Self and the Object World.* New York: International Universities Press, 1964.

Mahler, M., Pine, F., and Bergman, P. *The Psychological Birth of the Human Infant: Symbiosis and Individuation.* New York: Basic Books, 1975.

Mead, M. "A Cultural Anthropologist's Approach to Maternal Deprivation." In Public Health Papers No. 14, *Deprivation of Maternal Care: A Reassessment,* Geneva, World Health Organization, 1962.

Murphy, L. B., and Moriarty, A. E. *Vulnerability, Coping and Growth*. New Haven: Yale University Press, 1976.

Piaget, J., and Inhelder, B. *The Psychology of the Child*. New York: Basic Books, 1969.

Piaget, J. *Intelligence and Affectivity: Their Relationship during Child Development*. Palo Alto, Calif., Annual Reviews, 1981. (Originally published 1954.)

Polansky, N. A. *Damaged Parents*. Chicago: University of Chicago Press, 1981.

Provence, S. (ed.). "Infants and Parents: Case Studies," *Clinical Infant Reports*, No. 2. New York: International Universities Press, 1983.

Thomas, A., and Chess, S. *Temperament and Development*. New York: Brunner/Mazel. 1977.

Tompkins, S. *Affect, Imagery, Consciousness*, Vol. 1 and 2. New York: Springer-Verlag, 1962.

Vygotsky, L. *Thought and Language*. Boston: MIT Press, 1962.

Weil, A. "The Basic Core," *The Psychoanalytic Study of the Child*, 25:442–460, 1970.

White, R. W. "Ego and Reality in Psychoanalytic Theory," *Psychological Issues*, Monograph #11. New York: International Universities Press, 1963.

Yarrow, L. "Conceptualizing the Early Environment." In Chandler, C., Lourie, R., and Peters, A. (eds.), *Early Child Care: The New Perspectives*. New York: Atherton Press, 1968.

Historical

The following references may be useful in the historical observations, theories, and research on infants and young children.

Backwin, H. "Loneliness in Infants," *American Journal of Disabled Children*, 63:30, 1942.

Bender, L., and Yarnell, H. "An Observational Nursery," *American Journal of Psychiatry*, 97:1158, 1941.

Benedek, T. "Adaptation to Reality in Early Infancy," *Psychoanalytical Quarterly*, 7:200–215, 1938.

Bernfeld, S. *Psychology of the Infant*. London: Routledge and Sons, 1929.

Bowlby, J. "Maternal Care and Mental Health," *Bulletin of the World Health Organization*, 3:355, 1951.

Buhler, C. *The First Year of Life*. New York: John Day, 1930.

Burlingham, D., and Freud, A. *Young Children in Wartime*. London: Allen and Unwin, 1942.

Cameron, H. *The Nervous Child*. London: Oxford Medical Publications, 1919.

Darwin, C. *The Expression of Emotions in Man and Animals*. Chicago: University of Chicago Press, 1965.

Freud, A., and Burlingham, D. *Infants Without Families. Reports on the Hampstead Nurseries 1939–1945. The Writings of Anna Freud Vol. 3*. New York: International Universities Press, 1973.

Freud, S. "Beyond the Pleasure Principle" (1920), *Standard Edition*, 18:3–64. London: Hogarth Press, 1955.

Freud, S. "Instincts and Their Vicissitudes" (1915), *Standard Edition*, 14:111–140. London: Hogarth Press, 1968.

Gesell, A. L., and Amatruda, C. *The Embryology of Behavior: The Beginnings of the Human Mind.* New York: Harper & Bros., 1945.

Harlow, H. F., and Harlow, M. K. "Social Deprivation in Monkeys," *Scientific American*, 207:136–146, 1962.

Hartmann, H. *Ego Psychology and the Problem of Adaptation* (1939). Translated by David Rapaport. New York: International Universities Press, 1958.

Hartmann, H., Kris, E., and Loewenstein, R. M. "Comments on the Formation of Psychic Structure," *The Psychoanalytic Study of the Child*, 2:11–38, 1941.

Hunt, J. Mc. "Infants in an Orphanage," *Journal of Abnormal and Social Psychology*, 36:338, 1941.

Kanner, L. "Autistic Disturbance of Affective Contact," *Nervous Child*, 2:217–250, 1949.

Klein, M. *The Psychoanalysis of Children*, (1932). New York: Grove Press, 1960.

Levy, D. M. *Maternal Overprotecting*, New York: Norton, 1966.

Lourie, R. S. "The First Three Years of Life: An Overview of a New Frontier for Psychiatry," *American Journal of Psychiatry*, 127:1457, 1971.

Lourie, R. S. "Experience with Therapy of Psychosomatic Problems in Infants." In Hoch, P., and Zunin, J. (eds.). *Psychopathology of Children*, New York: Grune and Stratton, 1955.

Lowrey, L. G. "Personality Distortion and Early Institutional Care," *American Journal of Orthopsychiatry*, 10:546, 1940.

Middlemore, M. P. *The Nursing Couple.* London: Hamish-Hamilton, 1941.

Piaget, J. *The Origins of Intelligence in Children.* New York: Norton, 1952.

Piaget, J. *Play, Dreams and Imitation in Children.* New York: Norton, 1962.

Provence, S., and Lipton, R. C. *Infants in Institutions.* New York: International Universities Press, 1962.

Rachford, B. K. *Neurotic Disorders of Childhood.* New York: E. B. Treat and Co., 1905.

Spitz, R. *The First Year of Life.* New York: International Universities Press, 1965.

Spitz, R. "Hospitalism: An Inquiry into the Genesis of Psychiatric Conditions in Early Childhood," *The Psychoanalytic Study of the Child*, 1:53–74, 1945.

Winnicott, D. W. *The Maturational Processes and the Facilitating Processes and the Facilitating Environment* (1962). New York: International Universities Press, 1965.

Regulation and Interest in the World

These references all discuss in one form or another how babies learn to make visual and auditory discriminations, to respond to consequences of others, to distinguish between pleasure and displeasure, and to organize basic patterns of regulation such as alertness, sleeping/waking, eating, and elimination. These references also discuss how the baby's underlying physiologic functioning corresponds with growing and social and emotional functioning.

Bergman, P., and Escalona, S. K. "Unusual Sensitivities in Very Young Children," *Psychoanalytic Study of the Child*, 31:333–352, 1949.

Bower, T. B. "Visual World of Infants," *Scientific American*, 215:80–82, 1966.

Brazelton, T. B. *Neonatal Assessment Scale*. London and Philadelphia: Spastics International Medical Publishers, 1973.

Brazelton, T. "Precursors for the Development of Emotions in Early Infancy." In Plutchik, R., and Kellerman, H. (eds.), *Emotions in Early Development Vol. 2: The Emotions*. New York: Academic Press, 1983.

Bronson, G. W. "Structure, Status and Characteristics of the Nervous System at Birth." In Stratton, P. M. (ed.), *The Psychobiology of the Human Newborn*. London: Wiley, 1982.

Condon, W. S., and Sander, L. W. "Neonate Movement Is Synchronized with Adult Speech: Interactional Participation and Language Acquisition," *Science*, 183:99–101, 1974.

DeCasper, A., and Fifer, W. "Of Human Bonding: Newborns Prefer Their Mothers' Voices," *Science*, 208:1174–1176, 1980.

Eisenberg, R. B. *Auditory Competence in Early Life*. Baltimore: University Park Press, 1976.

Fantz, R. L. "Visual Perception from Birth as Shown by Pattern Selectivity," *Annals of the New York Academy of Sciences*, 118:793, 1965.

Field, T., Woodson, R., Greenberg, R., and Cohen, D. "Discrimination and Imitation of Facial Expressions by Neonates," *Science*, 218:179–181, 1982.

Freedman, D. A., Fox-Kolendal, B. J., Margileth, D. A., and Miller, D. H. "The Development of the Use of Sound as a Guide to Affective and Cognitive Behavior—A Two Phase Process." *Child Development*, 40:1099–1105, 1969.

Fries, M. E., and Woolf, P. J. "Some Hypotheses on the Role of Congenital Activity Type in Personality Development," *The Psychoanalytic Study of the Child*, 8:48–632, 1953.

Graves, Pirkko L., "The Functioning Fetus." In Greenspan, S., and Pollack, G. (eds.), *Course of Life, Vol. I, Early Infancy and Childhood*. Washington, D.C., DHHS Pub. No. (ADM) 80-999, U.S. Government Printing Office, 1980.

Humphrey, T. "The Development of Human Fetal Activity and Its Relation to Postnatal Behavior." In Reese, H., and Lipsitt, L. (eds.), *Advances in Child Development and Behavior*, Vol. 2, pp. 1–57, New York: Academic Press, 1970.

Klaus, M. H., and Kennell, J. H. (eds.). *Maternal Infant Bonding*. St. Louis: Mosby, 1976.

Korner, A. "Some Hypotheses Regarding the Significance of Individual Differences at Birth for Later Development," *The Psychoanalytic Study of the Child*, 19:58–72, 1964.

Liley, A. W. "The Foetus as a Personality," *Australian and New Zealand Journal of Psychiatry*," 6:99–105, 1972.

Lipsitt, L. "Learning Processes of Newborns," *Merrill-Palmer Quarterly*, 12:45, 1966.

Lipton, E. L., Steinschneider, A., and Richmond, J. D. "Autonomic Function in the Neonate," *Psychosomatic Medicine*, 22:57–65, 1960.

MacFarlane, A. "Olfaction in the Development of Social Preferences in the Human Neonate." In *Parent-Infant Interaction, CIBA Foundation Symposium* 33, pp. 103–117. Amsterdam: Elsevier Publishing Co., 1975.

Meltzoff, A., and Moore, K. "Imitation of Facial and Manual Gestures by Human Neonates," *Science*, 198:75–78. 1977.

Muir, D., and Field, J. "Newborn Infants Orient to Sounds," *Child Development*, 50:431–436, 1979.

Porges, S. W. "Heart Rate Patterns in Neonates: A Potential Window to the Brain." In Fields, T. M., and Sostek, A. M. (eds.), *Infants Born at Risk: Physiological and Perceptual Processes.* New York: Grune and Stratton, in press.

Sander, L. "Issues in Early Mother-Child Interaction," *Journal of the American Academy of Child Psychiatry*, 1:141, 1962.

Sander, L. "Primary Prevention and Some Aspects of Temporal Organization in Early Infant Caretaker Interaction." In Rexford, E., Sander, L., and Shapiro, T. (eds.), *Infant Psychiatry: A New Synthesis.* New Haven: Yale University Press, pp. 187–204, 1976.

Wolff, P. "The Causes, Controls, and Organization of Behavior in the Neonate," *Psychological Issues*, Monograph #17. New York: International Universities Press, 1966.

Falling in Love

That babies can form a selective interest in the human world and then develop reciprocal interaction patterns with their primary caregivers can be further explored in the works of:

Balint, A. "Love for the Mother and Mother Love," *International Journal of Psycho-Analysis*, 30:251–259, 1938.

Barrera, M., and Mauer, D. "The Perception of Facial Expressions by the Three Month Old," *Child Development*, 52:203–206, 1981.

Bowlby, J. *Attachment and Loss, Vol. I: Attachment.* New York: Basic Books, 1969.

Brazelton, T. B., Koslowski, B., and Main, N. "The Origins of Reciprocity: The Early Mother-Infant Interaction." In Lewis, M., and Rosenblum, L. (eds.), *The Effect of the Infant on Its Caregiver.* New York: Wiley, p. 49, 1974.

Cohn, J., and Tronick, E. "Communicative Rules and the Sequential Structure of Infant Behavior During Normal and Depressed Interaction." In Tronick, E. (ed.), *The Development of Human Communication and the Joint Regulation of Behavior.* Baltimore, Md.: University Park Press, 1982.

Cravioto, J., and Delicardie, E. "Environmental Correlates of Severe Clinical Malnutrition and Language Development in Survivors from Kwashiorkor or Marasmus." In PAHO Scientific Publication No. 251, *Nutrition, the Nervous System and Behavior*, Washington, D.C.: Pan American Health Organization, 1973.

Izard, C. E., Huebner, R. R., Risser, D., McGinnes, G., and Dougherty, L. "The Young Infant's Ability to Produce Discrete Emotion Expressions," *Developmental Psychology*, 16:132–140, 1980.

Oster, H., and Ewy, R. "Discrimination of Sad vs. Happy Faces by Four Month Olds." Cited in H. Oster, " 'Recognition' of Emotional Expression in Infancy?" In Lamb, M., and Sherrod, L. (eds.), *Infant Social Cognition.* Hillsdale, N.J.: Erlbaum, 1981.

Spitz, R. "Anaclitic Depression," *The Psychoanalytic Study of the Child*, 2:313–342, 1946.

Stern, D. "Mother and Infant at Play: The Dyadic Interaction Involving Facial, Vocal, and Gaze Behaviors." In Lewis, M., and Rosenblum, L. (eds.), *The Effect of the Infant on its Caregiver*. New York: Wiley, 1974, pp. 187–213.

Developing Intentional Communication

As infants reach the second half of the first year of life their interactions become more intentional, in both the impersonal sphere as well as the emotional sphere. Studies include:

Bronson, G. W., and Pankey, W. "On the Distinction Between Fear and Wariness," *Child Development*, 48:1167–1183, 1977.

Bruner, J. "Early Social Interaction and Language Acquisition." In Schaeffer, H. (ed.), *Studies in Mother-Infant Interaction*. New York: Academic Press, 1977.

Campos, J., and Stenberg, C. "Perception, Appraisal, and Emotion: The Onset of Social Referencing." In Lamb, M., and Sherrod, L. (eds.), *Infancy Social Cognition*. Hillsdale, N.J.: Erlbaum, 1981.

Charlesworth, W. R. "The Role of Surprise in Cognitive Development." In Elkind, D., and Flavell, J. (eds.), *Studies in Cognitive Development*. Oxford: Oxford University Press, 1969.

Fraiberg, S. H., and Freedman, D. A. "Studies in Ego Development of the Congenitally Blind Child," *The Psychoanalytic Study of the Child*, 19:113–169, 1964.

Katan, A. "The Infant's First Reaction to Strangers: Distress or Anxiety?" *International Journal of Psycho-Analysis*, 53:501–503, 1972.

McCall, R. B. "Smiling and Vocalization in Infants as Indices of Perceptual-Cognitive Processes," *Merrill-Palmer Quarterly*, 18:341–347, 1972.

Scarr, S., and Salapatek, P. "Patterns of Fear Development During Infancy," *Merrill-Palmer Quarterly*, 16:53–90, 1970.

Sroufe, L., Waters, E., and Matas, L. "Contextual Determinants of Infant Affective Response." In Lewis, M., and Rosenblum, L. (eds.), *The Origins of Fear*. New York: Wiley, 1974, pp. 49–72.

Stenberg, C., Campos, J., and Emde, R. "The Facial Expressions of Anger in Seven Month Old Infants," *Child Development*, 54:178–184, 1983.

The Emergence of a Complex Sense of Self

The infant achieves more organized behavioral and emotional patterns as he progresses from nine months up through sixteen or seventeen months. These capacities for greater organization affect his behavior as well as his emotions and his interaction patterns. During this phase the child also learns to understand the functional properties of objects, as a precursor to learning to use ideas.

Ainsworth, M., and Wittig, B. "Attachment and Exploratory Behavior of One Year Olds in a Strange Situation." In Foss, B. M. (ed.), *Determinants of Infant Behavior (Vol. 4)*. New York: Wiley, 1969.

Bell, S. M. "The Development of the Concept of the Object as Related to Infant-Mother Attachment," *Child Development*, 41:291–311, 1970.

Bronson, W. "Toddler's Behaviors with Agemates: Issues of Interaction, Cognition, and Affect." In Lipsitt, L. (ed.), *Monographs on Infancy*. Norwood, N.Y.: Ablex, 1981.

Feinman, S., and Lewis, M. "Social Referencing and Second Order Effects in Ten Month Old Infants," *Child Development*, 54:878–887, 1983.

Kagan, J. *The Second Year*. Cambridge, Mass.: Harvard University Press, 1981.

Klinnert, M. D., Campos, J., Sorce, J. F., Emde, R. N., and Svejda, M. J. "Social Referencing: Emotional Expressions as Behavior Regulators." In Plutchik, R., and Kellerman, H. (eds.), *Emotions in Early Development*. New York: Academic Press, 1983.

Matas, L., Arend, R., and Sroufe, L. A. "Continuity of Adaption in the Second Year: The Relationship Between Quality of Attachment and Later Competent Functioning," *Child Development*, 49:547–556, 1978.

Press, B., and Greenspan, S. "Toddler Friendships: The Development of Emotional Relationships in the Second Year," prepublication manuscript.

Werner, H., and Kaplan, B. *Symbol Formation*. New York: Wiley, 1963.

Winnicott, D. W. "Transitional Objects and Transitional Phenomena," *International Journal of Psycho-Analysis*, 1953. Reprinted in *Collected Papers: Through Pediatrics to Psycho-Analysis*. New York: Basic Books, 1960, pp. 229–242.

Zahn-Waxler, C., Radke-Yarrow, M., and King, R. A. "Child-rearing and Children's Prosocial Initiations Towards Victims of Distress," *Child Development*, 50:319–330, 1979.

Creating Emotional Ideas and Emotional Thinking

The ability to construct ideas and use ideas to guide pretend play, language, the formation and labeling of feelings, and more complex interpersonal interactions can be further studied in the works of:

Dudek, S., and Dyer, S. A. "Longitudinal Study of Piaget's Developmental Stages and the Concept of Regression," *Journal of Personality Assessment*, 36:1025–1034, 1972.

Erikson, E. H. "Configurations in Play—Clinical Notes," *Psychoanalytic Quarterly*, 6:139–214, 1937.

Flavell, J., Botkin, P., Fry, C., Wright, J., and Jarvis, P. *The Development of Role-Taking and Communication Skills in Children* New York: Wiley, 1968.

Fraiberg, S. "Libidinal Object Constancy and Mental Representation," *Psychoanalytic Study of the Child*, 24:9–47, 1969.

Freud, S. "The Ego and the Id" (1923–1924), *Standard Edition*, 19:3–66. London: Hogarth Press, 1959, p. 160.

Gouin-Decarie, T. *Intelligence and Affectivity in Early Childhood: An Experimental Study of Jean Piaget's Object Concept and Object Relations*. New York: International University Press, 1965.

Greenspan, S. I. "Intelligence and Adaptation: An Integration of Psychoanalytic and

Piagetian Developmental Psychology," *Psychological Issues*, Monograph, 47–48. New York: International Universities Press, 1979.

Hoffman, M. L. "Development of Prosocial Motivation: Empathy and Guilt." In Eidenberg, N. (ed.), *The Development of Prosocial Behavior*, New York: Academic Press, 1982, pp. 281–313.

Kohlberg, L. "Stage and Sequence: The Cognitive-Developmental Approach to Socialization." In Goslin, D. A. (ed.), *Handbook of Socialization Theory and Research*. Chicago: Rand McNally, 1969, pp. 347–480.

McDevitt, J., and Mahler, M. "Object Constancy, Individuality, and Internalization." In Greenspan, S., and Pollack, G. (eds.), *The Course of Life, Vol. I, Infancy and Early Childhood*, Washingon, D.C., DHHS Pub. No. (ADM) 80-999, U.S. Government Printing Office, 1980.

Mahler, M. S. "On the Current Status of the Infantile Neurosis," *Journal of the American Psychoanalytic Association*, 23(2):327–333, 1975.

Nagera, H. *Early Childhood Disturbances, the Infantile Neurosis, and the Adulthood Disturbances (Problems of a Developmental Psychoanalytical Psychology)*. New York: International Universities Press, 1966.

Nicholich, L. "Towards Symbolic Functioning: Structure of Early Pretend Games and Potential Parallels with Language," *Child Development*, 52:386–388, 1981.

Peller, L. "Libidinal Phases, Ego Development and Play," *The Psychoanalytical Study of the Child*, 9:178–198, 1954.

Provence, S. "Direct Observation and Psychoanalytic Developmental Psychology; The Child From One to Three." In Greenspan, S., and Pollack, G. (eds.), *The Course of Life, Vol. I., Infancy and Early Childhood*, Washington, D.C. DHHS Pub. No. (ADM) 80-999, U.S. Government Printing Office, 1980.

Sandler, J., and Rosenblatt, B. "The Concept of the Representational World," *The Psychoanalytic Study of the Child*, 17:128–145, 1962.

Waelder, R. "The Psychoanalytical Theory of Play," *Psychoanalytical Quarterly*, 2:208–224, 1933.

Index

Aggression, 98, 118–19, 140–41, 146, 164, 168, 202–203
Anger, 8, 9, 50, 64–65, 84, 90, 97, 110, 112, 118, 142, 143, 144, 146, 167, 201, 202–203, 208
Assertiveness. *See* Curiosity and assertiveness

Babies. *See* Infants and children
Babysitters, 43–44, 49, 51, 52, 58, 129, 148, 200–201
Behavior of infants and children:
  accepting limits on, 91, 103–104, 106, 108–109
  aggressive, 98, 140–41, 146, 168
  angry, 9, 50, 64, 84, 143–44, 146, 162
  assertive, 9, 65, 114–15, 146
  attentive, 14
  calm, 4, 14, 15, 17, 26, 39
  clinging, 134, 138–39, 200–201
  colicky, 20
  communicative, 4–5, 15, 62–82, 97–100, 108
  competitive, 9, 168
  creative, 5–6, 129–31
  crying, 14, 15
  defiant, 98
  destructive, 2, 9
  differentiating fantasy from reality, 6, 165, 173, 193–94, 214–15
  emotional limitations on, 9
  explorative, 4, 14, 16, 17, 87–89
  expressing ideas with, 129–34
  fearful, 148–49

flexible, 157–62
fussy, 14, 32, 42, 57, 61
hyper-excitable, 2, 20–21, 23, 25, 43, 67, 68
hypo-arousable, 20, 21–23, 24, 25, 65–66
imitative, 41, 50, 86–87, 88–89
impulsive, control of, 177
independent, 87–88, 99, 102–103, 115, 124, 128, 200–201, 224
interested in world, 4, 14, 16, 17, 24, 26
irritable, 20, 21, 50, 61, 77
language. *See* verbal
loving, 9, 40–41, 42, 56, 65
memory, 179–81
nightmares, 206–209
organized (patterned), 5, 84–126, 131, 176
originality of, 88, 93
overexcited, 20–21, 23, 25, 43. *See also* hyper-excitable
passive, 1–2, 47, 67, 78, 99, 144
planning for future, 178
reality testing, 177
recovery from stress, 100–101, 108–109, 149 50
regressive, 138
self-regulated, 4, 11, 14, 15, 17, 24, 29, 74, 157
sensory, 13–14, 15–16, 18–26. *See also* Sensory development
stability of mood, 177–78
taking initiative, 87, 101–102, 124
temper tantrums, 2, 9, 11, 108, 134, 143–44, 187, 203

In every corner of the world, on every subject under the sun, Penguin represents quality and variety—the very best in publishing today.

For complete information about books available from Penguin—including Puffins, Penguin Classics, and Arkana—and how to order them, write to us at the appropriate address below. Please note that for copyright reasons the selection of books varies from country to country.

In the United Kingdom: Please write to *Dept. JC, Penguin Books Ltd, FREEPOST, West Drayton, Middlesex UB7 0BR.*

If you have any difficulty in obtaining a title, please send your order with the correct money, plus ten percent for postage and packaging, to *P.O. Box No. 11, West Drayton, Middlesex UB7 0BR*

In the United States: Please write to *Consumer Sales, Penguin USA, P.O. Box 999, Dept. 17109, Bergenfield, New Jersey 07621-0120.* VISA and MasterCard holders call 1-800-253-6476 to order all Penguin titles

In Canada: Please write to *Penguin Books Canada Ltd, 10 Alcorn Avenue, Suite 300, Toronto, Ontario M4V 3B2*

In Australia: Please write to *Penguin Books Australia Ltd, P.O. Box 257, Ringwood, Victoria 3134*

In New Zealand: Please write to *Penguin Books (NZ) Ltd, Private Bag 102902, North Shore Mail Centre, Auckland 10*

In India: Please write to *Penguin Books India Pvt Ltd, 706 Eros Apartments, 56 Nehru Place, New Delhi 110 019*

In the Netherlands: Please write to *Penguin Books Netherlands bv, Postbus 3507, NL-1001 AH Amsterdam*

In Germany: Please write to *Penguin Books Deutschland GmbH, Metzlerstrasse 26, 60594 Frankfurt am Main*

In Spain: Please write to *Penguin Books S. A., Bravo Murillo 19, 1° B, 28015 Madrid*

In Italy: Please write to *Penguin Italia s.r.l., Via Felice Casati 20, I-20124 Milano*

In France: Please write to *Penguin France S. A., 17 rue Lejeune, F–31000 Toulouse*

In Japan: Please write to *Penguin Books Japan, Ishikiribashi Building, 2–5–4, Suido, Bunkyo-ku, Tokyo 112*

In Greece: Please write to *Penguin Hellas Ltd, Dimocritou 3, GR–106 71 Athens*

In South Africa: Please write to *Longman Penguin Southern Africa (Pty) Ltd, Private Bag X08, Bertsham 2013*